IMAGES
of America

SEMINOLE

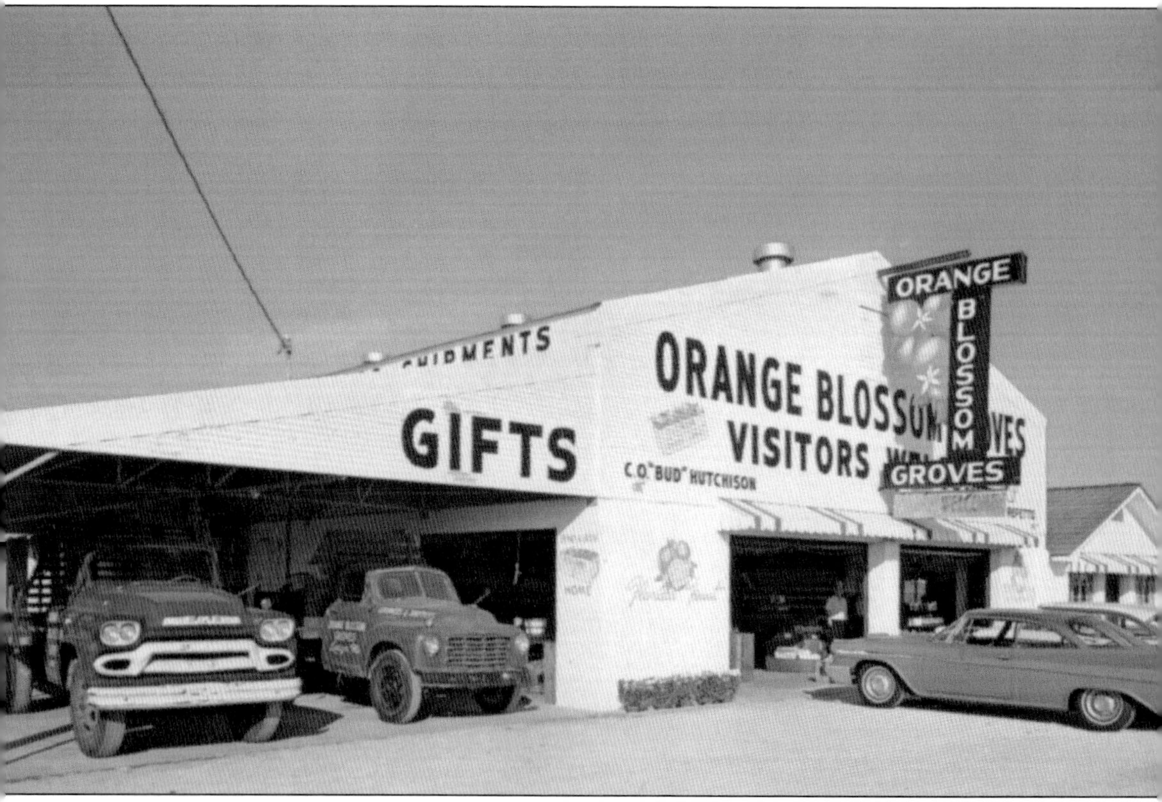

Al Repetto spent his childhood in Seminole groves. After returning from service during World War II, Repetto and his brother-in-law C.O. Hutchinson opened Orange Blossom Groves in 1946. As suburban developments appeared near their business at 5800 Seminole Boulevard, they purchased new groves in other areas of Pinellas County. Repetto maintained the business until 2005. The longtime rancher and citrus entrepreneur died in 2012. (Courtesy of Heritage Village.)

On the Cover: As new subdivisions such as Ridgewood Groves appeared in unincorporated Seminole, people began to outnumber the orange trees. This publicity photograph, taken in the late 1950s, captures a promotional social gathering held in the groves. The "Ridgewood Mountain Village" moniker seemed deceptive on the surface, considering that the highest "peak" in the Seminole area sits below 80 feet in elevation. (Courtesy of the Jack Swenningsen Collection.)

IMAGES
of America

SEMINOLE

James Anthony Schnur

ARCADIA
PUBLISHING

ISBN 978-1-4671-1483-7

Published by Arcadia Publishing
Charleston, South Carolina

Printed in the United States of America

Library of Congress Control Number: 2015938265

For all general information, please contact Arcadia Publishing:
Telephone 843-853-2070
Fax 843-853-0044
E-mail sales@arcadiapublishing.com
For customer service and orders:
Toll-Free 1-888-313-2665

Visit us on the Internet at www.arcadiapublishing.com

To the members of the Seminole Historical Society for their efforts to preserve our community's history.

Contents

ACKNOWLEDGMENTS

The author wishes to express his appreciation to the executive board and officers of both the Seminole Historical Society (SHS) and the Pinellas County Historical Society (PCHS). SHS moved into refurbished headquarters at the former city hall in May 2015, where it embarks on a new chapter of its history. PCHS has reaffirmed its commitment to preserving Heritage Village, a cultural treasure for the entire county located in the Seminole area. The staff, volunteers, and docents at Heritage Village, as well as Ellen Babb, the village's operations manager, regularly offered their encouragement whenever I visited the archives and library.

I have received guidance and support from friends and family. Sandy Holloway, immediate past president of SHS, frequently encouraged members to share memories with me. Carolyn Schnur Hoffman and Patricia M. Landon patiently suggested edits and assisted with the selection of images. Without their assistance, this book would never have come together. Liz Gurley at Arcadia Publishing guided me throughout the process, and her efforts are deeply appreciated. I also extend a deep debt of appreciation to Michele Abramo, Glenda Archer, Nancy Barlow, Bill Bowman, Michael Bryan, Gretchen Cain, Penny Cooke, Gloria Douglas, Terry Hooker, Lou LaGrande, James Olliver, Bob Spoto, Katheryn Spoto, Jack Swenningsen, and Jimmy Vines. Most thankfully, Phuongdung Schnur, my wife, forgave me for my many late nights in front of a computer monitor.

Except for images supplied by the author or otherwise credited, all images in this volume appear courtesy of the Archives and Library of Heritage Village (HV), the Seminole Historical Society (SHS), the Burgert Brothers Photographic Collection of the Tampa–Hillsborough County Public Library System (THPL), and the Nelson Poynter Memorial Library at the University of South Florida St. Petersburg (USFSP).

Introduction

The City of Seminole came into existence on November 15, 1970. Although incorporated Seminole carries the distinction of being the "youngest" municipality in Pinellas County, the Seminole area of west-central Pinellas County along Florida's west coast has a history of documented settlement since the mid-19th century. This book examines the history of the greater Seminole area, not just events within the confines of the present-day city itself. The opening chapter traces early pioneer pathways at a time when "neighbors" lived miles away. Subsequent chapters describe the development of agribusiness and groves as methods of transportation improved, the early subdivisions and suburbs that replaced citrus trees in the decades following World War II, the incorporation of the city, and recent events in an urbanized region.

The city's name honors Native Americans from the Creek and other early nations who came into Florida from other areas of the present-day southeastern United States between the mid-1750s and early 1800s. Although the Seminoles played a large role in the history and settlement of Florida before the Civil War, few members of the Seminole nation actually lived along the Pinellas Peninsula. For thousands of years, however, earlier Native American communities flourished in this area. Their populations declined after the arrival of early Spanish conquistadors in Florida, such as the visit by the Pánfilo de Narváez expedition that landed near the Seminole area in early 1528. Between the mid-1500s and mid-1800s, few people lived here.

Newcomers began to arrive in small numbers after the Civil War, attracted by the excellent drainage and higher elevation along the ridge. While many visitors and residents find coastal and beachfront destinations attractive today, the dark swarms of mosquitoes, a lack of freshwater, and limited infrastructure left most of the central Pinellas Gulf Beaches uninhabited until the mid-1910s. A few of the early families that had settled in Anona, a settlement along the Intracoastal Waterway near present-day Largo, migrated south and southeastward in the 1860s and 1870s. They established farms near and along Ridge Road, Oakhurst Road, and Seminole Boulevard, tending to prefer locations along the ridge that provided breezes and fewer mosquitoes. They enjoyed a bounty of deer and other wildlife, built small cabins, and began to farm.

Other settlers began to live in the areas near Long Bayou, present-day Bay Pines, and areas south of Park Boulevard by the 1870s. Small farms dotted the landscape, but larger groves did not appear until regular railroad service came to the area. In the area between Largo and Long Bayou, truck farmers began to cultivate larger tracts of land by the early 1900s. Their agricultural bounties fed the growing populations of St. Petersburg and other nearby cities during the Florida land boom after World War I, while also sustaining the growing agribusiness centered in Seminole.

Early names given to the area include both Oakhurst and Johns Pass. Members of the Meares family settled around the lake at Seminole City Park, then known as Meares Lake, and soon called the area Oakhurst. At this site in 1879, settlers also established a post office known as Johns Pass, which was miles away from the actual Johns Pass that was carved between the current cities of Madeira Beach and Treasure Island by a powerful 1848 hurricane. Nobody lived on those islands during most of the late 1800s, though pioneers traveling along Seminole Point, now Bay Pines, occasionally sailed out to the island to fish.

Agricultural and business opportunities expanded with the opening of the Tampa & Gulf Coast Railway in late 1914. This railroad offered a direct connection between Tampa and the newly created Pinellas County, an entity that became independent of Hillsborough County on January 1, 1912. The Tampa & Gulf Coast Line followed the present-day route of the Fred Marquis Pinellas Trail from Taylor Lake Park southward through Seminole, across Long Bayou, and into St. Petersburg. In addition to the railroad, the opening of the first bridge across Long Bayou along present-day Bay Pines Boulevard in 1911 allowed for a shorter drive between St. Petersburg and Seminole. When that bridge failed shortly after opening, workers built a replacement span.

As citrus groves appeared throughout the Seminole area in the 1920s and 1930s, nearby residential developments brought more business. Albert Archibald and David Welch developed Madeira Beach, while Charles Redington opened beaches north of Madeira that brought more visitors to the fruit stands and groves in Seminole. The decision by federal authorities to build a soldiers' home at Bay Pines and the continued expansion of the veterans' hospital at this location since the 1930s brought greater interest to the region. Although locals began to refer to the area more frequently as "Seminole" instead of "Oakhurst," they still had Largo mailing addresses and lived in unincorporated Pinellas.

The shift from agricultural to residential development began after World War II. An important event occurred during the summer of 1949, when work crews constructed an earthen dam along Long Bayou at the present site of Park Boulevard. Prior to that time, Long Bayou continued northward and included all of what is now Lake Seminole. Farmers and cattle ranchers in the area, including Jay B. Starkey, wanted to transform part of the saltwater marsh into the freshwater estuary of Lake Seminole. Built at a cost of approximately $160,000, this dam created Lake Seminole north of Park Boulevard and allowed for a new roadway that connected the Seminole area with Pinellas Park.

Although many old-timers never considered the eastern shoreline of Lake Seminole to be part of Seminole, the extension of Park Boulevard and the decision by Starkey to sell his substantial land holdings along that side to developers led to new communities during the mid-1950s along a narrow country path known as Starkey Road. After the Bryan family sold their dairy (along Bryan Dairy Road) and the US Department of Energy opened the Pinellas Plant operated by General Electric on that site (now the Young-Rainey Star Center), more subdivisions appeared between Park Boulevard and Ulmerton Road along the area near Starkey Road.

During the 1950s and 1960s, new businesses appeared along both sides of Seminole Boulevard, formerly Missouri Avenue, between Fifty-Fourth Avenue and Ulmerton Road. Planned subdivisions and mobile home communities also replaced groves and trees as developers built homes that attracted retirees and transplants. Although commercial districts did exist, the community lacked a downtown. The opening of the first phase of what would become Seminole Mall in 1965 laid the groundwork for future expansion in the area. Indeed, much of the history of Seminole after its incorporation in the fall of 1970 centered around the mall and nearby businesses. Since then, the opportunities have expanded as rapidly as the city limits and the population.

One

Early Pathways along the Ridge 1800s–1910s

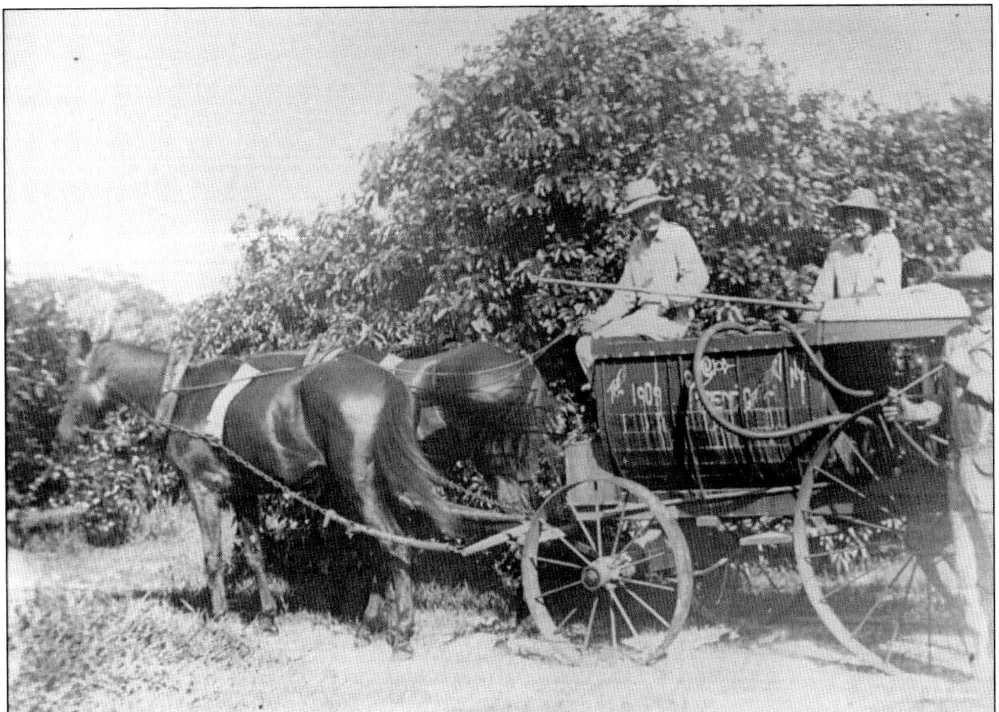

Workers regularly tended to citrus groves in the Oakhurst area during the early and mid-1900s. More than a century ago, this crew traveled around a family-owned property on a small horse-drawn wagon spraying trees both to protect them from fruit flies and to increase yields. Groves and other agricultural enterprises once predominated in an area now known for its suburban residential communities. (HV.)

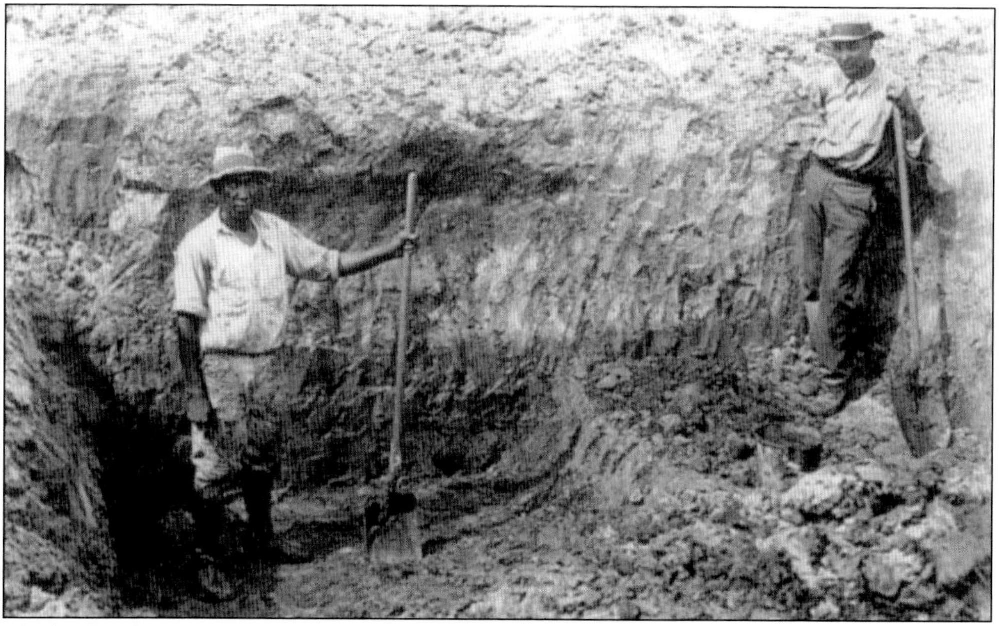

The land and estuaries around Seminole, Bay Pines, Long Bayou, and Joe's Creek have offered many archaeological finds. Workers in this image carefully remove a molar of a Columbian mammoth during an excavation in March 1929. In addition to fossils, archaeologists have also discovered potsherds (fragments of pottery), lithic and shell tools, and other artifacts from pre-Columbian cultures during their explorations along the coastal areas. (State Archives of Florida.)

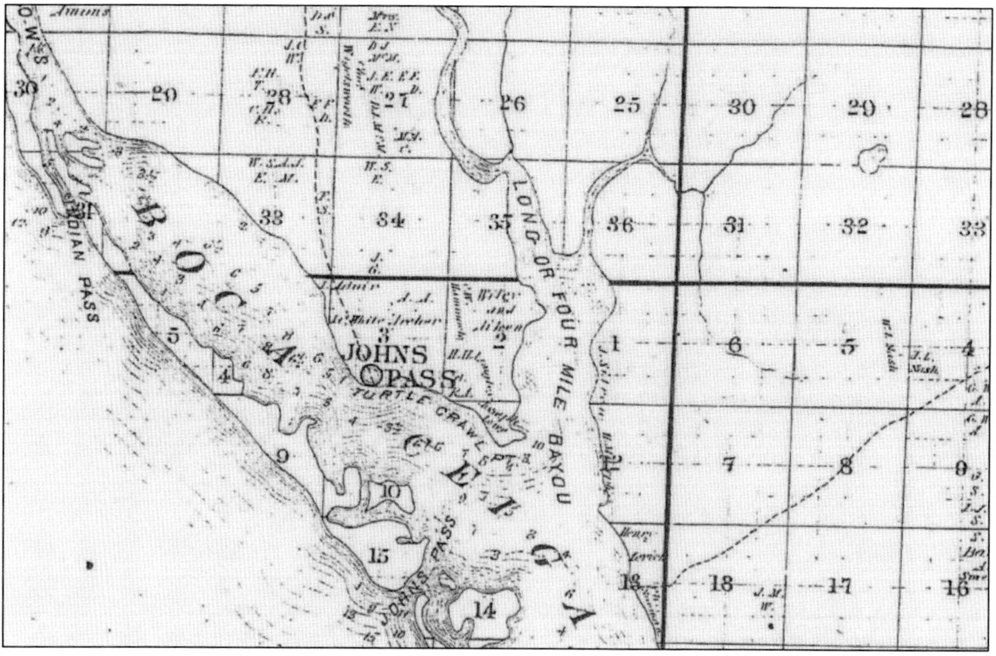

Part of a map drawn for Hamilton Disston, an investor who purchased four million acres of Florida land for $1 million in February 1881, offers an early view of the Seminole area. Published in November 1882, this map places the Johns Pass settlement on the mainland, near Hurricane Hole and Turtle Crawl Point. A hurricane in September 1848 carved the channel at Johns Pass. (USFSP.)

A lack of potable water and an overabundance of mosquitoes along the barrier islands kept residents of the Johns Pass settlement on the mainland except for occasional fishing expeditions. A handful of families lived on Seminole Point, the land currently shared by War Veterans' Memorial Park and the Bay Pines Veterans Affairs Healthcare System. Dedicated in 1974, War Veterans' Memorial Park occupies 122 acres of surplus land donated by the Department of Veterans Affairs. (Author.)

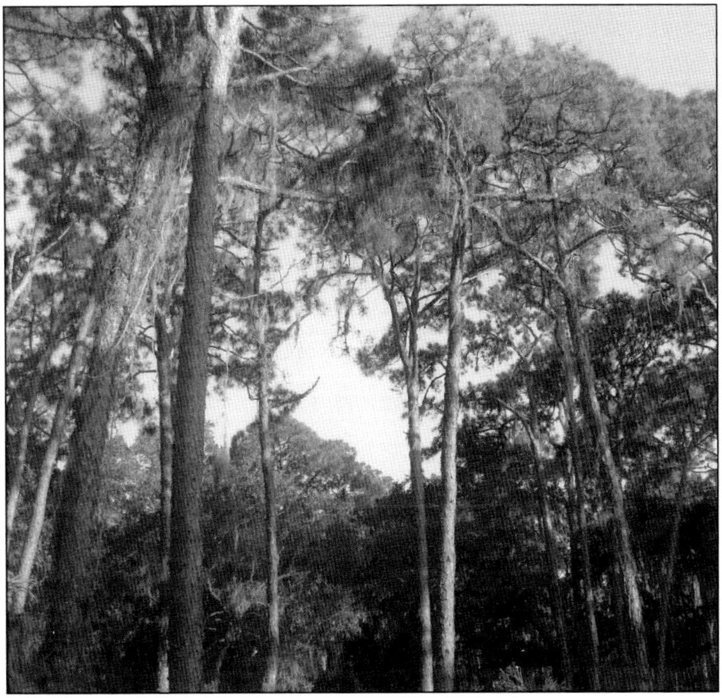

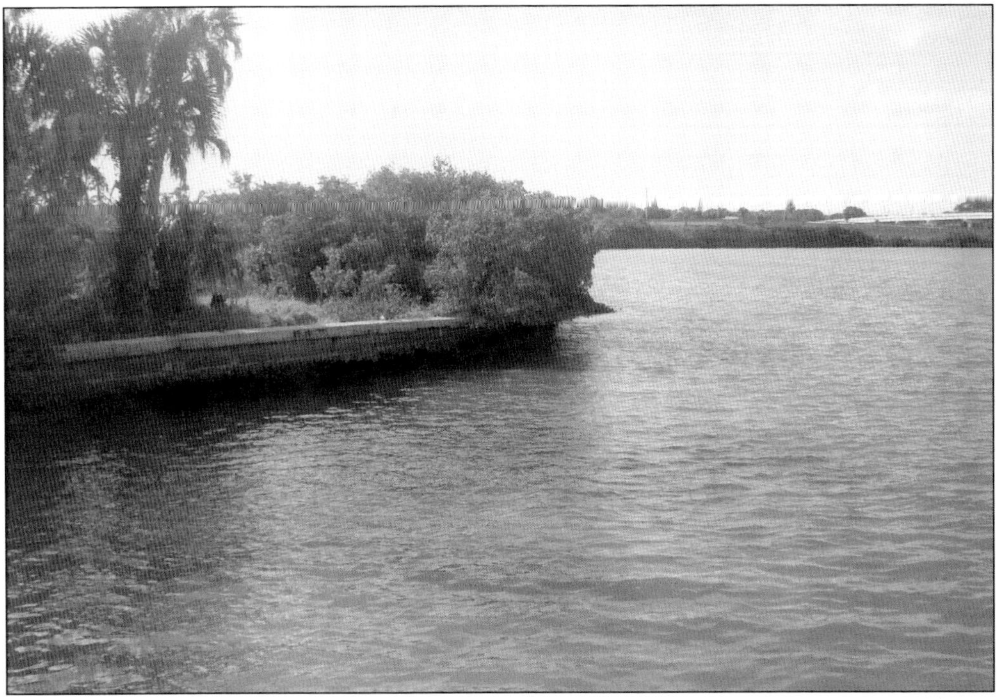

This 2015 springtime view at the mouth of Hurricane Hole looks from the Bay Pines VA Healthcare System property northward into the inlet. Capt. George Arthur grew oranges near this spot. John White built a small boat landing and operated a fish camp near the elementary campus of Madeira Beach Fundamental School. Augustus "Gus" Archer became postmaster when Seminole's post office opened just north of Hurricane Hole in 1886. (Author.)

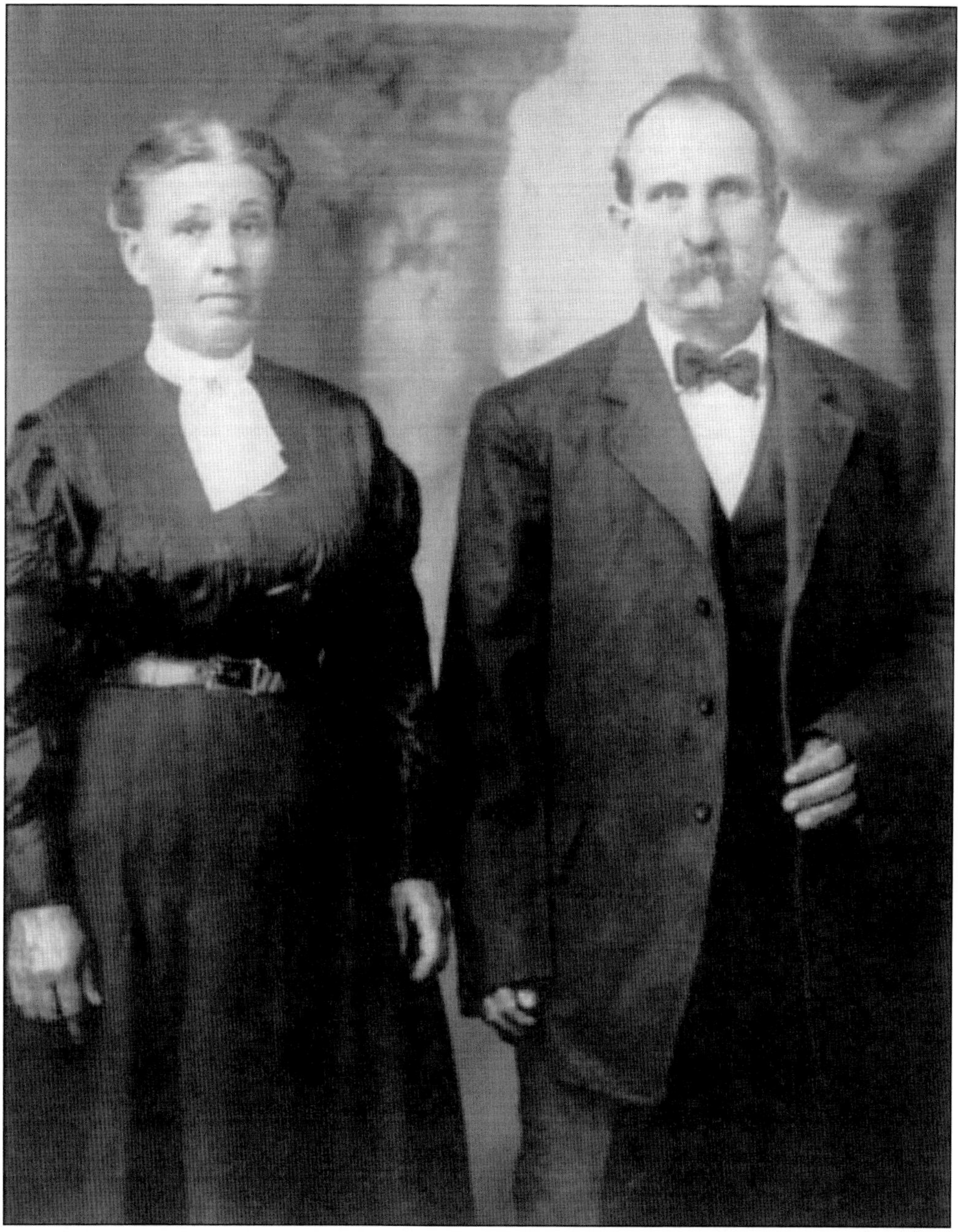

The Archer family came to the Anona area near present-day Largo from Key West in the 1850s. They settled there north of the John T. Lowe homestead. They later moved near the Seminole/Bay Pines interchange, once known as the Bay Pines Triangle, developed orange groves, and built a small general store. Augustus "Gus" Archer, the patriarch, passed away in December 1904. This photograph shows William Augustus Archer, the eldest of his sons, and William's wife, Harriet "Hattie" D. Brown Archer. William was not the only Archer son to marry a daughter from the Brown family. Oliver E. Archer wed Sarah "Sallie" Brown and Charles W. Archer exchanged vows with Idella "Della" Brown. The Archers lived in the Bay Pines and southern Seminole area at a time when neighbors lived as far away as Anona. (Courtesy of Glenda Archer.)

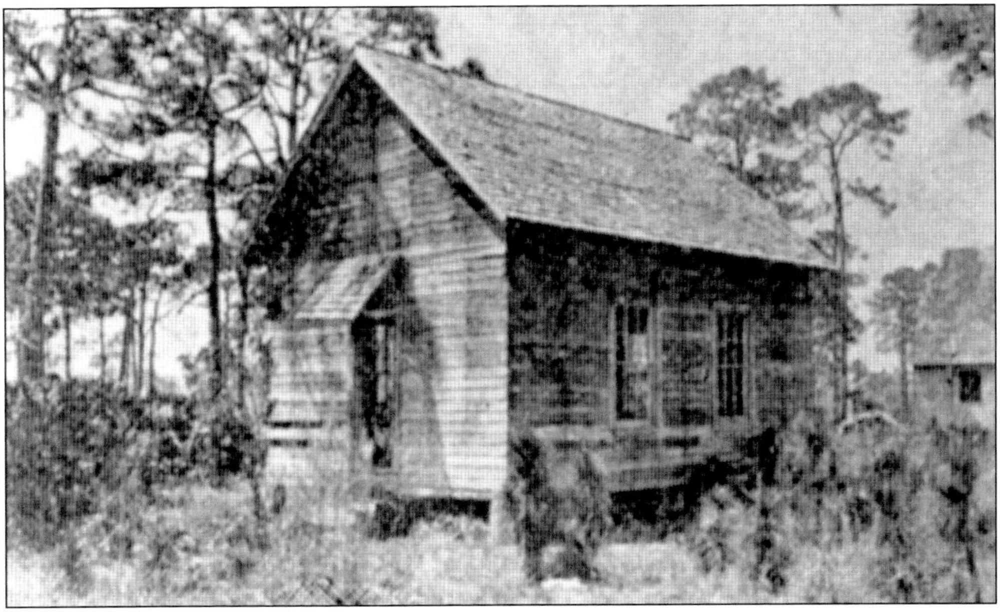

The Archers had originally joined the Lowe and Meares families as they sailed from Key West to Anona in the late 1850s. Gus Archer and members of the Thevenet family constructed this small school on an acre of the Thevenets' land near Seminole Boulevard and Fifty-Fourth Avenue by the early 1880s. Other Seminole schools, often small and used only briefly, opened on the remote bluffs before 1915. (HV.)

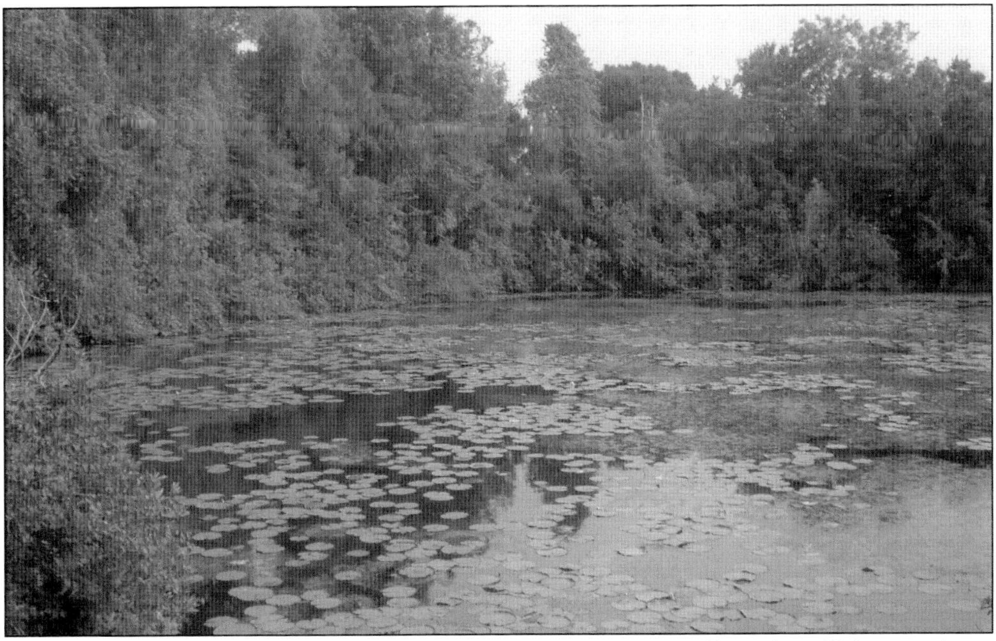

Early settlers encountered abundant sources of freshwater. Many small ponds and lakes, similar to the one shown here at the southeast corner of Walsingham Park near 102nd Avenue, quenched the thirst of indigenous populations, and by the 1800s, pioneer settlers. Larger bodies of water also existed, including Lake Largo, a lake of nearly 500 acres north of Ulmerton Road that locals drained in 1915–1916 for agricultural purposes. (Author.)

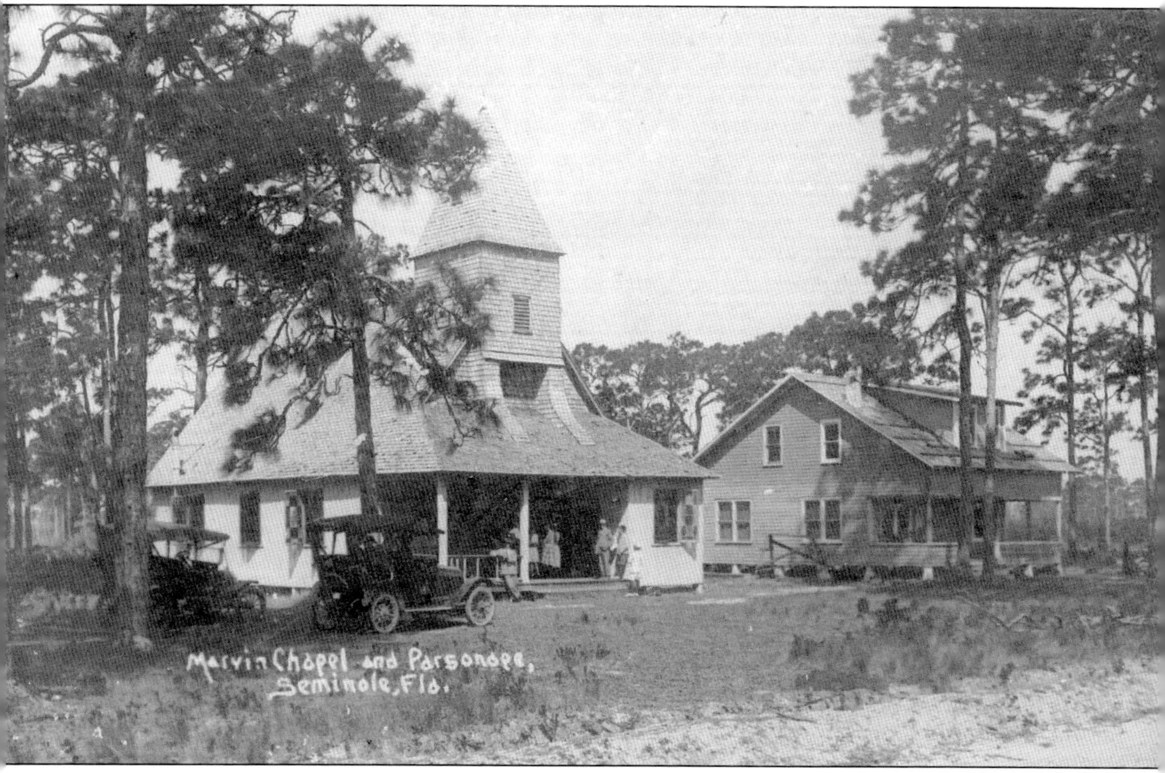

Thirteen members of the Archer, Cobb, Grable, Meares, and Whittle families came together, raised $300, and built this church on one acre of land donated by Capt. Augustus Archer. Members of the Campbell family joined in large numbers as well. Some lumber came across small dirt paths from a sawmill in the Dunedin area. Services began at the tan-colored wooden sanctuary under Rev. E.H. Giles in 1891. Known as Marvin's Chapel for Reverend Giles's son, this church had high ceilings and windows on all sides to provide cross-ventilation during warm summers. William Marshall Cobb served as the first superintendent of the Sunday school and held this position for more than 40 years. Charlotte Grable played the organ for services. Members of Marvin's Chapel established the Women's Missionary Society in 1913, Epworth League in 1914, and parsonage in 1916. (SHS.)

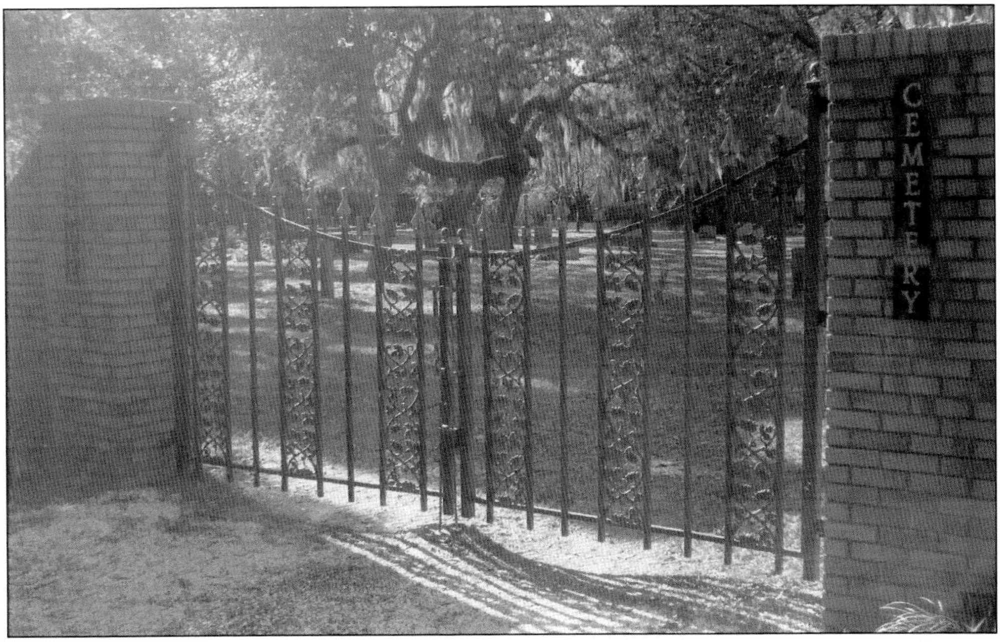

Prior to the creation of the Seminole Cemetery, pioneers buried their dead on family lands. Located on a slight ridge where Fiftieth Avenue North meets 109th Way, the Seminole Cemetery began when local Methodists approved bylaws in September 1894, thereby establishing a Seminole Civic Association that managed the original one-acre parcel. The cemetery grew in size after John S. Taylor Sr. sold adjacent land to the association. Arnett Lamar Brown, the unofficial historian of the cemetery, once told a reporter in 1983 that members of the Seminole United Methodist Church could acquire plots for $3 in its early years. Members of many pioneer families, including settlers with surnames such as Campbell, Cobb, Grable, Leach, Meares, Thevenet, and Whittle have their final resting place in this cemetery now surrounded by homes built after World War II. (Both, author.)

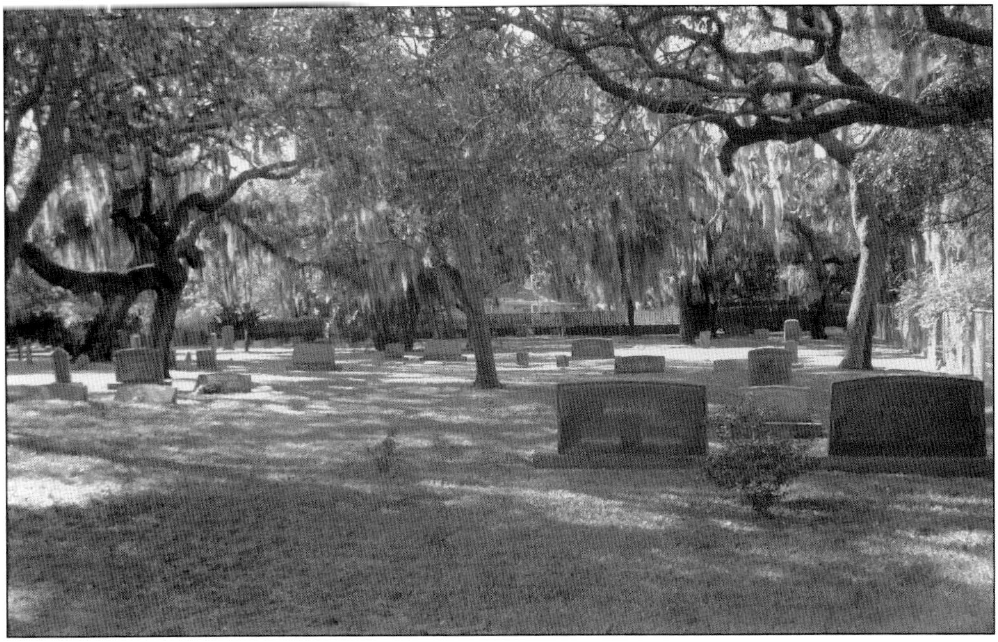

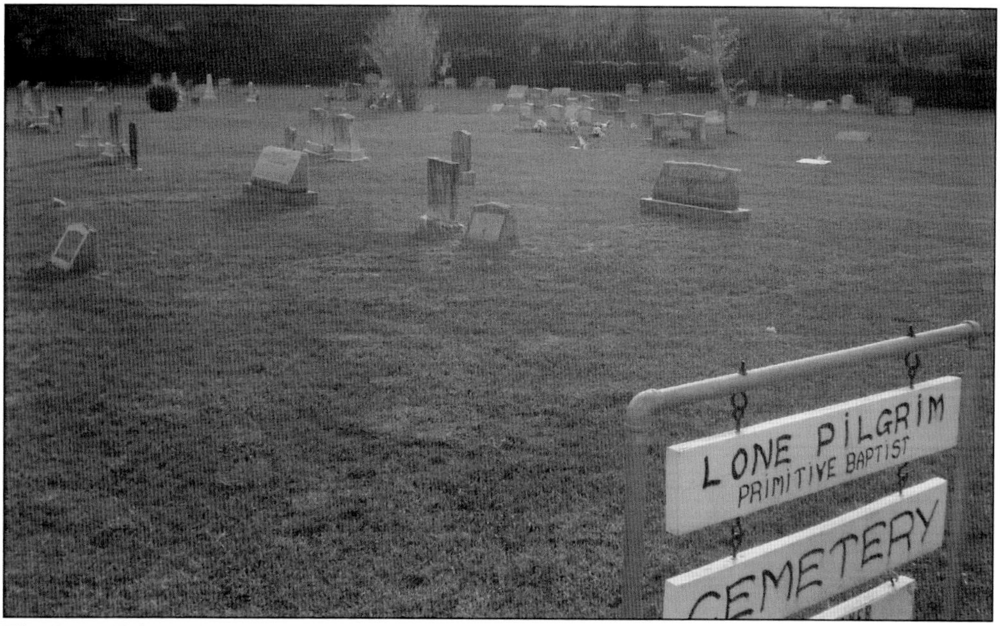

The Lone Pilgrim Primitive Baptist Church, established in the Largo area in 1887, started a cemetery a few miles north of the Seminole area in 1896. The cemetery occupies land along 102nd Avenue North, just west of Ridge Road and across the street from the Thurston Groves residential community. Notable settlers interred at Lone Pilgrim Primitive Baptist Cemetery include members of the Hussey, McMullen, O'Quinn, and Walsingham families. (Author.)

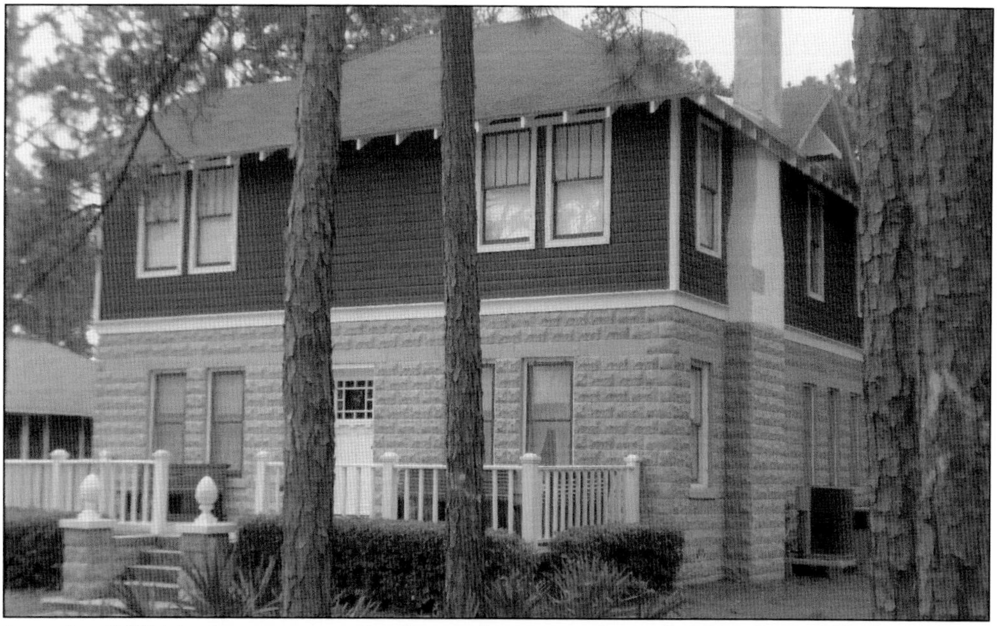
Jesse Ancil Walsingham came to the Seminole area in the mid-1890s. Originally from Taylor County in north Florida, the one-time strawberry farmer soon harvested a diverse array of crops near the road, lake, and park that presently bear the Walsingham name. In 1915, Walsingham oversaw the construction of this large house along Ridge Road north of present-day Walsingham Road. Crews moved the structure to Heritage Village in June 1984. (Author.)

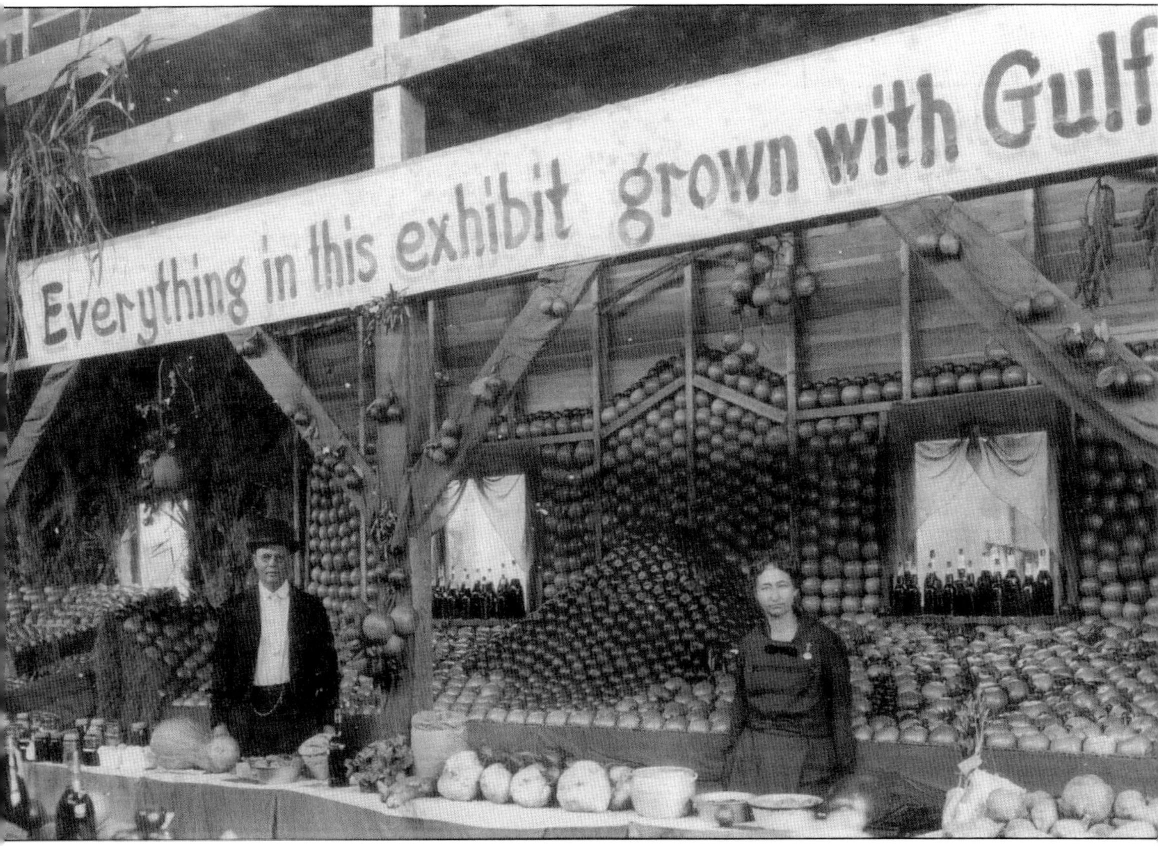

Jesse Ancil Walsingham bolstered agricultural activities in the Seminole area. Shown here with his wife, Mary Adona O'Quinn Walsingham, at an early Pinellas County Fair in Largo, he became a leading truck farmer who harvested crops for sale at local markets. Through his marriage, Walsingham had strong connections with the Lowe, McMullen, and O'Quinn pioneer families. During the early 1900s, he harvested an array of crops and citrus, served as a leader among the truck farmers and others involved in agriculture in Seminole and Largo, became a champion for the draining of Lake Largo, worked with the Woman's Club of Largo to begin an annual county fair in the 1910s, and also served as a butcher for his neighbors. (HV.)

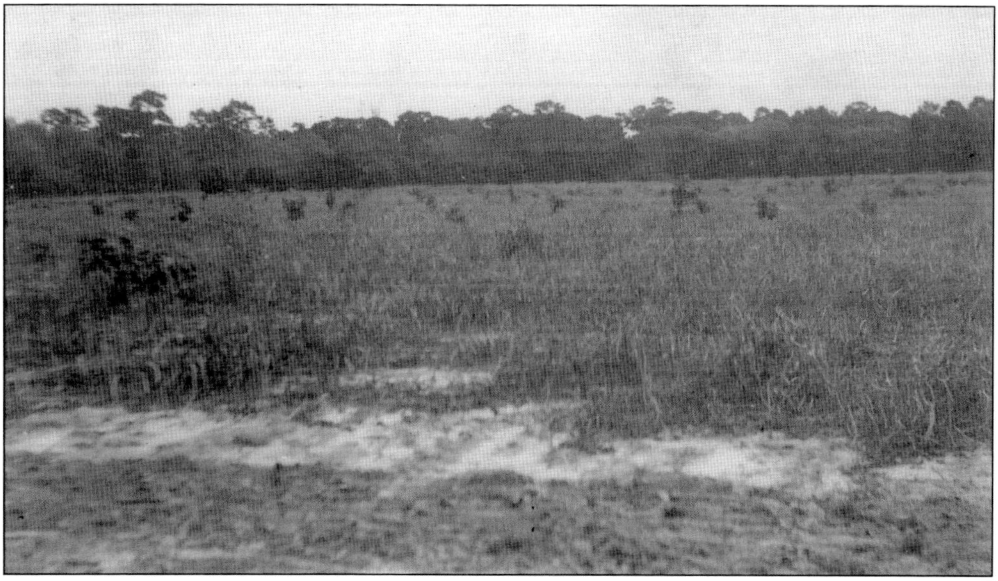

Newcomers spent much of their time removing trees from the land and fertilizing the soil for cultivation. Farmers preferred lands along the ridge at higher elevations because low-lying tracts frequently had sandy soils that yielded fewer crops. This photograph shows recently cleared acreage near Ridge Road in the early 1910s. (HV.)

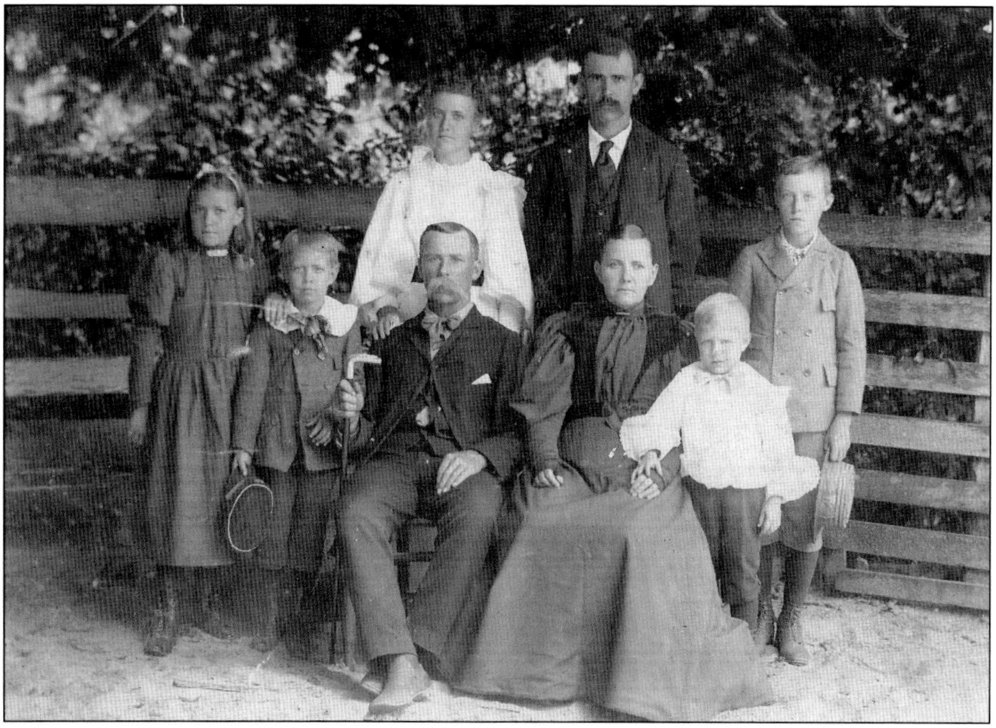

Clayton and Anna Whittle settled with their seven children just west of Ridge Road, near present-day Park Boulevard. Similar to other pioneer families, they spent much of their time harvesting crops. This posed portrait captures most of the family members in fancy clothes usually saved for special occasions. (HV.)

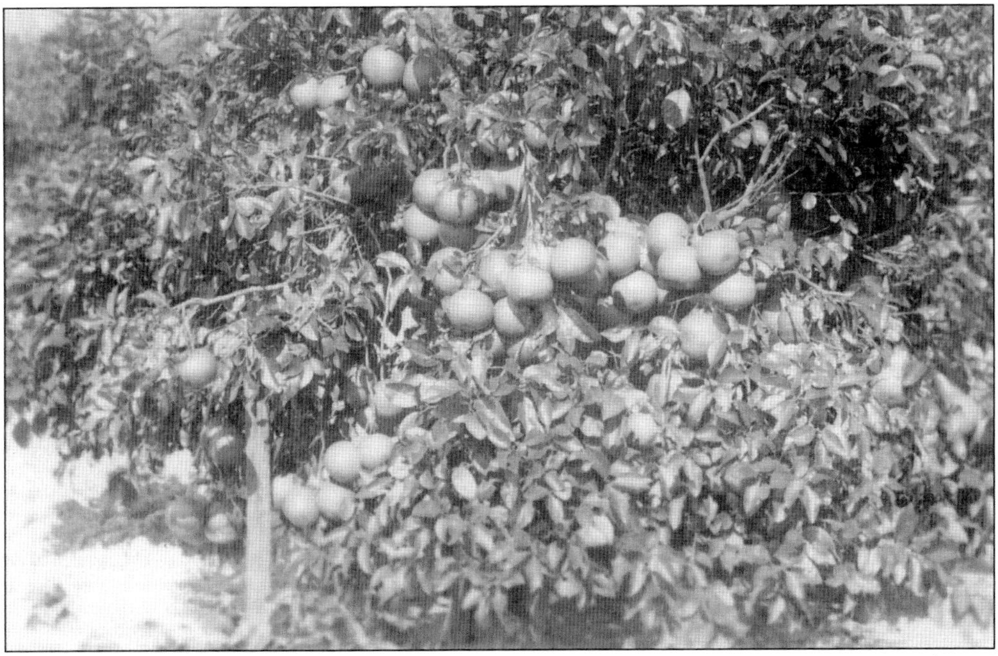

Introduced to the Americas by Spanish conquistadors and early settlers, citrus trees adapted well to the climate and soils of peninsular Florida from the 1500s forward. By the late 1800s, substantial groves appeared near railroad lines as local farmers harvested citrus for transport to distant markets. These ripe trees in Oakhurst awaited harvesting in the early 1910s. (HV.)

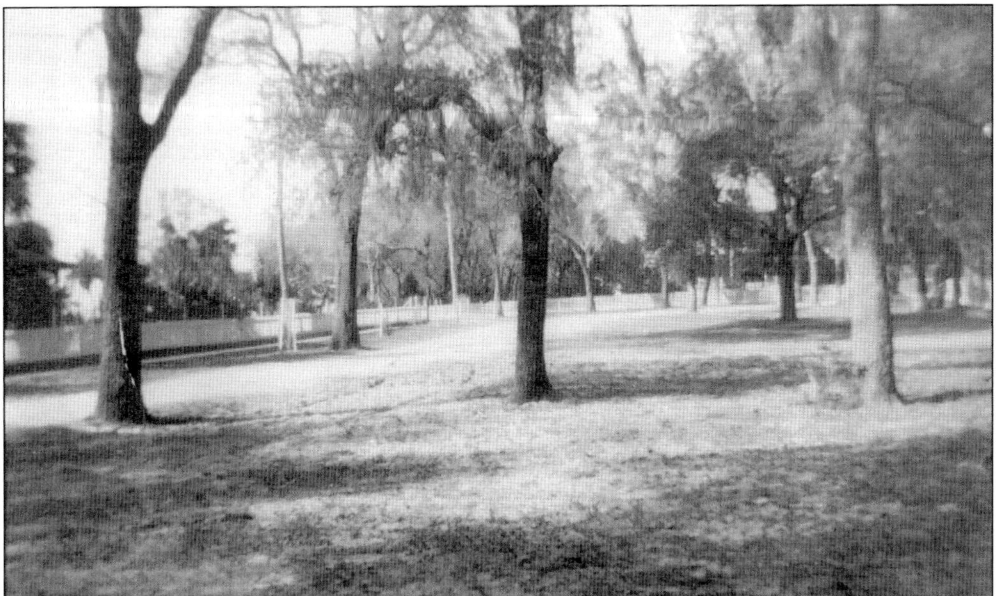

Much of Florida remained an open range until Gov. Fuller Warren signed into law a bill that prohibited "livestock running at large or straying upon public roads" in June 1949. During the 1800s and early 1900s, cattle and other animals often roamed freely in sparsely settled areas. To protect their crops from grazing animals, some settlers in the Oakhurst area near Meares Lake erected fences by 1912. (HV.)

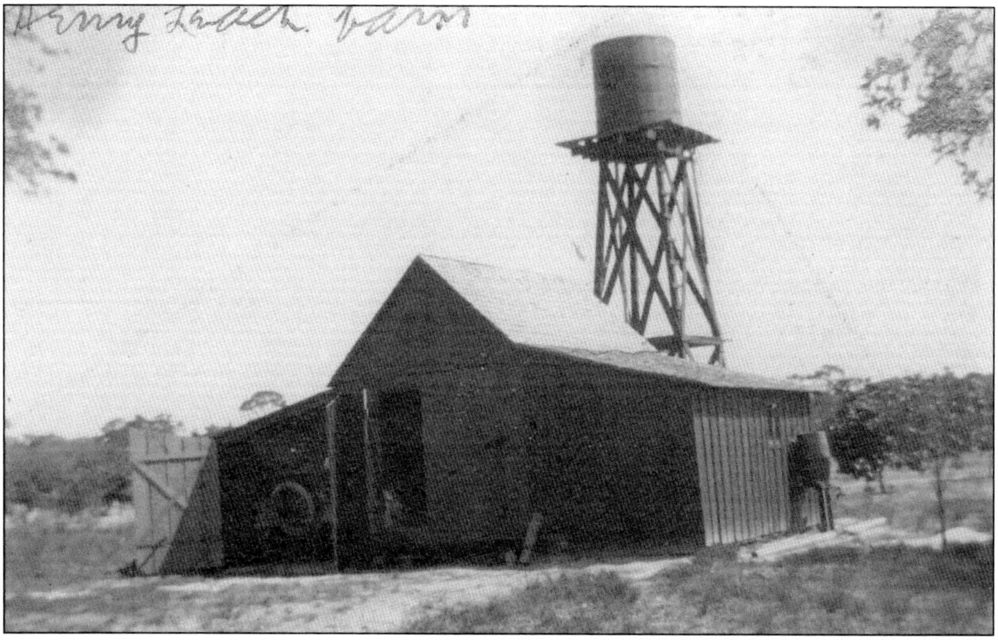

Pioneer members of the Meares and Leach families originally hailed from England. Albert S. Meares arrived in 1872 and settled near Meares Lake, now Seminole City Park. Robert Leach, a native of Somerset County, left England with a dream of growing oranges in Florida. He departed from New York on a railroad journey in 1887 that brought him to Tampa on Henry Plant's recently established railroad line. After gathering supplies, Leach hired a horse and wagon for an arduous journey over sandy paths to present-day Clearwater, then a settlement known as Clear Water Harbor with barely 100 residents. He soon moved to Oakhurst, established a grove, and married the former Katherine Brumby in 1902. The Brumbys had arrived on the Pinellas Peninsula in 1886. Robert and Katherine settled along Old Oakhurst road where it intersects Leach Road. (Both, HV.)

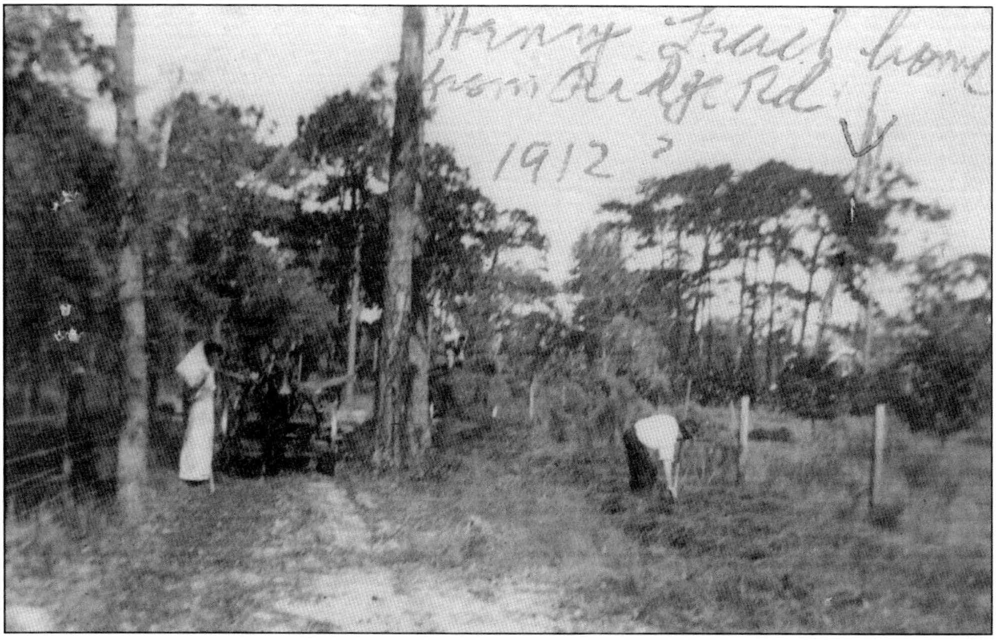

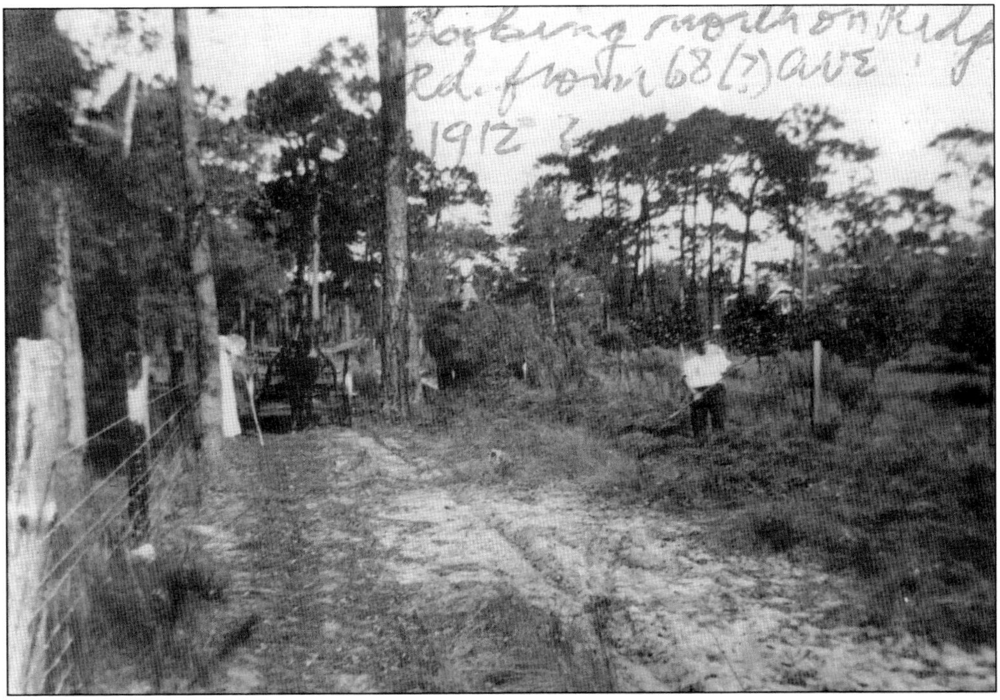

Although the arrival of the Orange Belt Railway in the spring of 1888 opened the frontier around Largo and areas north of present-day Ulmerton Road to widespread agricultural development, the Oakhurst area remained remote. This view of Ridge Road near the Meares and Leach property in 1912 reveals that little had changed in the 40 years since Albert Meares first arrived. (HV.)

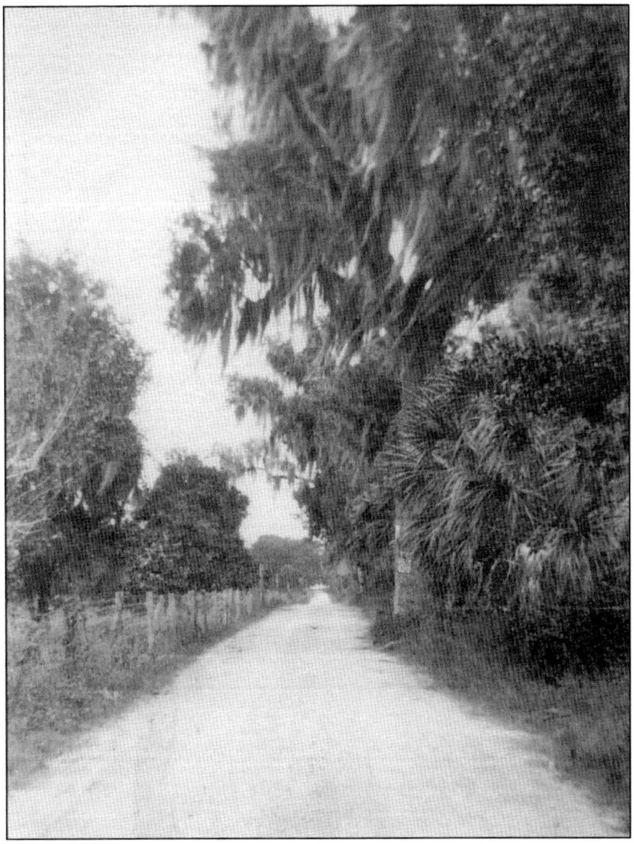

The Campbell family originally settled east of the Meares family in the late 1870s. A native of South Carolina and a Civil War veteran, Benjamin Franklin "Ben" Campbell married Margaret Ann Taylor, daughter of Pinellas pioneer John Stansel Taylor, in what was then the western section of Hillsborough County on May 20, 1868. While waiting for their groves to produce, cattle became their "money crop." (HV.)

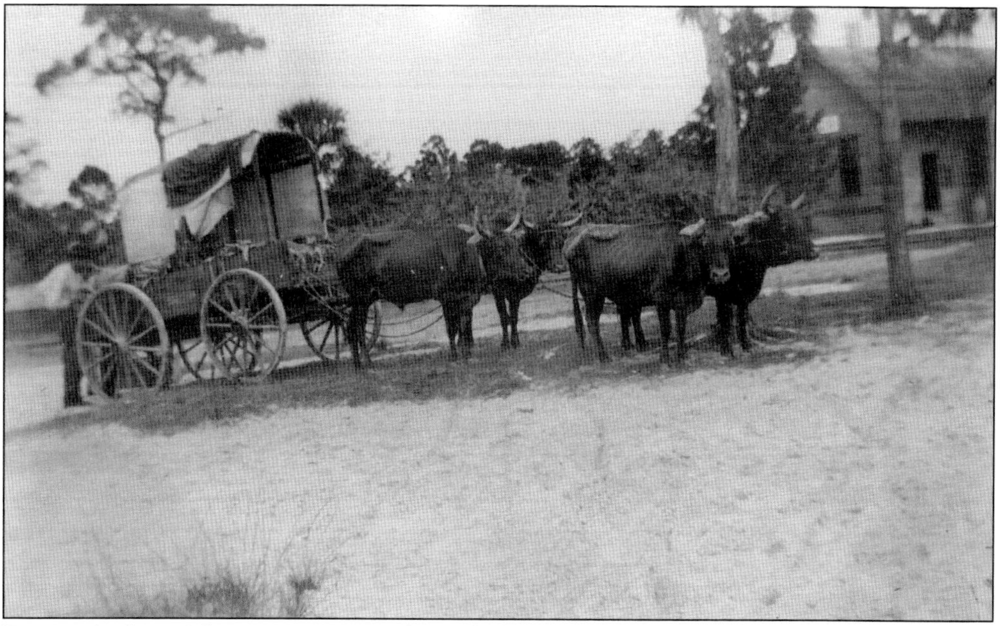

During the late 19th century, wagons drawn by horses and oxen provided the primary mode of transport across dirt and sand trails to other parts of the Pinellas Peninsula. Some of these small horse paths, often the shortest distance between the heart of the Oakhurst settlement and outlying areas, later became the arterial network that would develop into Oakhurst Road (Seventy-Fourth Avenue), Ridge Road, and Seminole Boulevard. (HV.)

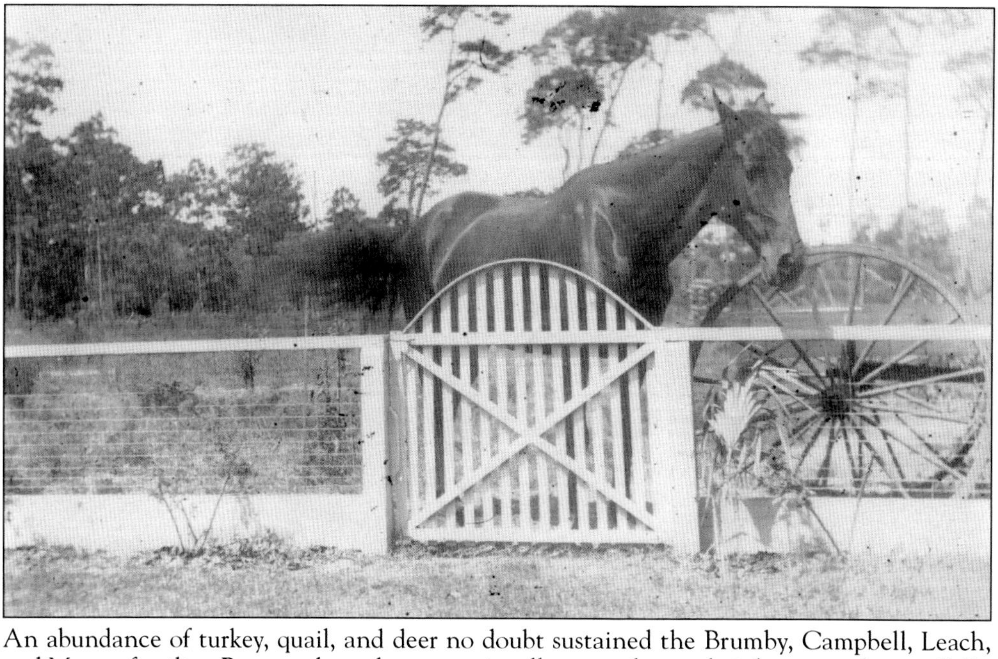

An abundance of turkey, quail, and deer no doubt sustained the Brumby, Campbell, Leach, and Meares families. Bears and panthers occasionally roamed near their homesteads as well. By the 1890s, Robert Leach had started to ship fruits from the Oakhurst area through the port at Clearwater to a relative in Mobile, Alabama. In exchange, Leach received shipments of wheat and vegetables that he sold on the Pinellas Peninsula. (HV.)

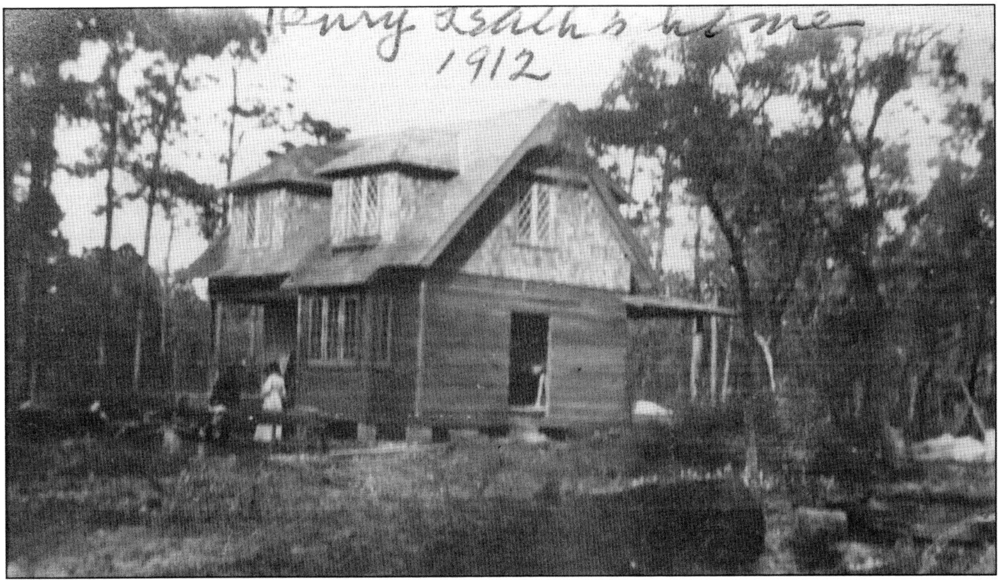

Henry Leach built this home near Leach Road, southwest of Meares Lake. Terrible freezes in December 1894 and February 1895 damaged many of the crops and groves in this area when temperatures fell below 20 degrees Fahrenheit. Undeterred, the Leach family constructed a packinghouse in the Oakhurst area and soon hauled wagonloads of their agricultural products to the railroad depot in Largo for shipping to locations such as New York and Boston. Later, the Leaches purchased one of the first motorized vehicles in the Oakhurst area. Encountering automobiles remained a rare occurrence along the ridges of Seminole and Oakhurst until the mid-1910s, when road improvements started in the region. Although an automobile allowed family members to get to distant locations with less hassle, the poor condition of roads made short drives sometimes feel like long headaches. (Both, HV.)

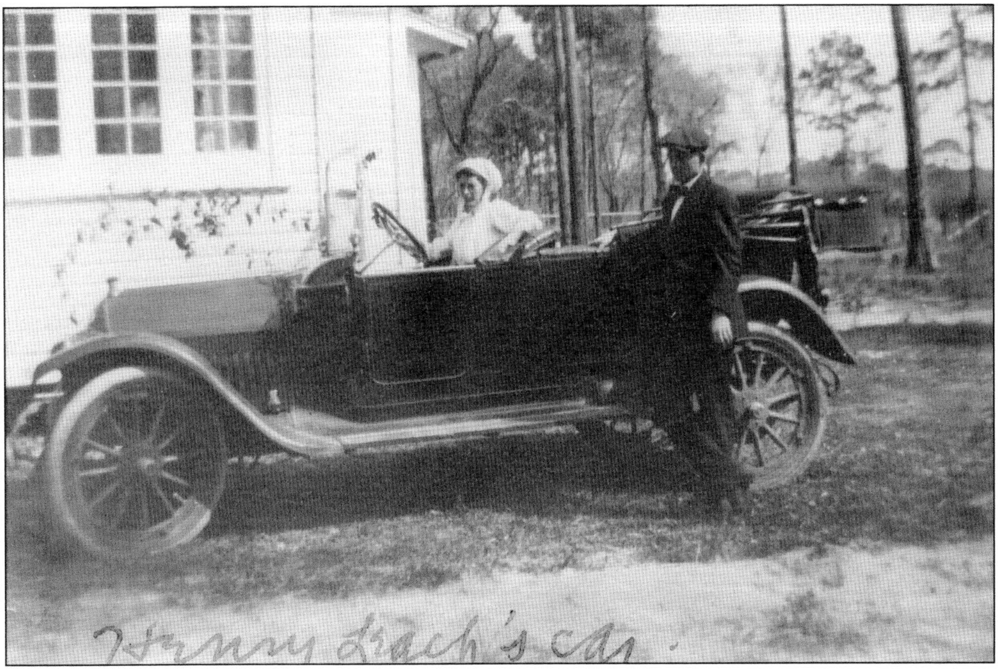

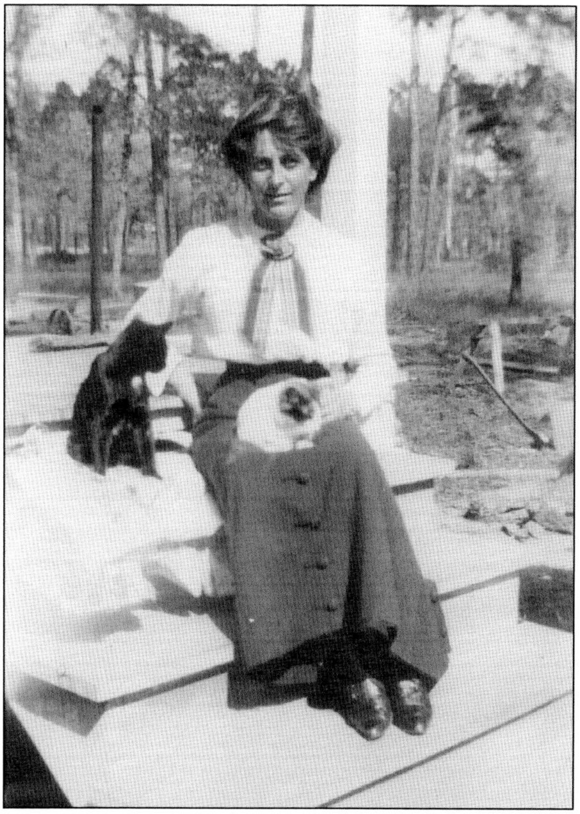

This posed photograph of Kathleen Leach, Henry's wife, captures a relaxing moment with her on the family porch with her cats during the early 1910s. Henry and Kathleen's daughter Elizabeth left Oakhurst for Tallahassee to attend the Florida State College for Women—now Florida State University—during the 1930s. Elizabeth lived on land north of the present-day location of Blessed Sacrament Catholic Church. (HV.)

The home that Robert and Katherine Leach constructed at Oakhurst became a popular gathering place for others in the area, including members of the Brumby and Meares families. This residence, once located in the area of the Leach Estates subdivision near 116th Street, had somewhat of an English style though it sat upon the subtropical Florida frontier. (HV.)

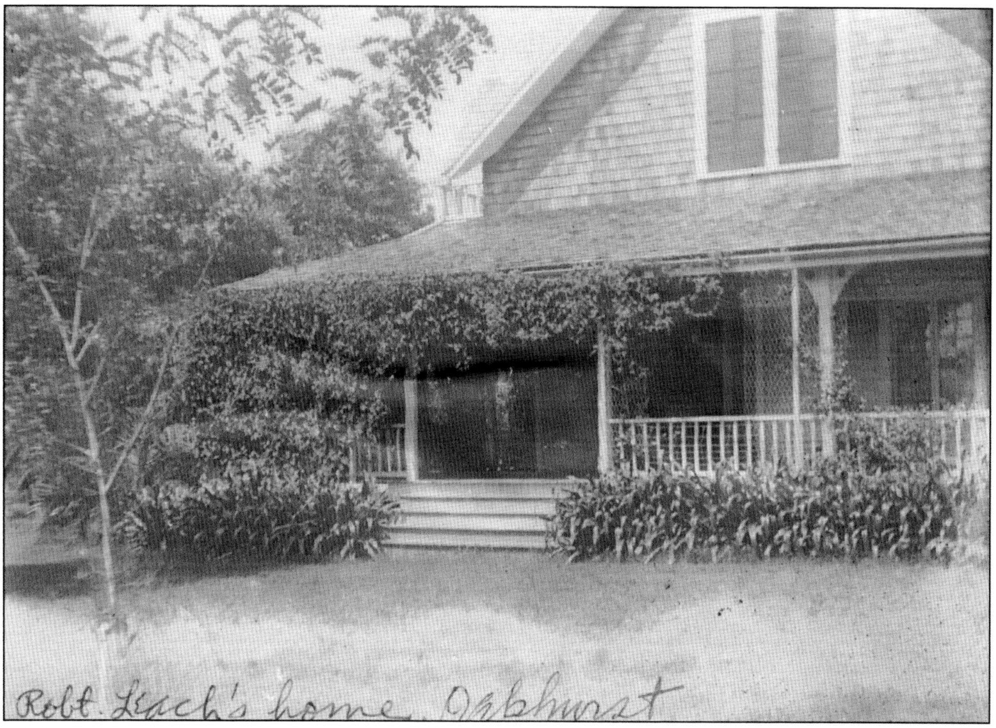

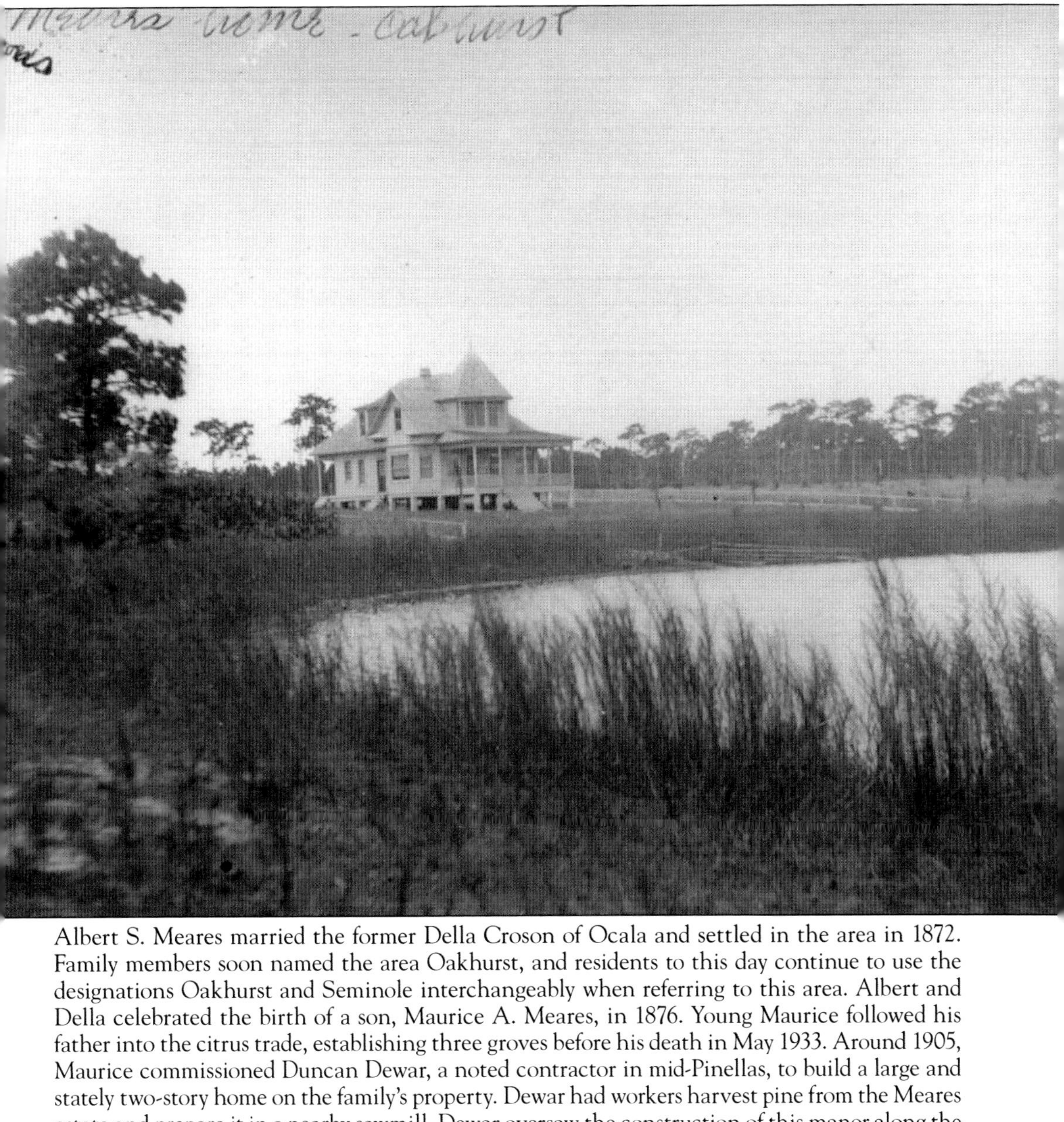

Albert S. Meares married the former Della Croson of Ocala and settled in the area in 1872. Family members soon named the area Oakhurst, and residents to this day continue to use the designations Oakhurst and Seminole interchangeably when referring to this area. Albert and Della celebrated the birth of a son, Maurice A. Meares, in 1876. Young Maurice followed his father into the citrus trade, establishing three groves before his death in May 1933. Around 1905, Maurice commissioned Duncan Dewar, a noted contractor in mid-Pinellas, to build a large and stately two-story home on the family's property. Dewar had workers harvest pine from the Meares estate and prepare it in a nearby sawmill. Dewar oversaw the construction of this manor along the western side of the lake. The view from this image looks westward from the site of the southern part of the lake, near the location of the band shell. (HV.)

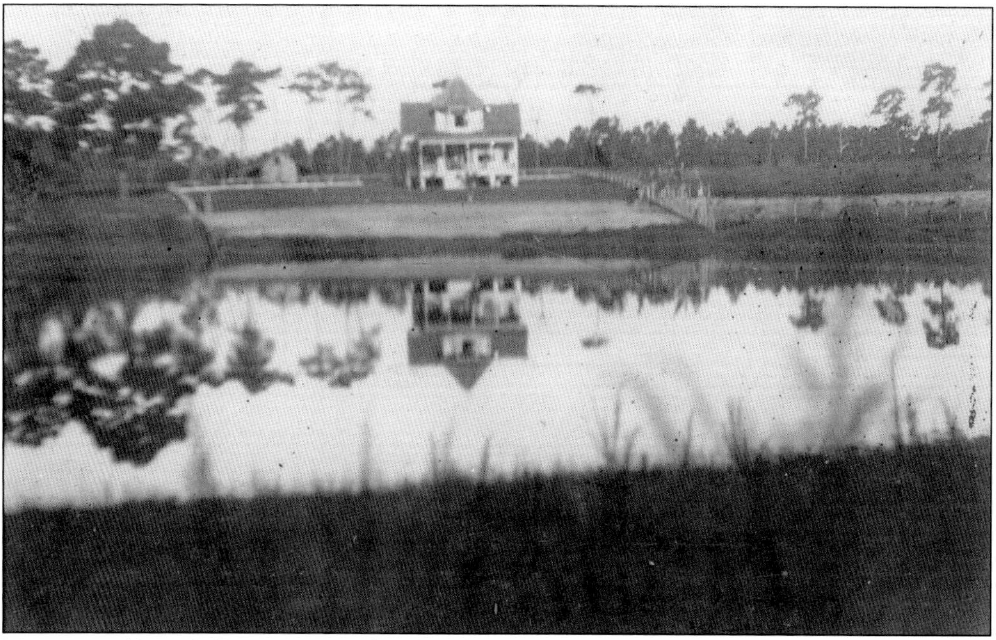

Maurice and Maude Brown Meares lived in this manor made of local cypress and pine as groves sprouted around their lands. Their only child, Vance, grew up here before attending the Georgia School of Technology—now Georgia Tech—in the 1930s. Vance returned to Oakhurst and lived in the home his parents built until his death in the early 1960s. Between the time of Vance's death and the spring of 1974, when the city acquired the Meares Lake tract from Vance Jr. and other family members for $200,000, this once beautiful structure suffered from neglect and vandalism. As the city took possession of this home, workers found a structure with trash strewn about, overturned appliances, holes throughout the walls, and extensive graffiti. Unfortunately, crews had to demolish the residence, shown here as it appeared in the 1910s. (Both, HV.)

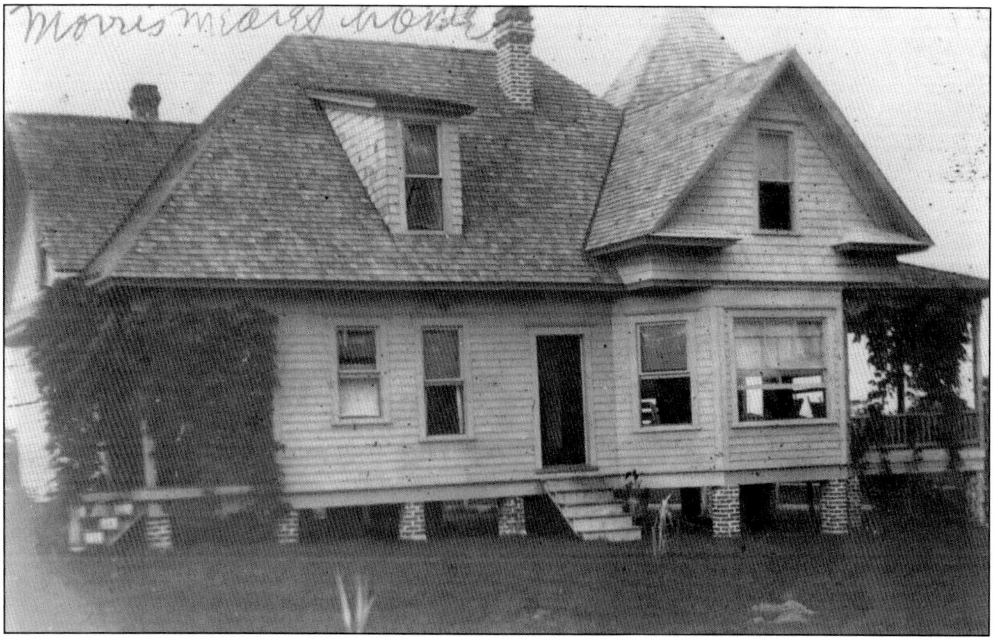

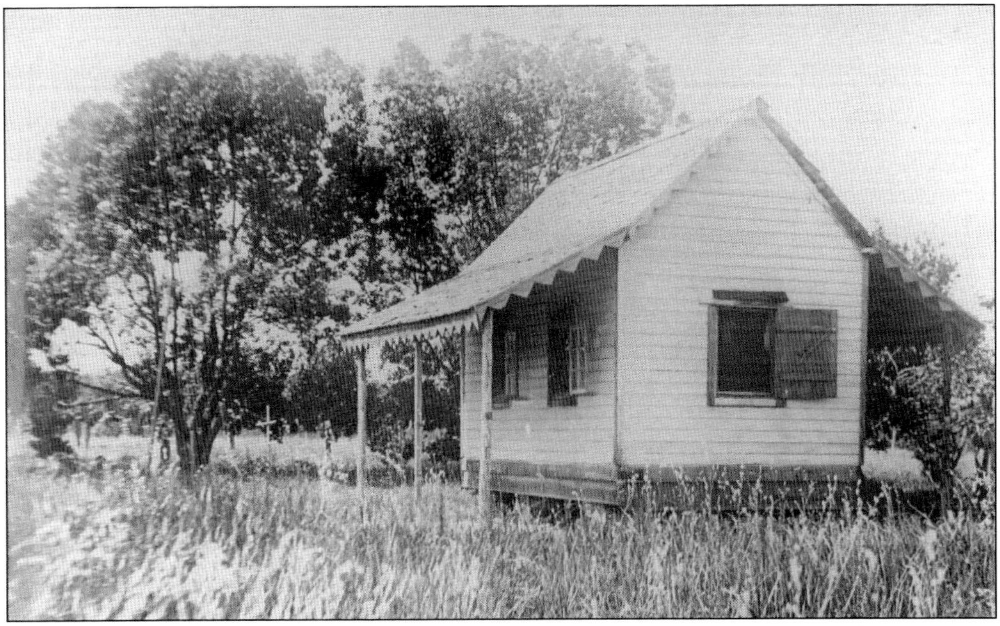

Smaller cabins, such as the residence of Stuart Meares southwest of the Leach property, were more representative of early residential dwellings found in the Seminole area than the manor built for Maurice and Maude Meares. Simple cabins lacked indoor plumbing or other utilities by their very nature, yet they offered suitable shelter during the regular rainstorms and mosquito swarms that pioneers contended with at the time. (HV.)

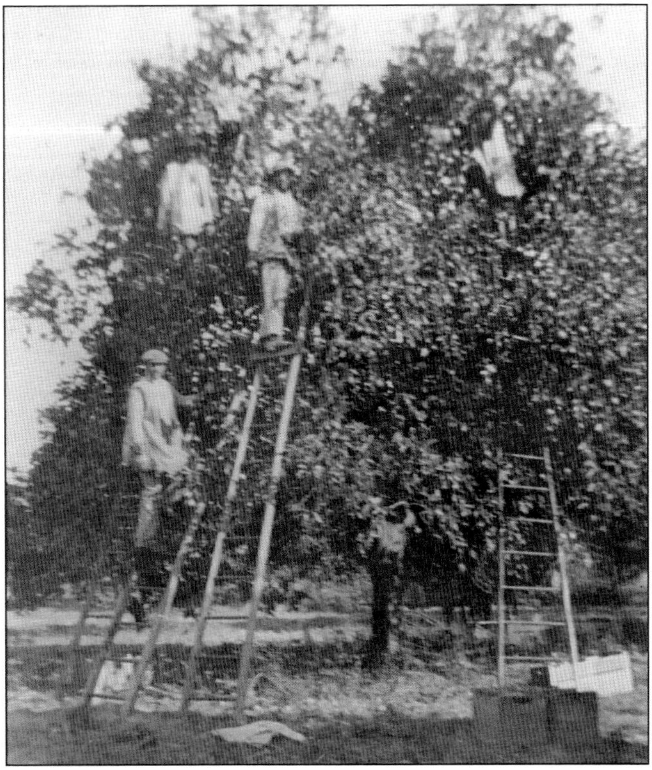

Migrant grove workers assisted during peak harvest times. Until the 1920s, they often lived in itinerant camps or temporary housing. Located in unincorporated Pinellas County, small African American settlements, such as Baskins Crossing, Dansville, and Ridgecrest, took shape after 1920 and provided a stable labor force. Dan and Lloyd Henry, brothers from Georgia, began acquiring land near Jesse Walsingham's groves in 1928 and developed the Dansville community. (HV.)

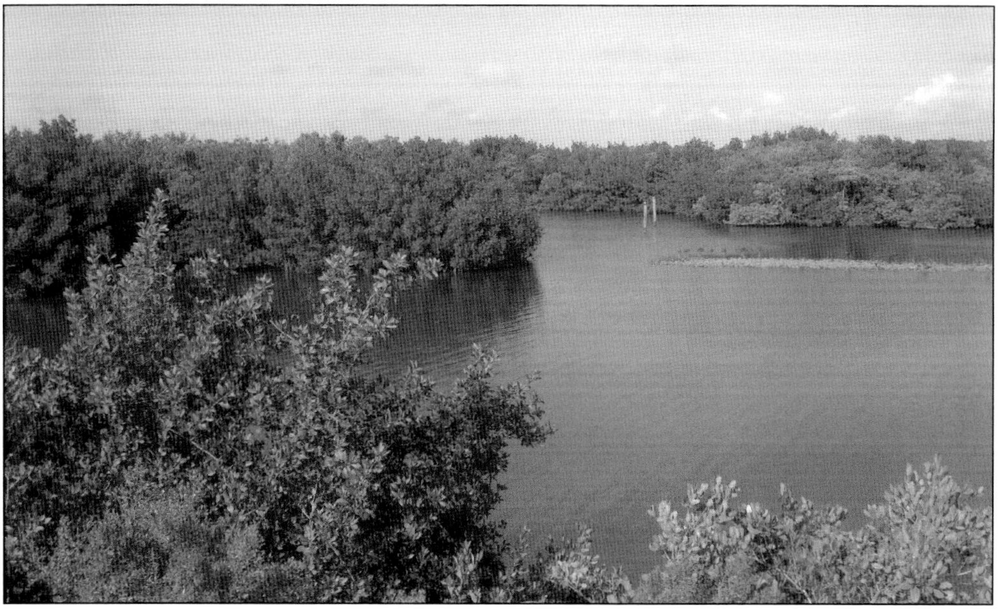

Changes in transportation along Boca Ciega Bay, Long Bayou, and Seminole Point redefined the region. Native Americans and early visitors to this area prior to the mid-1800s often arrived and continued to travel along the coastline by canoes or small boats. Pathways and dirt trails formed as remote settlements appeared in the late 1800s. After years of waiting, a small bridge spanned the bayou in 1911 to connect the Seminole area to St. Petersburg, though it lasted only a few months before suffering damage. A replacement span opened in 1914. That same year, a railroad trestle across the bayou north of the bridge allowed for regular railroad service between Seminole and distant destinations. By 1915, crews carved the Cross Bayou Canal that connected Boca Ciega Bay and Tampa Bay, allowing for the drainage of lands and expanded agriculture. (Above, author; below, HV.)

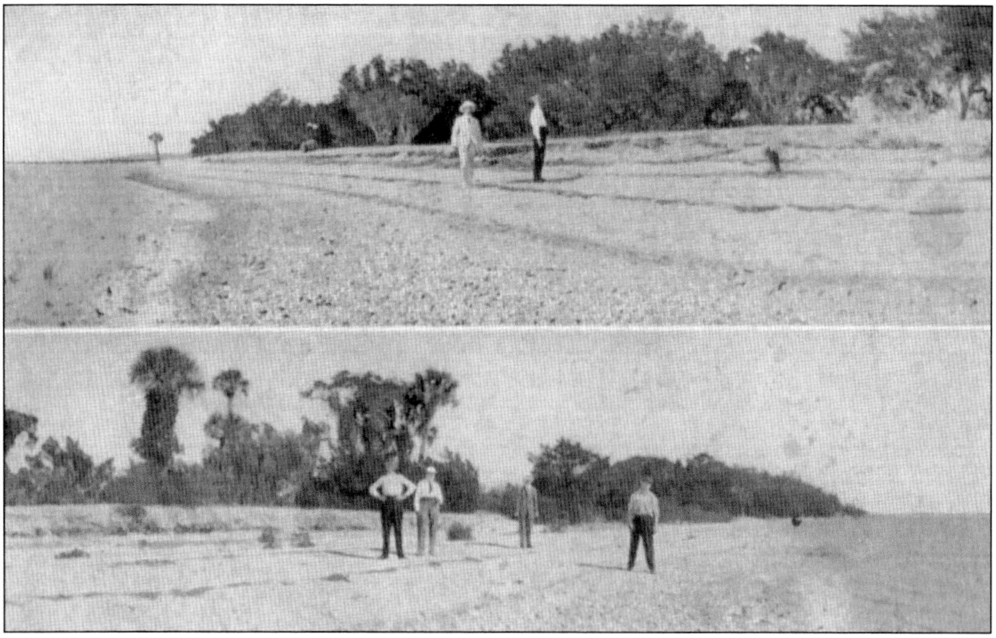

Two

Rails, Roads, and Groves 1910s–1940s

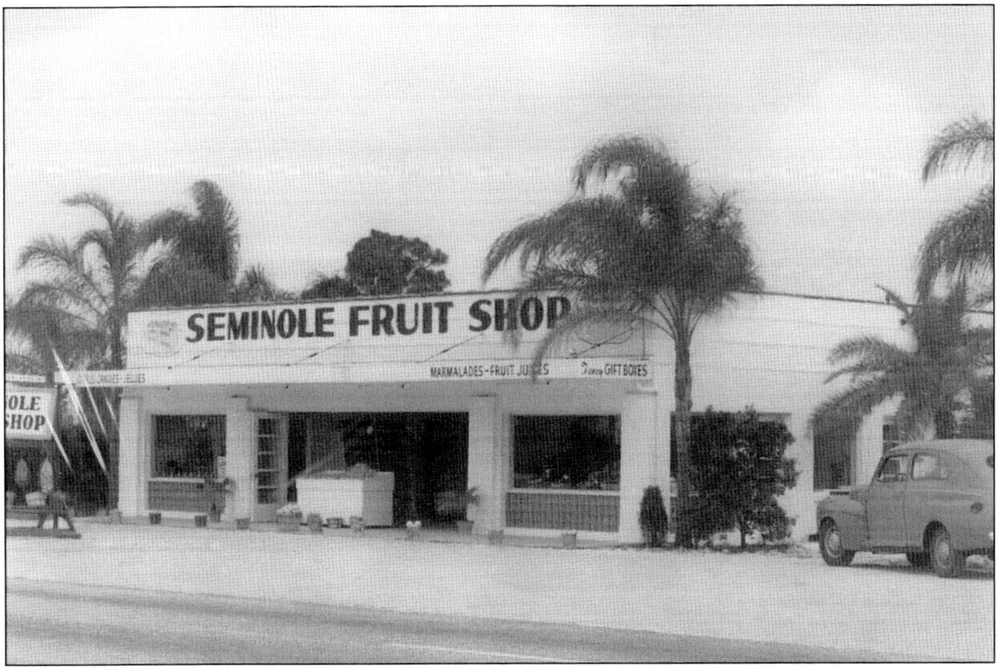

The proliferation of groves in the Seminole area sustained the economy and encouraged new businesses. Jesse Johnson and other family members had developed the Seminole Nurseries in 1929 near the present-day intersection of Park Boulevard and Seminole Boulevard. By the late 1940s, newspaper advertisements encouraged customers to visit the Grove Gift Shop, across from the nursery, "in a tropical garden" setting. (SHS.)

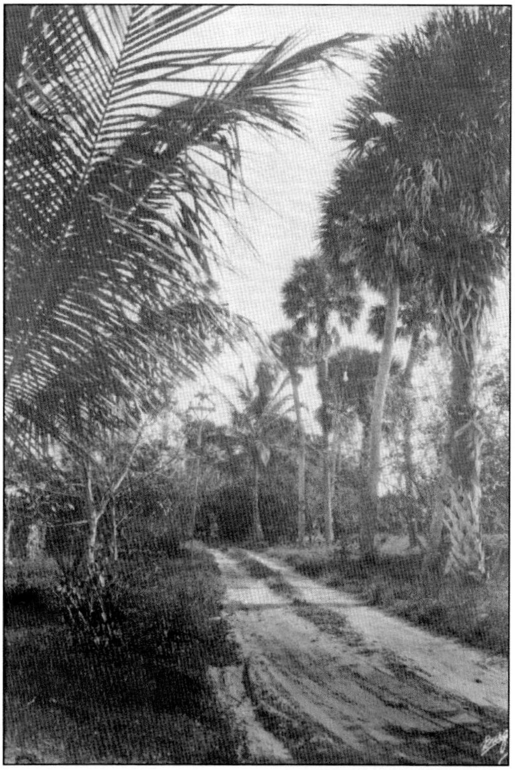

The invention of the bicycle in the 1800s and mass-produced automobile by the early 1900s led to the Good Roads Movement, a concerted effort to improve the quality of paths and roadways, especially in rural areas. Dirt and sand roads, such as this rough and rutted pathway in Seminole, took their toll on cars, carriages, wagons, and other wheeled vehicles. (HV.)

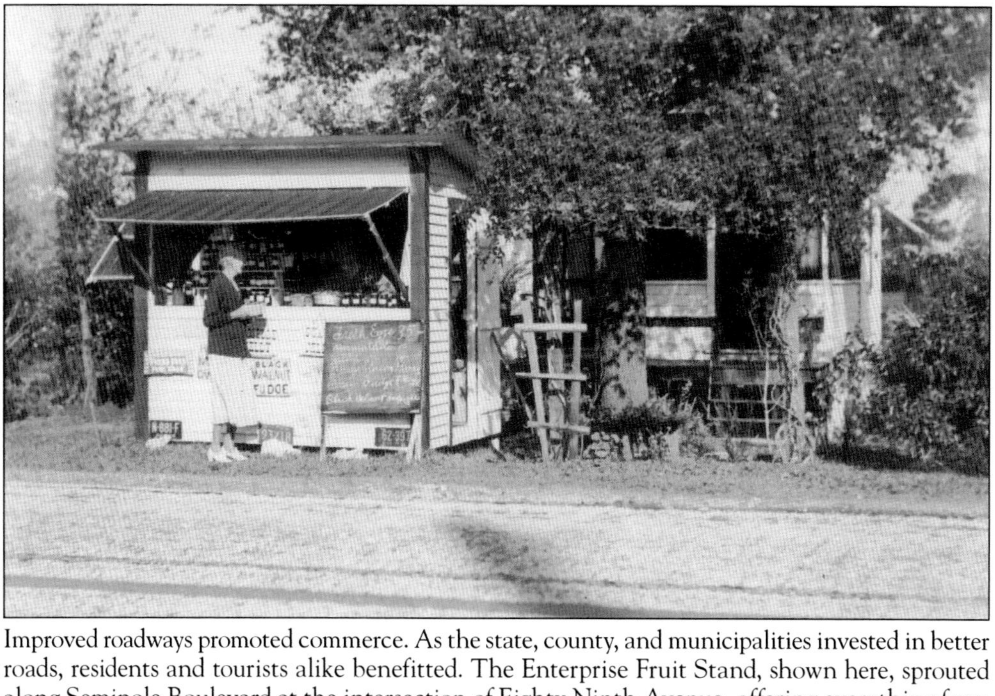

Improved roadways promoted commerce. As the state, county, and municipalities invested in better roads, residents and tourists alike benefitted. The Enterprise Fruit Stand, shown here, sprouted along Seminole Boulevard at the intersection of Eighty-Ninth Avenue, offering everything from fruits and jams to fudge and eggs. Roadside stands such as this frequently sold locally grown produce and offered homemade recipes for marmalades and other prepared products. (HV.)

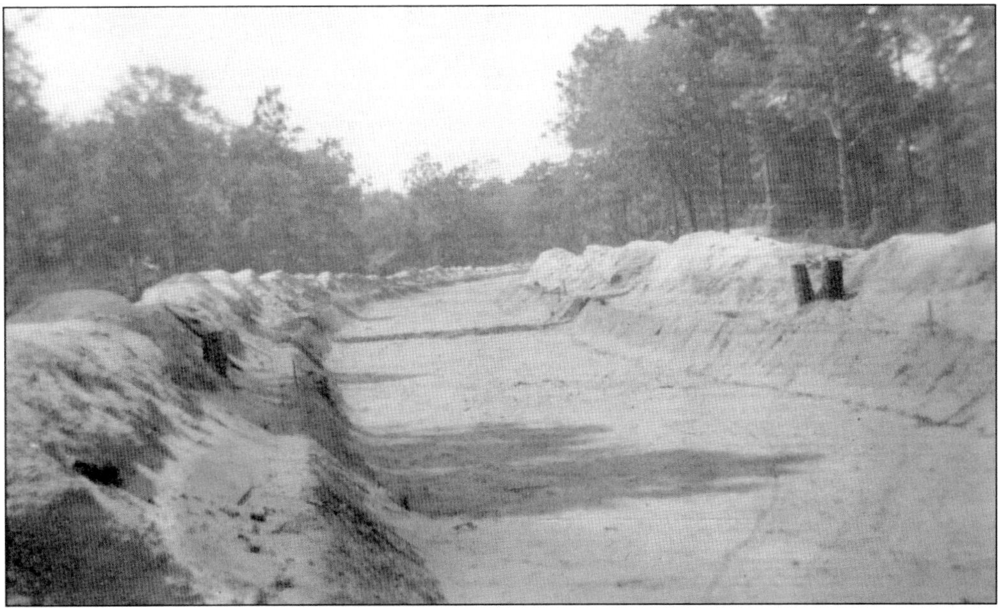

The Orange Belt Railway connected the Pinellas Peninsula with the outside world as it reached the small settlement that later became St. Petersburg in 1888 by cutting across the central peninsula from Largo toward St. Petersburg on the east side of present-day Lake Seminole. At that time, the Largo depot located near the intersection of Seminole Boulevard and Bay Drive offered the closest place where residents of the Oakhurst area could catch a train or ship their goods. A second line, the Tampa & Gulf Coast Railway, launched service connecting Seminole and other areas along the lower portion of the present-day Pinellas Trail beginning in 1914. This view shows the portion of the Tampa & Gulf Coast under construction near the current location of Seminole City Park as it appeared in 1914 and 2014. (Above, HV; below, author.)

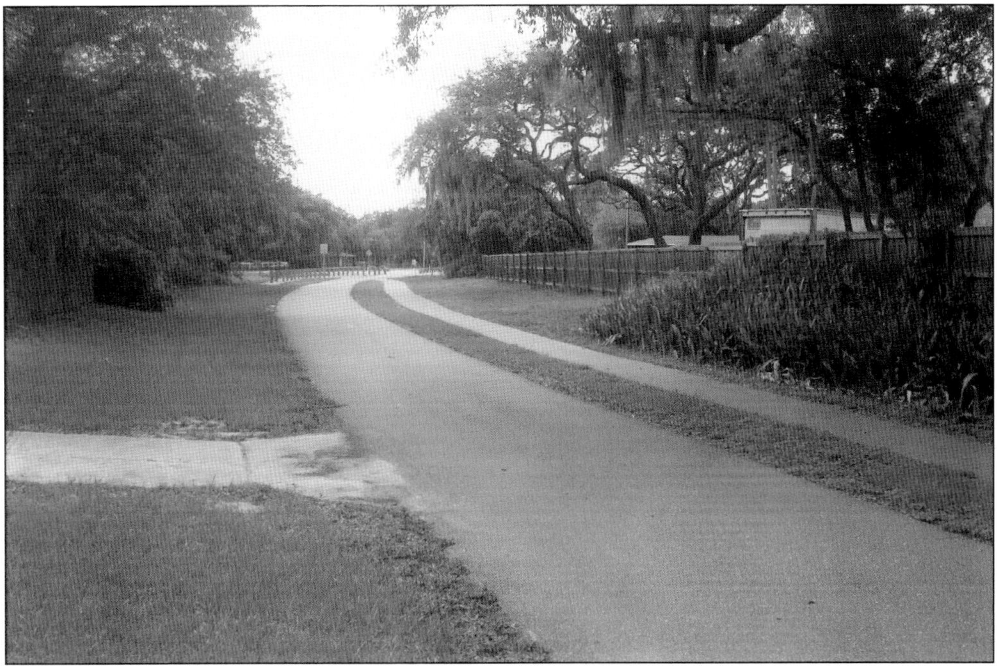

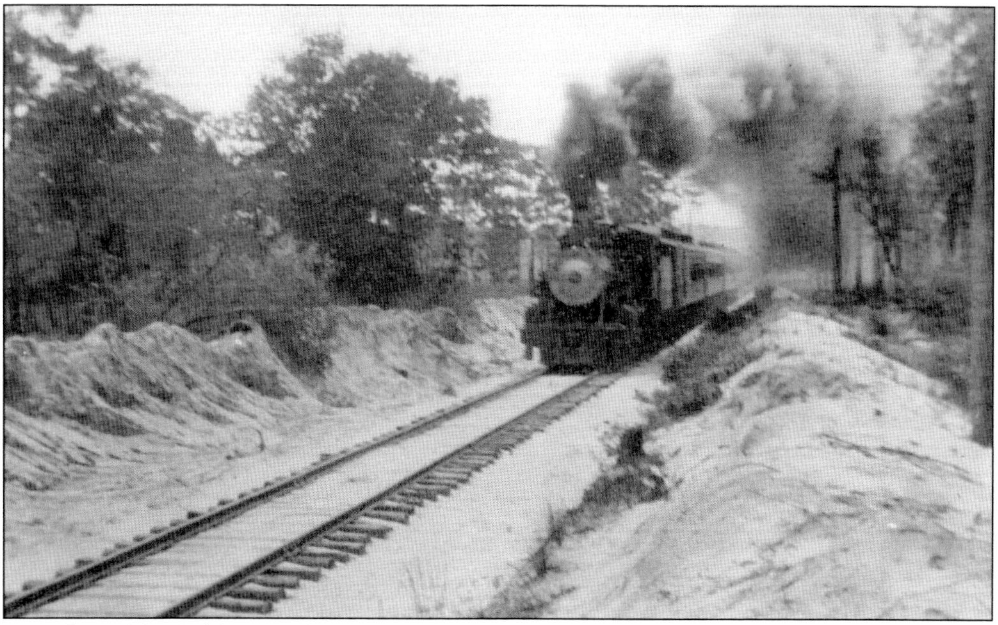

A resident of the Oakhurst and Seminole areas captured this image of the first Tampa & Gulf Coast locomotive near Meares Lake in 1914. The presence of the railroad accelerated the development of groves, as landowners had a reliable and convenient way to ship crops to faraway markets. A depot opened at Oakhurst, near the Seminole City Park, and another small one appeared alongside Seminole Boulevard. (HV.)

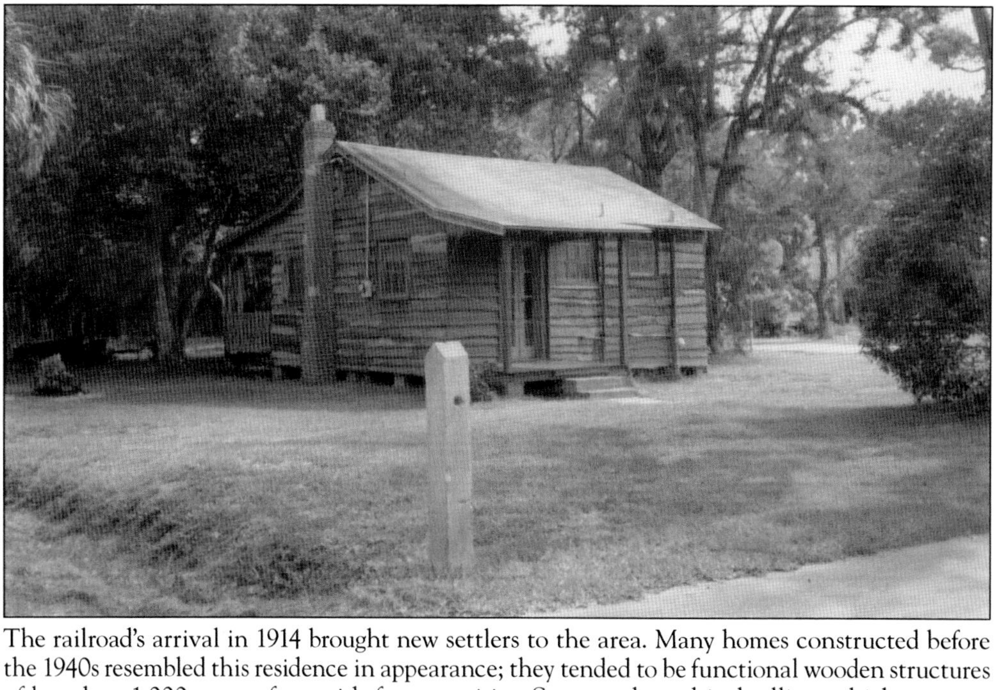

The railroad's arrival in 1914 brought new settlers to the area. Many homes constructed before the 1940s resembled this residence in appearance; they tended to be functional wooden structures of less than 1,000 square feet, with few amenities. Some such as this dwelling, which once sat along 128th Street south of Park Boulevard, remained in use long after larger homes appeared alongside them. (Lyn Friedt Collection, HV.)

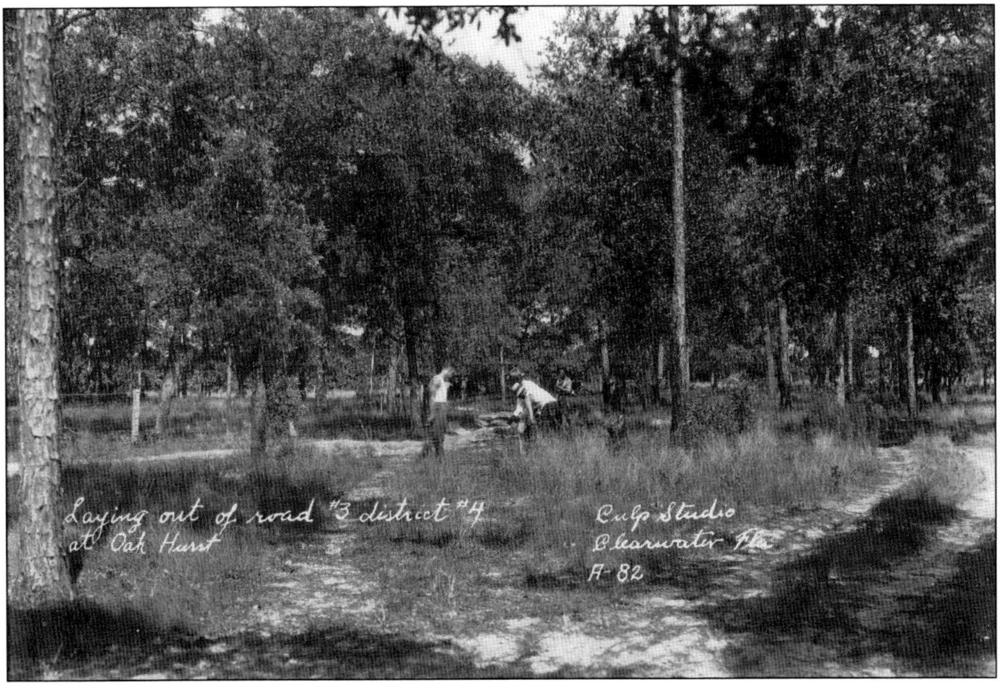

On June 5, 1923, voters countywide approved the issuing of bonds to develop a network of arterial roads throughout Pinellas County. Road No. 1 ran from Largo into western St. Petersburg at Park Street, including present-day Seminole and Bay Pines Boulevards as segments. Other projects, such as the creation of Welch Causeway and the opening of the first bridge in July 1926 to the small but developing settlements along and just north of Johns Pass that would later become Madeira Beach, brought more traffic to the Seminole area. These images illustrate the sweaty and gritty work involved in establishing rights-of-way, blasting trees, clearing the land, grading the roadway, and preparing thoroughfares for vehicular traffic in the Oakhurst area. (Both, HV.)

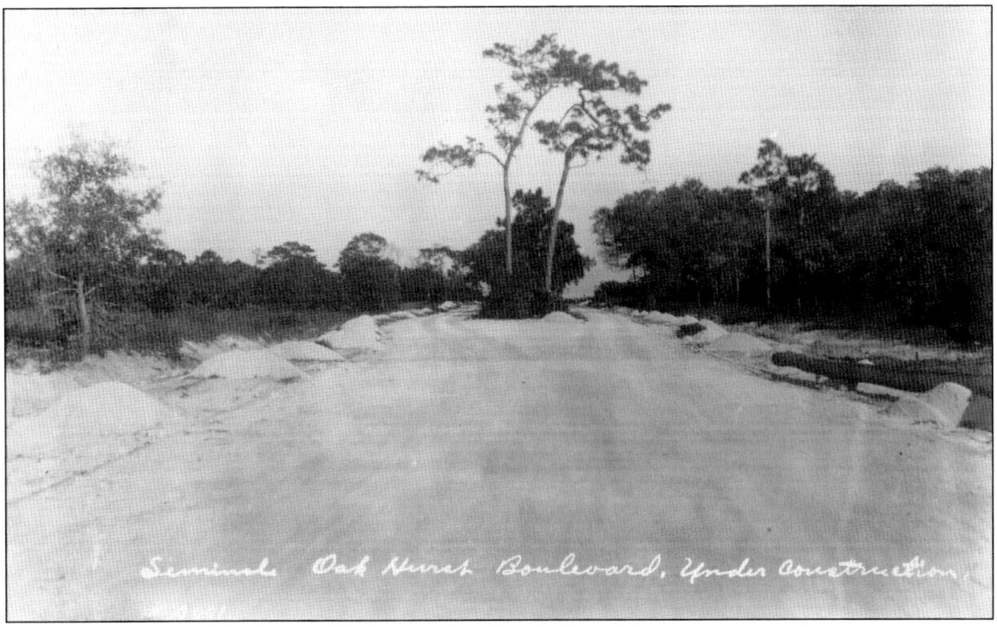

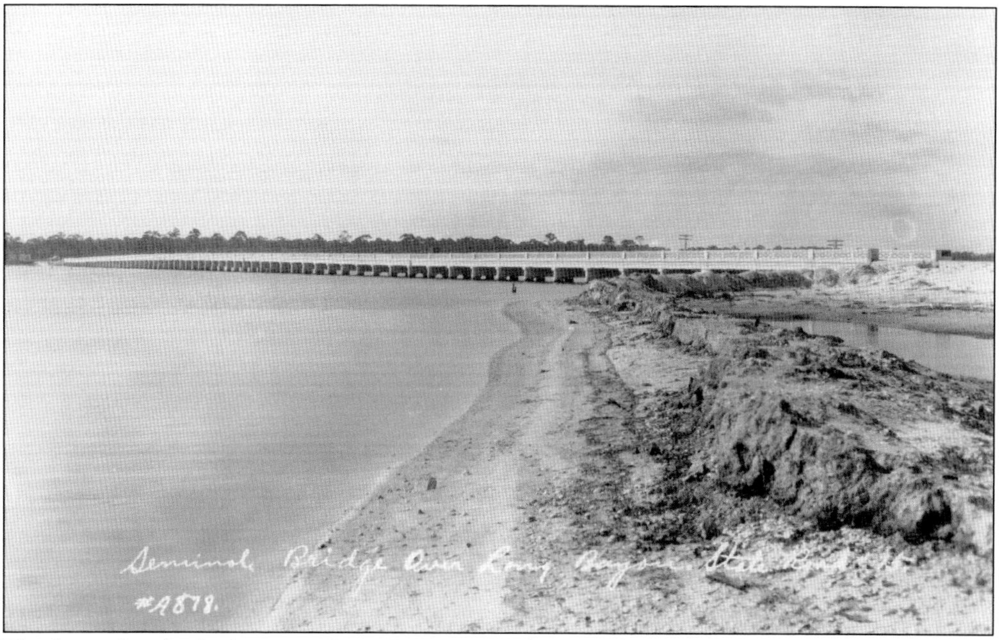

The first vehicular bridge across Long Bayou opened in 1911 but collapsed only a few months later when a man and his team of mules crossed the span in September. Indifference from the other side of Tampa Bay and in the county seat of Tampa regarding the bridge's poor construction helped to garner support for the movement to create Pinellas County. In a November 1911 referendum, voters along the Pinellas Peninsula approved a measure to secede from Hillsborough County, effective January 1, 1912. The vote in the Seminole area for independence from Hillsborough was unanimous (46-0). A replacement span opened in May 1914 but suffered irreparable damage after the October 1921 hurricane. The bridge shown here opened in 1924. The view above looks toward the northwest, and the view below looks toward Bay Pines. (Above, HV; below, THPL.)

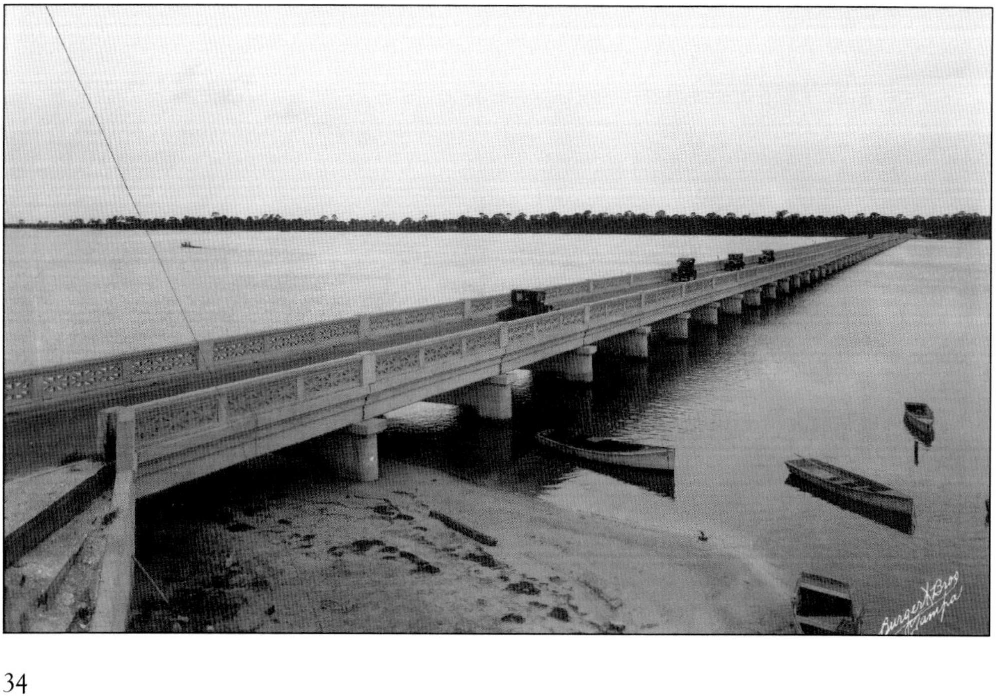

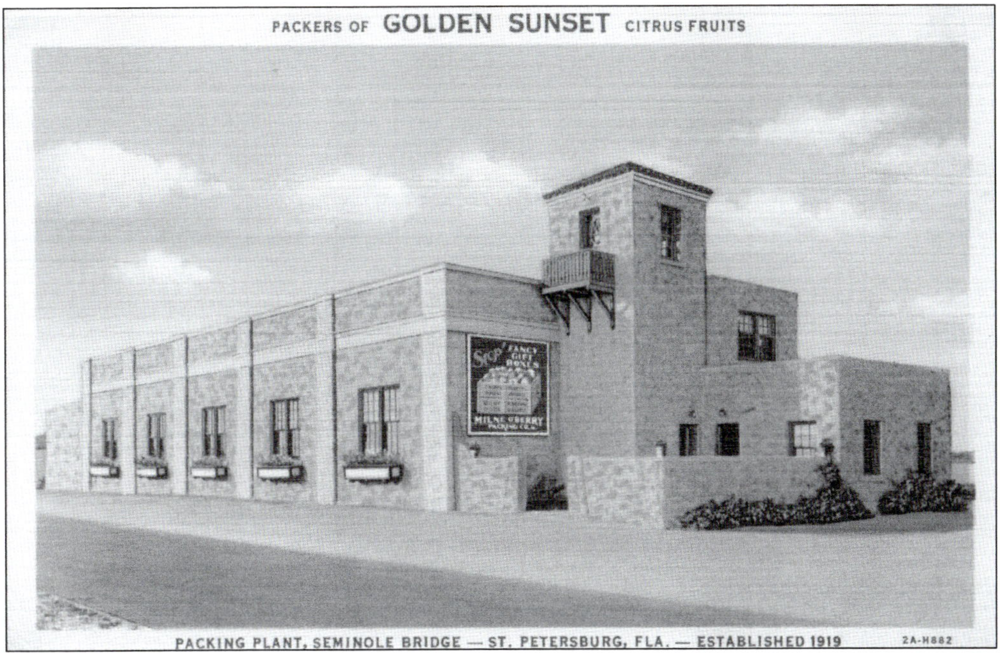

Improved roadways promoted access to an area that developers often referred to as "Seminole country" during the land boom of the late 1910s and 1920s. Promotional materials and advertisements touted the rich soils and abundant groves in Seminole at a time when Tampa and St. Petersburg enjoyed robust real estate markets. As agricultural products from Seminole and Largo filled kitchens in homes and restaurants, the citrus industry also expanded. A total of 34 packinghouses operated in Pinellas by 1927, including a large one in the Seminole area. Al Milne and Warren Holman O'Berry established the Milne-O'Berry Packing Company in St. Petersburg and erected this building at the eastern end of the Seminole Bridge. A loading dock sat along the railroad line in the rear of this mid-1920s building, one that serves a different commercial purpose 90 years later. (Above, HV; below, author.)

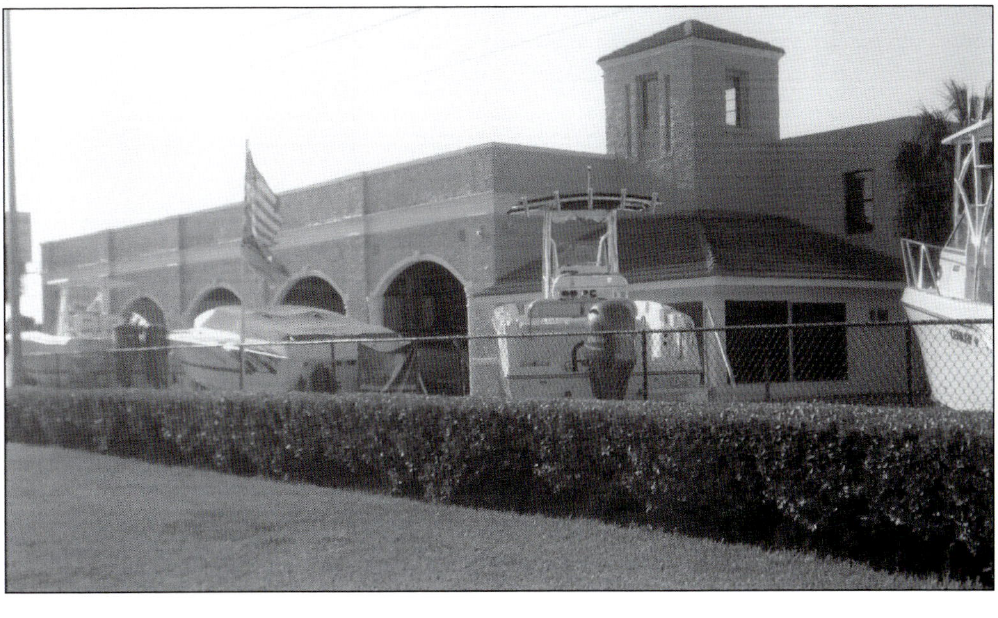

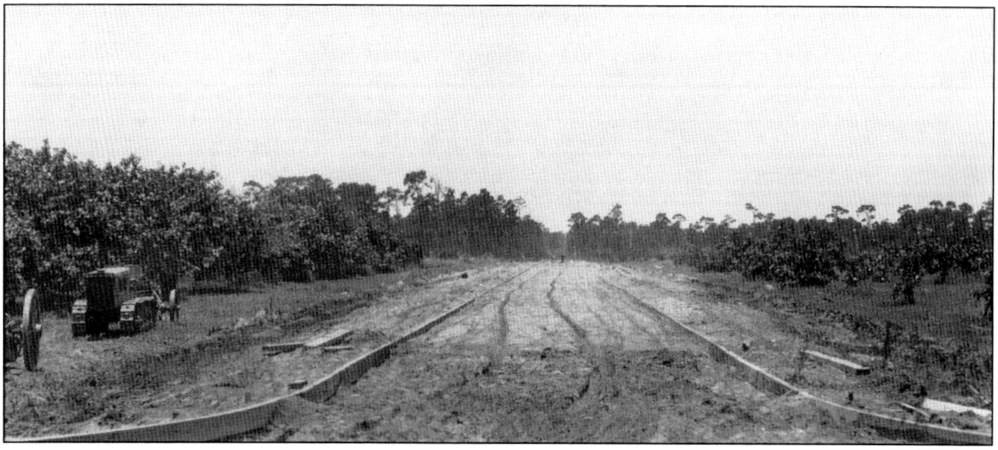

As the land boom surged in Pinellas, the firm of Anderson, Smith, and Klein announced the creation of the Seminole Estates planned community in June 1925. During the late summer and fall of 1925, advertisements saturated local newspapers here and in New England that touted this area as the next great investment in Florida. The image below shows part of a full-page ad in the September 20, 1925, issue of the *St. Petersburg Times* mentioning Seminole Estates. Also appearing at the top of the drawing is "Seminole Beach," a community planned by John Sturgis Bradbury and Thomas F. Pearce in 1914, long before Madeira Beach existed. Seminole Beach later became part of the developments created by Charles E. Redington in the 1930s. The promotion of Seminole Estates ended as the land boom faltered. (Above, HV; below, USFSP.)

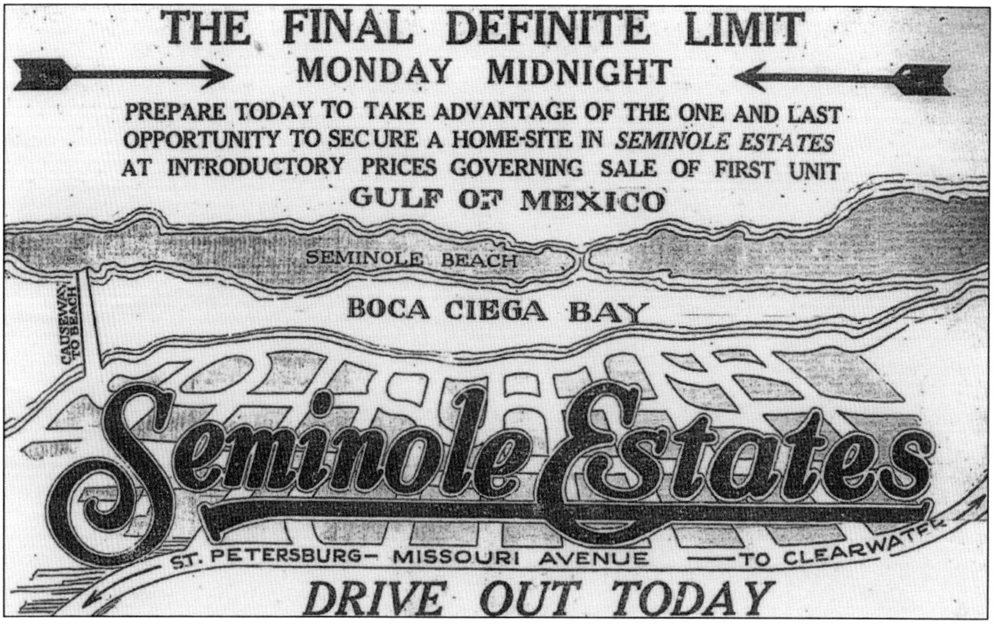

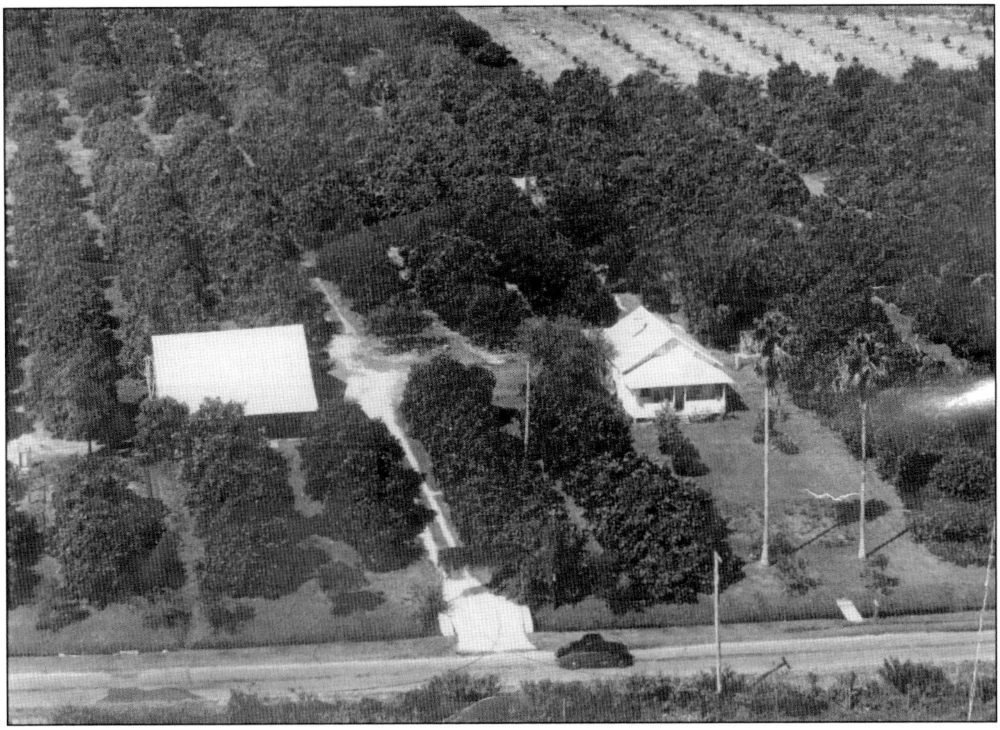

The Thurstons began cultivating groves west of the intersection of Ridge Road and 102nd Avenue in 1917. They had acquired the land from pioneer families and developed a successful business. The image above from the 1930s looks westward with Ridge Road in the foreground. The Thurston homestead along Ridge Road appears below, with the railroad tracks—now a section of the Pinellas Trail—dividing the property. By the 1960s, developers started to ask Marguerritte Thurston if she wanted to sell the property. She chased them away. As Thurston told a reporter in 1989, "My land's going to stay right here, just like it is, like it always has been." However, after she passed away in 1998, her family had no choice but to dispose of the remaining 37-acre tract to cover estate taxes. (Both, HV.)

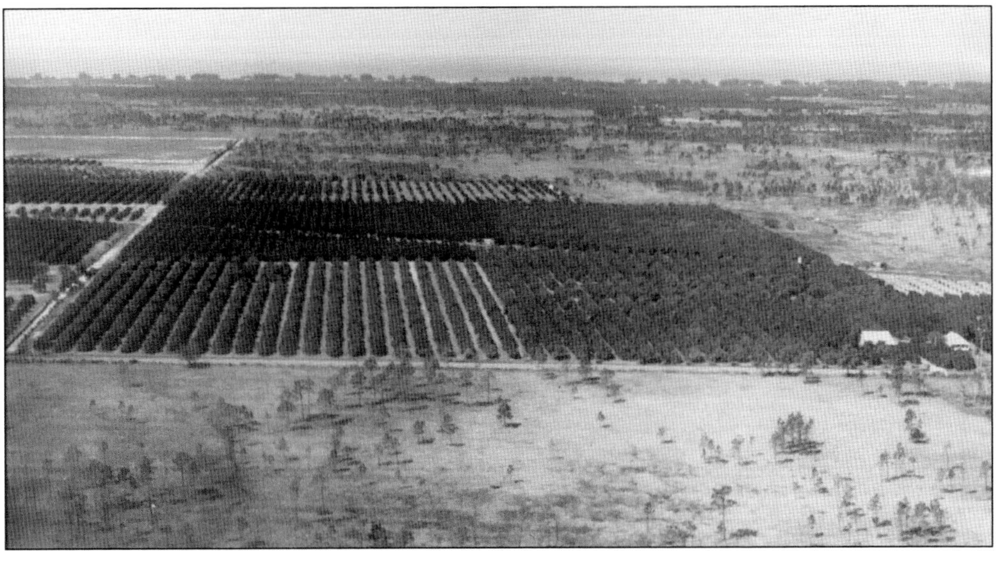

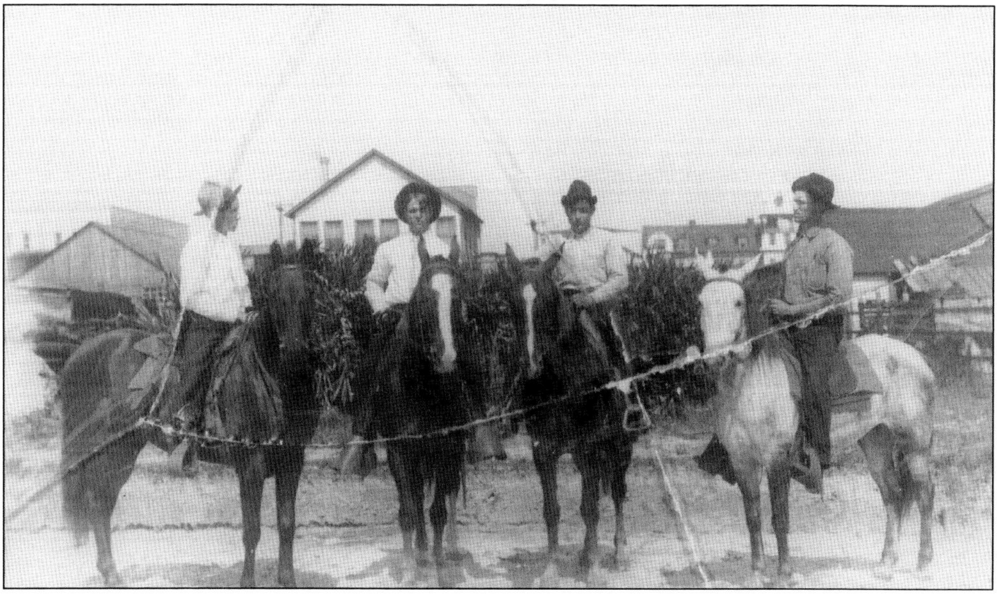

Although a Minnesota native, Jay B. Starkey had deep roots as a rancher along Florida's west coast. Born in 1895, he moved with his family to the small village of St. Petersburg as a child in March 1899. During his childhood and as a young adult, he learned about tending cattle from much older members of the McMullen and Booth families. The World War I veteran walked away from a career with the post office in St. Petersburg, trading it for 10 acres south of Largo he had acquired for a horse, cow, and $50 down payment. Above, Starkey, at far left, rides with other cowboys in downtown St. Petersburg in the early 1900s. The Detroit Hotel appears in the rear. Below, Starkey (marked with an "X" at right) joined others at his Ulmerton Ranch. (Both, HV.)

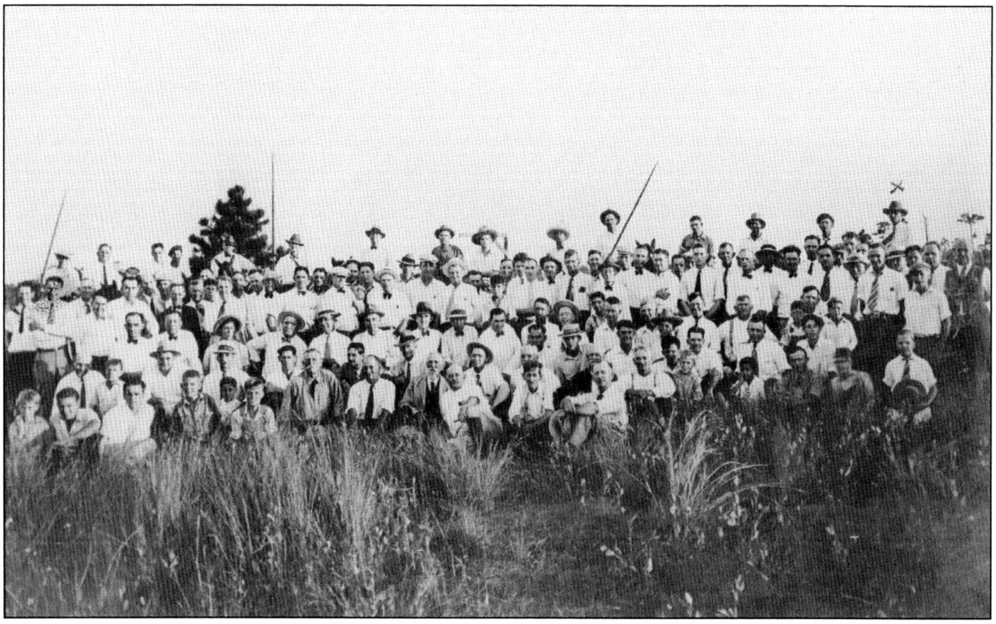

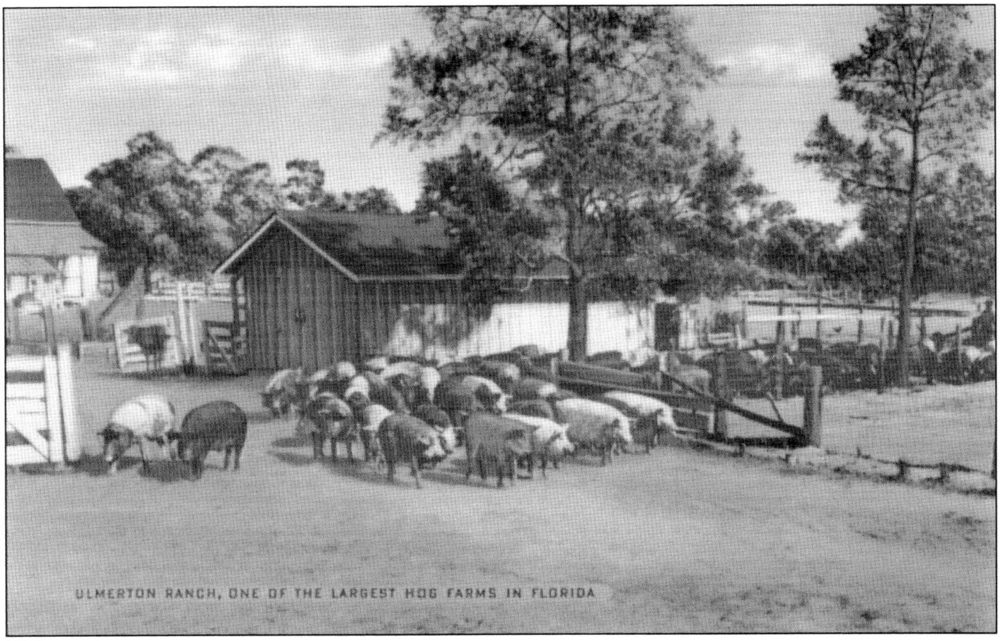

By the early 1920s, Jay B. Starkey forded livestock and horses across Long Bayou during low tide. Portions of what is now Lake Seminole were usually less than three feet deep at that time. He paid off the $1,650 owed on his land, expanded his holdings to over 300 acres by 1928, and developed Ulmerton Ranch with Dave Cunningham and his family as a 665-acre enterprise by the 1950s. The ranch began on September 1, 1924, when Starkey moved the first 300 hogs to his acreage along the eastern side of Lake Seminole. The number of hogs doubled before the end of the year. Cunningham joined him as a partner in 1927. By 1929, Starkey had introduced the first Angus, Brahman, and purebred Hereford bulls to Pinellas County. These postcards show the Ulmerton Ranch during the mid-20th century. (Both, HV.)

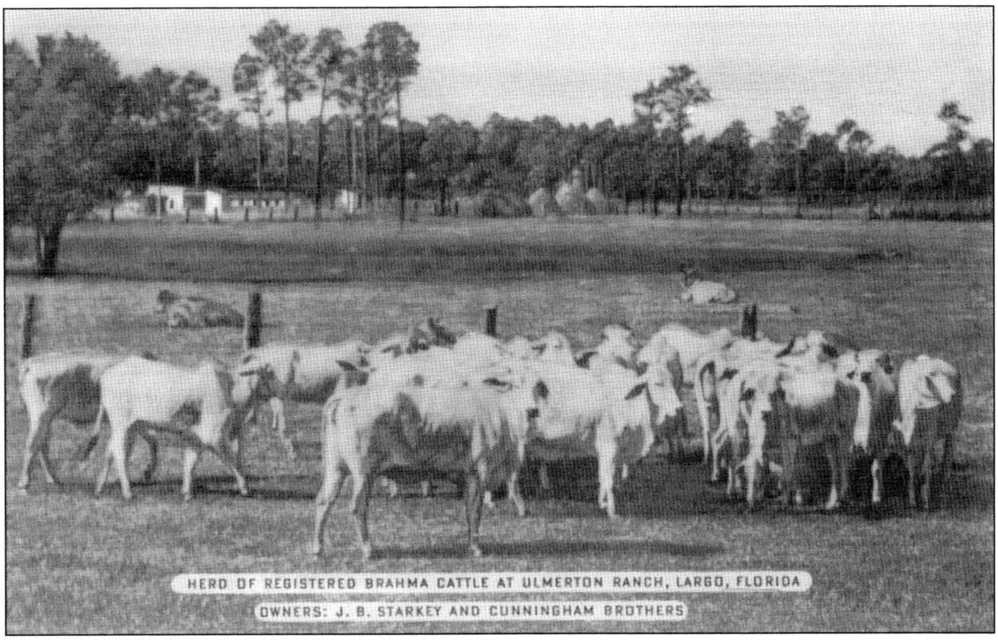

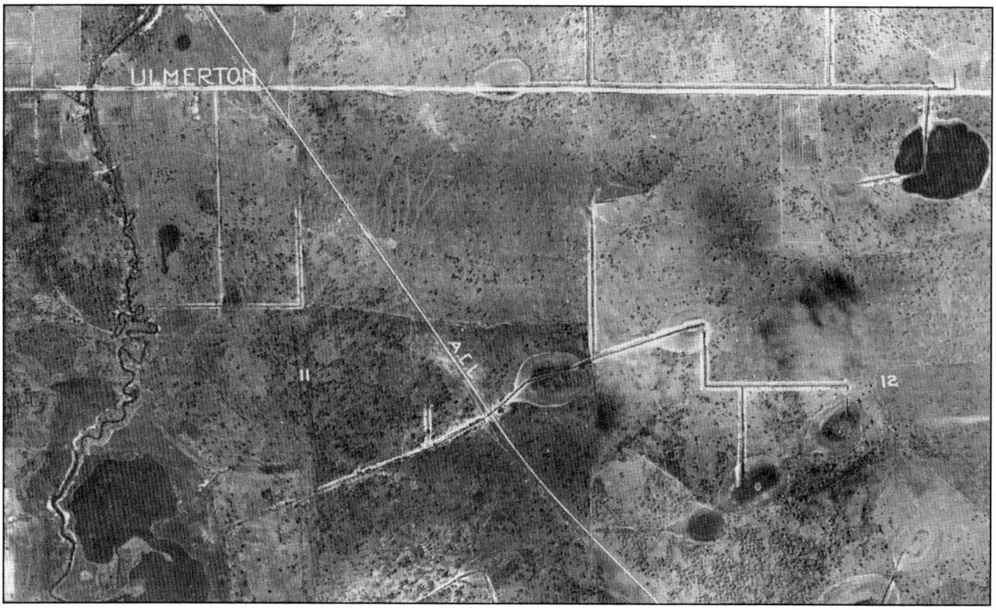

This aerial photograph from the mid-1920s follows Ulmerton Road from the eastern tip of Largo Mall (upper left), past Starkey Road, toward Belcher Road, as it appeared at that time. Tracks of the Atlantic Coast Line Railroad, formerly the Orange Belt Railway, bisect Ulmerton Road near present-day Lake Avenue. As Starkey acquired and settled on this land east of the bayou, he had few neighbors. (HV.)

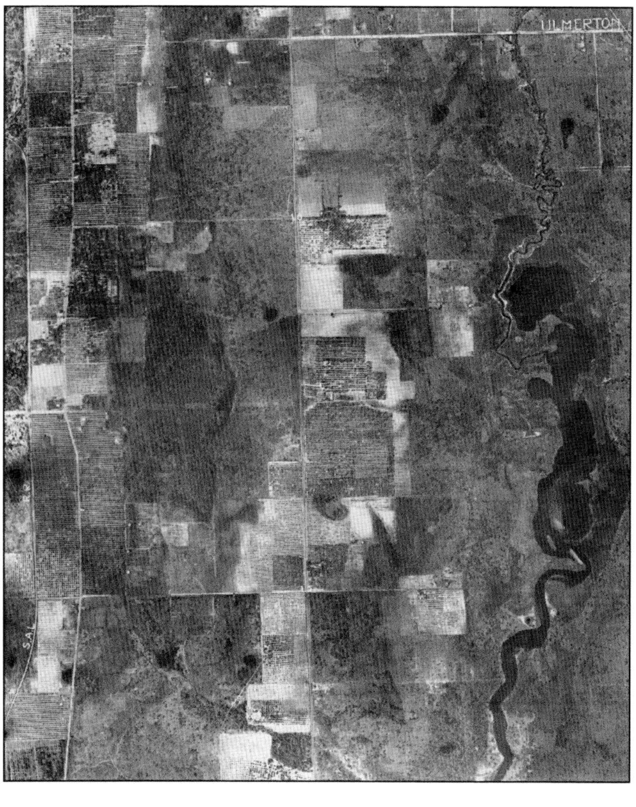

A view along the western side of Long Bayou before it became Lake Seminole from the same flight reveals large groves and few homes between Ulmerton Road, the bayou (right), 102nd Avenue North, and the Seaboard Air Line Railroad tracks (now the Pinellas Trail, left). Seminole Boulevard, still known as Missouri Avenue in the Seminole area at that time, bisects the image as the primary north-south route. (HV.)

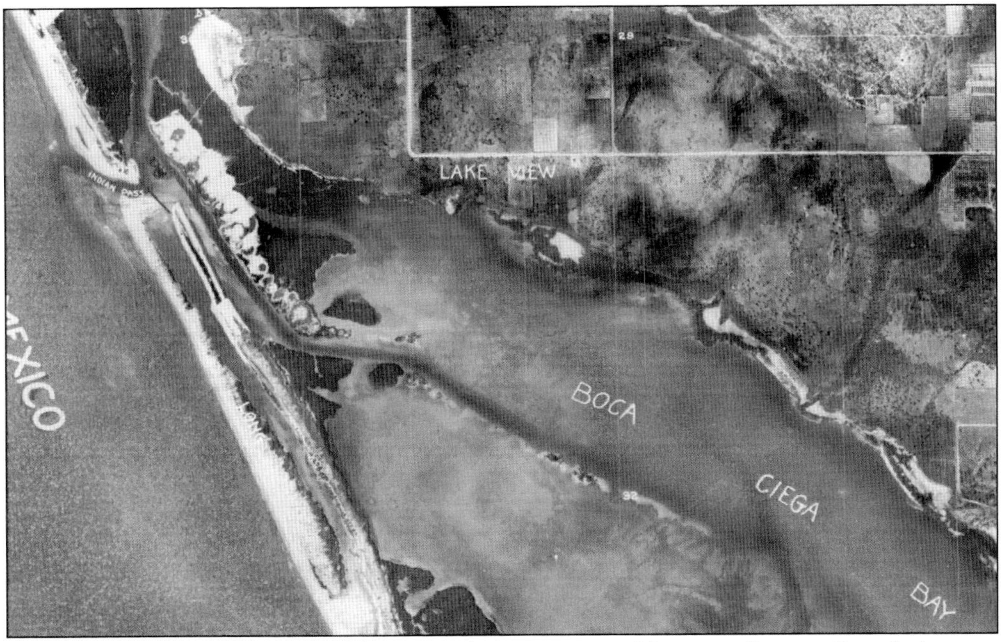

This 1926 aerial view follows Oakhurst Road as it curves and becomes Seventy-Fourth Avenue. A few groves flourished along this older section of Oakhurst Road/Seventy-Fourth Avenue near Vonn Road (now known as 131st Street). Indian Pass is clearly visible near where Boca Ciega Bay meets "the Narrows." In June 1929, engineers decided to use dredge-and-fill operations to close Indian Pass, near the present boundary of Redington Shores and Indian Shores. (HV.)

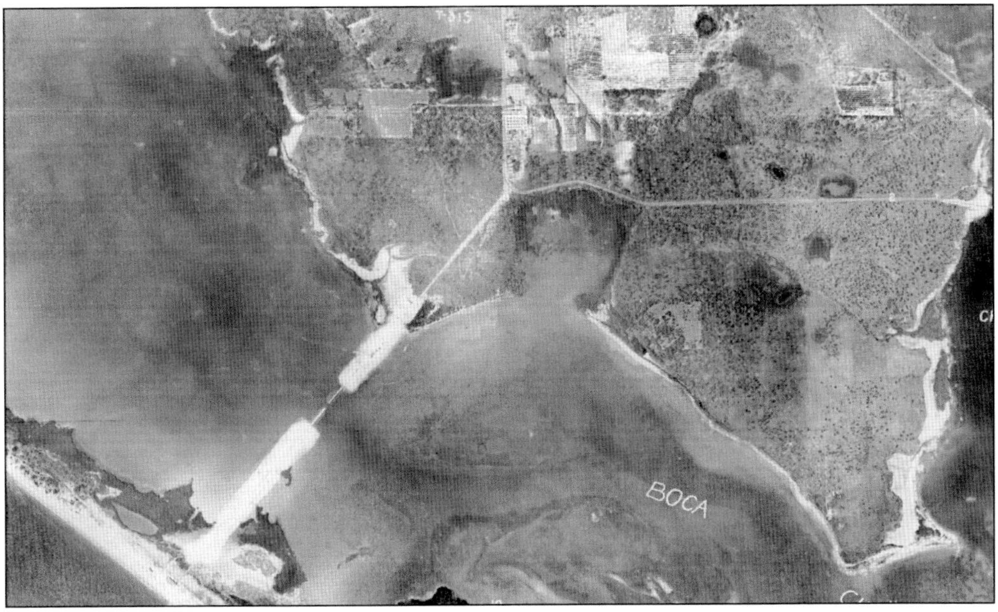

This 1926 overflight revealed groves along Fifty-Fourth Avenue at the top of the image, on both sides of Missouri Avenue, now Seminole Boulevard. Dredges had pumped sand on both approaches to Welch Causeway, allowing motor vehicles to take the toll-free bridge to lands under development by Albert Archibald and David Welch that later became Madeira Beach. Note that the present location of Madeira Beach Fundamental School remained underwater. (HV.)

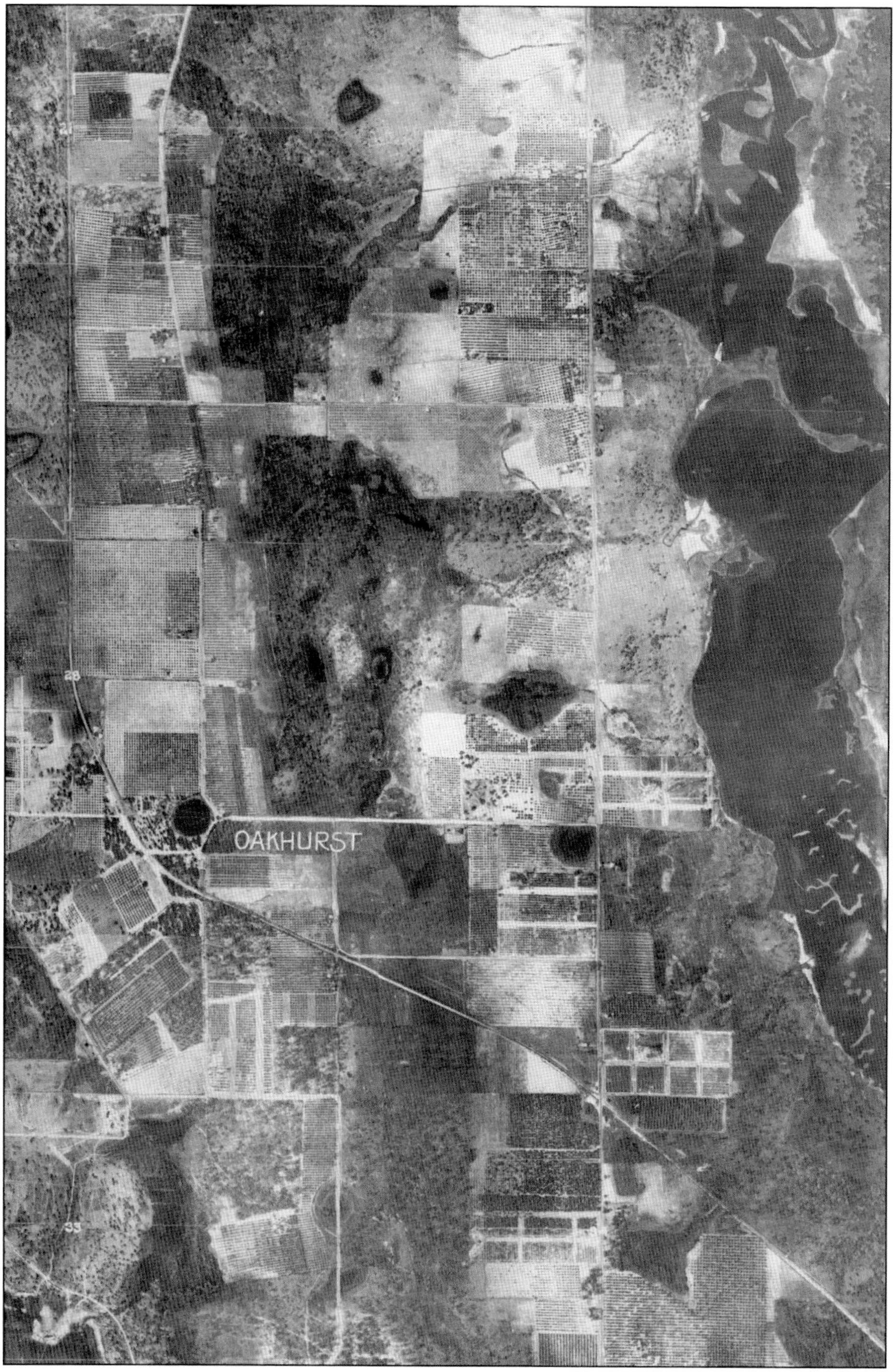

A glance at the region between Fifty-Fourth and 102nd Avenues reveals the importance of groves and agriculture in the Seminole area during the mid-1920s. Substantial groves with trees neatly planted in rows and columns predominated. Before Park Boulevard cut across Long Bayou to form Lake Seminole, shallow areas were found throughout the saltwater marshland. (HV.)

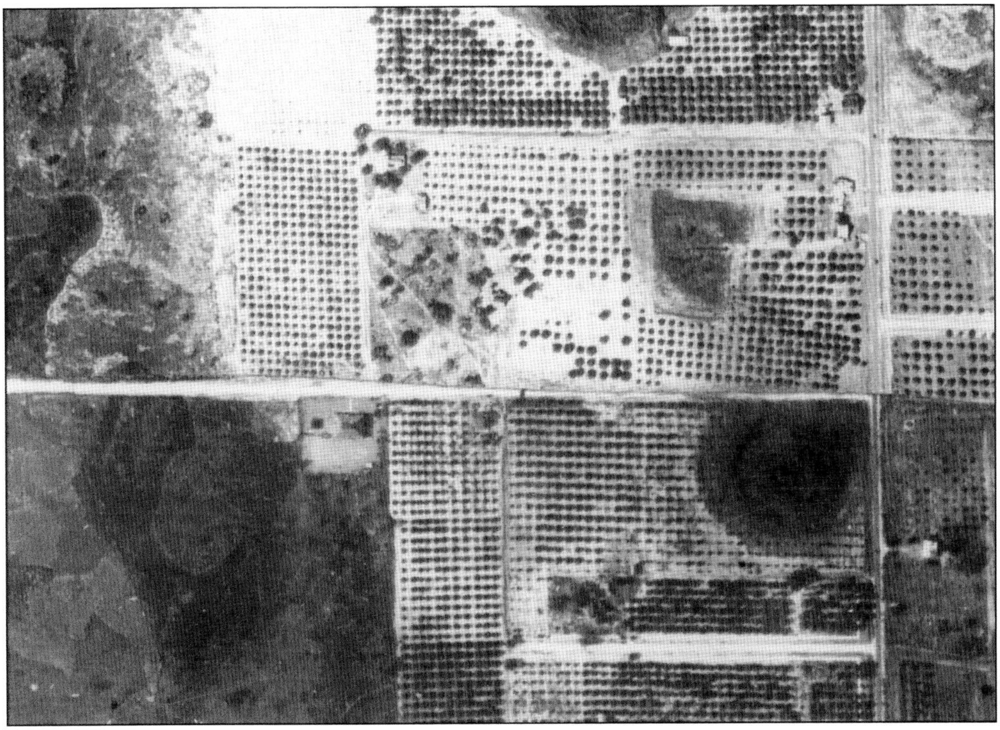

Seminole Elementary School opened in 1915 at its present site along Park Boulevard, then a dirt path extension of Oakhurst Road. The campus moved from an earlier site on the Thevenets' land (see page 13) near the present location of the Seminole cabin. Members of the Campbell, Meares, and Thevenet families served as the school's trustees in 1914 when planning began for the redbrick building with two classrooms and two restrooms. The 1926 aerial view above shows the school campus, left center, with groves to the north and east. Fundraisers during the early years included popular fish and oyster suppers, along with ice cream socials. The campus has expanded since the 1950s, with more classrooms and other facilities added. In preparation for the original building's centennial, workers restored the exterior in 2014–2015, as shown below. (Above, HV; below, author.)

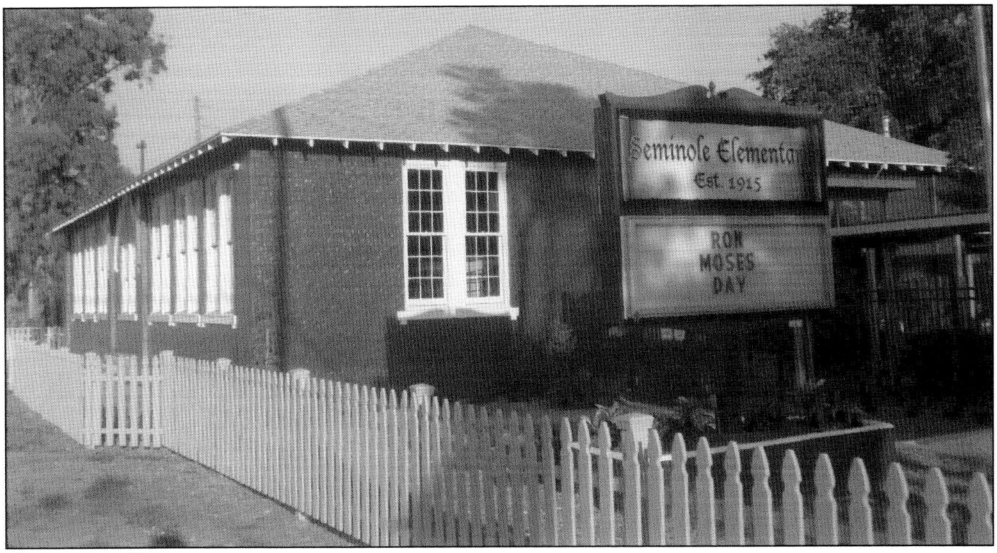

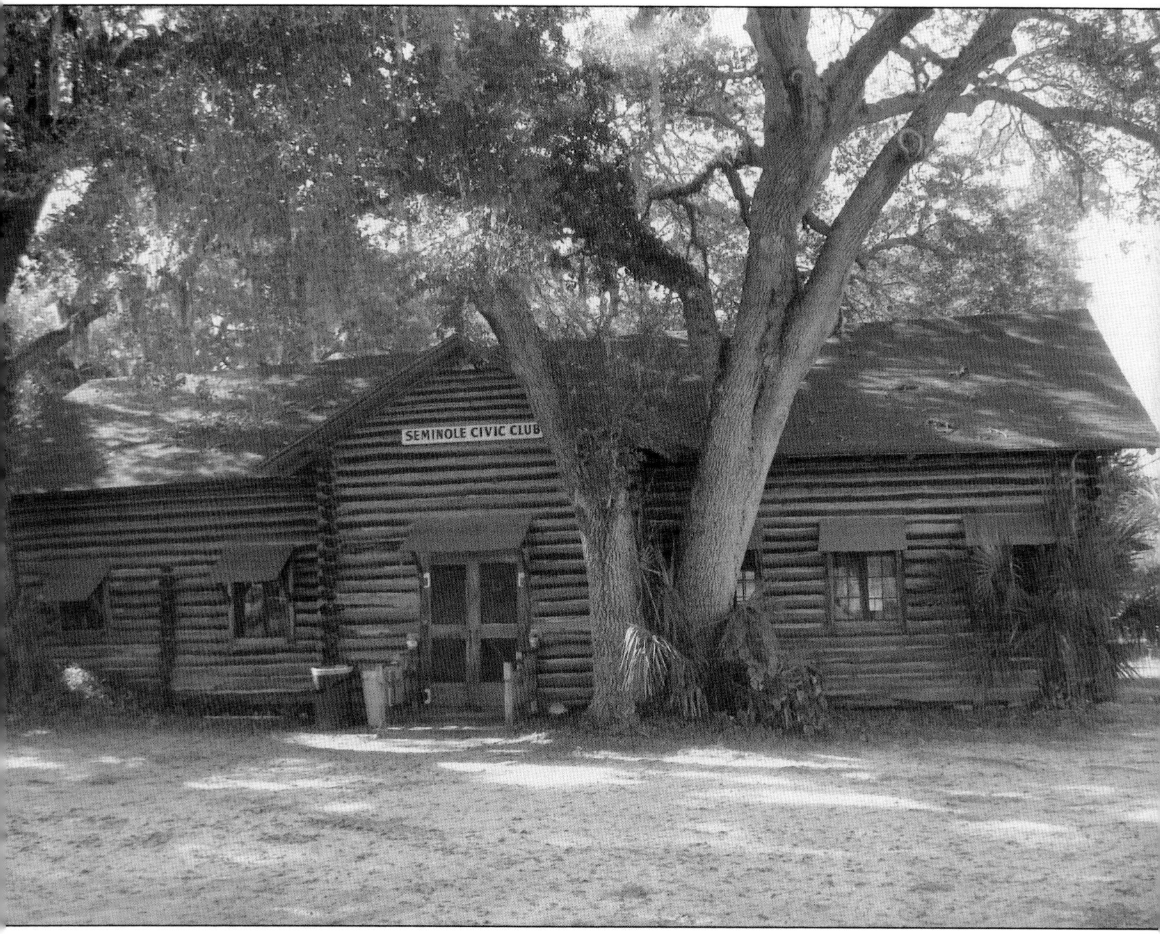

Many residents believe that the Seminole Cabin, located across Fifty-Fourth Avenue from the Seminole Methodist Church and near the intersection with Seminole Boulevard, dates back to the 1800s. Rustic in appearance, the cabin's origins are actually in the mid-1930s as a federal works project during the Great Depression. With congressional funding as part of President Franklin D. Roosevelt's New Deal, workers prepared the site in 1934 under the auspices of the Federal Emergency Relief Administration, predecessor to the Works Progress Administration. During the summer, they ran into a delay due to some difficulties in securing logs. Francis Leon (F. Leon) Campbell took a lead in the project. Jesse Johnson, connected by marriage to the Campbells since 1925, provided logs from his land near the Seminole Mall area to move things forward and end the delay. Finishing touches took place in 1935 as members of the Seminole Civic Club celebrated the completion of this cabin. (Author.)

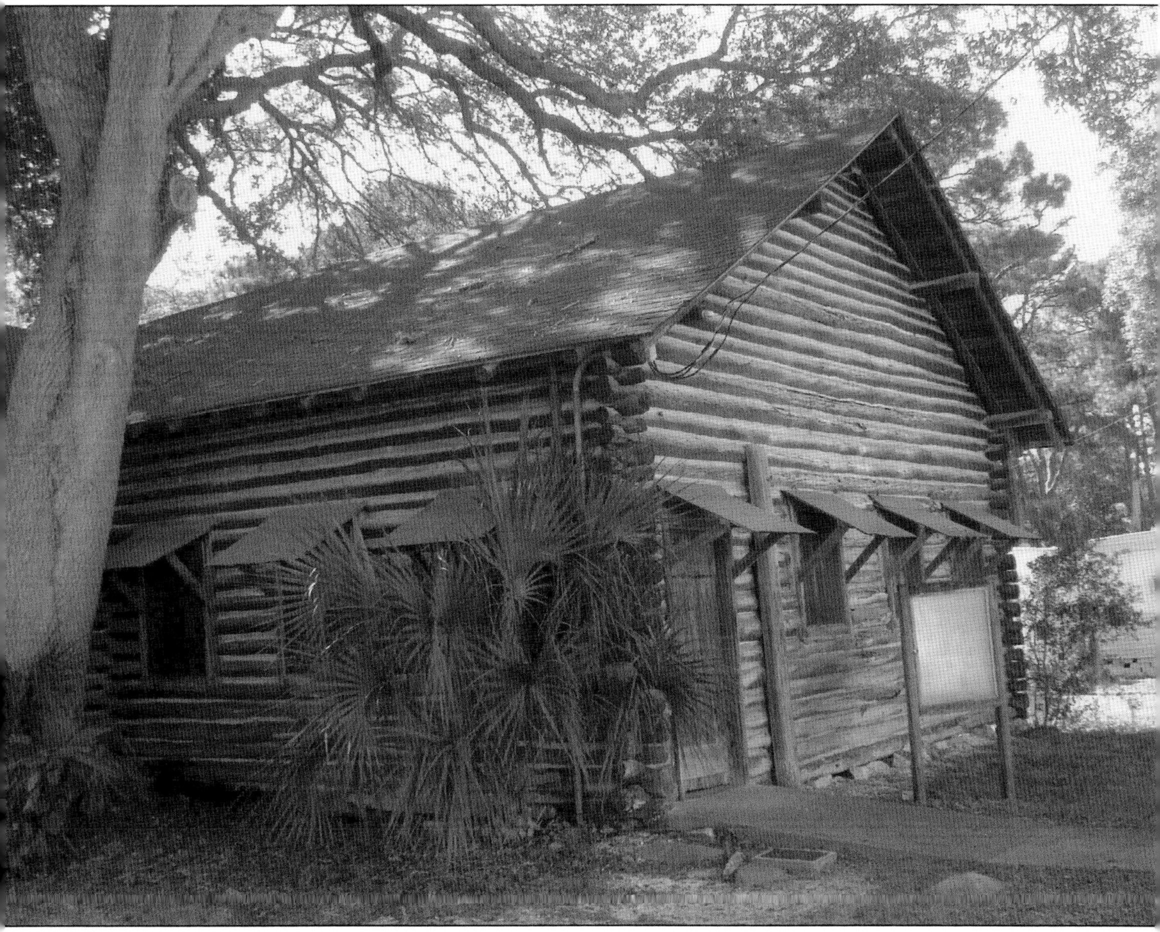

From the mid-1930s forward, the Seminole Cabin has hosted social events and gatherings for the families in the area. Sometimes known as the Seminole Community House, the cabin has hosted fish fries, potluck suppers, Boy Scout troop meetings, and a variety of other events. A polling place for the Seminole area during its early years, the cabin became the headquarters for women in the Seminole chapter of the American Red Cross who congregated to assemble surgical dressings as part of the domestic effort during World War II. Reunions of the Campbells and other pioneer families overcrowded the structure. In mid-1954, the leadership of the Seminole Civic Club approved a measure to turn the structure over to Seminole Methodist Church. Civic Club board members Ray Nash, Leon Campbell, Jesse Johnson, Bill Johnson, Arnett Brown, and Carlton Beard voted unanimously to deed the club to the church. Now more than 80 years old, the cabin continues to serve the community into the new millennium. (Author.)

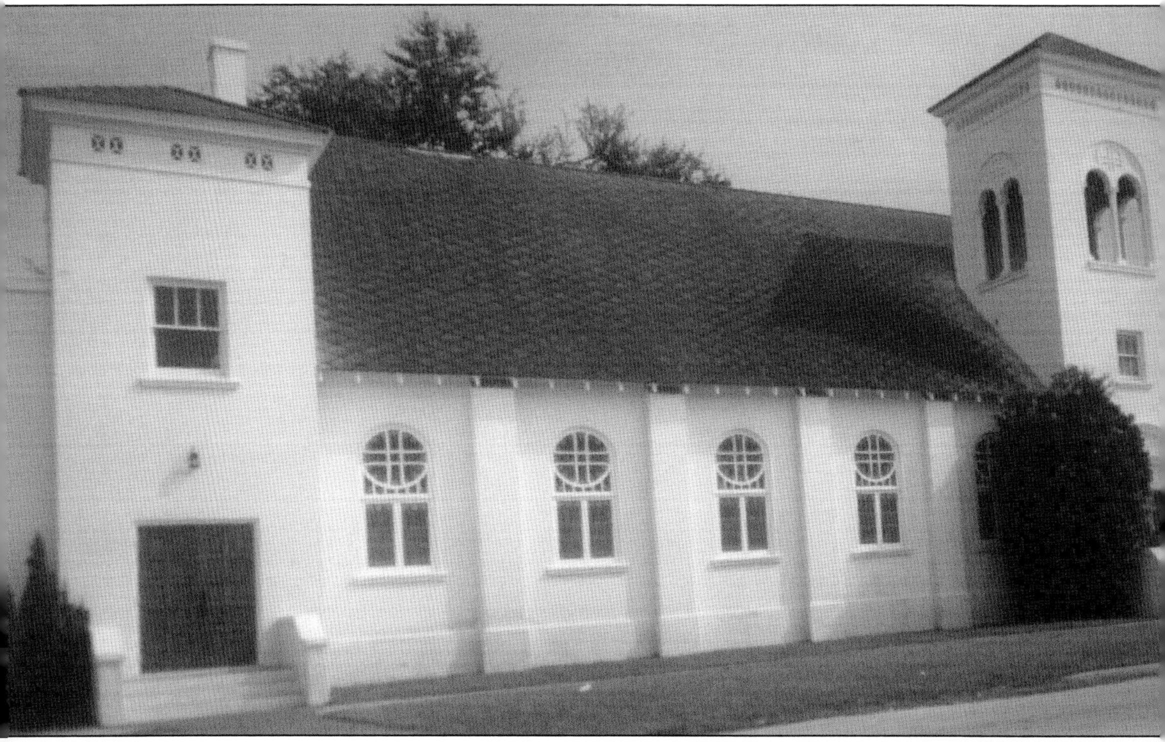

The violent hurricane of October 1921 leveled Marvin's Chapel, shown on page 14, though the adjacent parsonage survived the storm. The members temporarily held services at the 1915 Seminole schoolhouse until they erected a bungalow structure as their second church, with the first service by Rev. C.W. Cotton on Thanksgiving Day 1924. The new structure took on the name Seminole United Methodist Church. As the congregation grew, an effort to expand the chapel began in July 1937. Members of the Cobb, Campbell, Johnson, and Whittle families took the lead. The chapel at the intersection of Seminole Boulevard and Fifty-Fourth Avenue opened in 1938, connected to the 1924 building. A new sanctuary for Seminole United Methodist Church took shape to the immediate west in the late 1950s, with subsequent additions to the campus added thereafter. (SHS.)

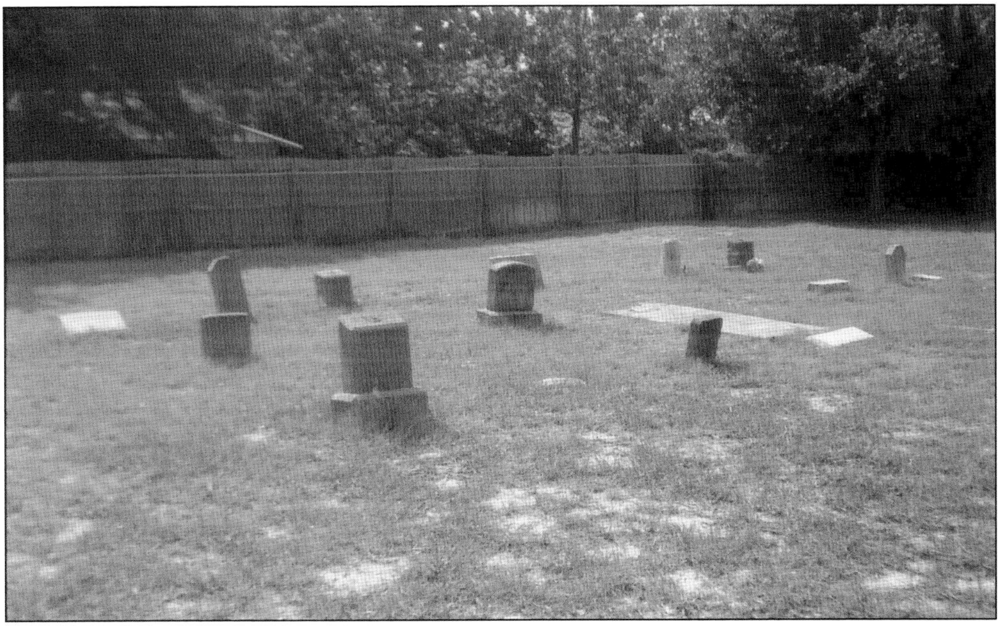

Visitors to Garden Sanctuary, south of Eighty-Second Avenue and west of 131st Street, may wonder about the small group of older headstones on the west end of the property (above). Although racial segregation prevented African Americans from living in much of the Oakhurst area, a five-acre plot on this site became known as "Memorial Cemetery (Colored)" or Oakhurst Cemetery during the late 1920s. Black families from St. Petersburg buried loved ones here, though few records were kept and many sites were unmarked. In November 1953, bulldozers leveled headstones in Oakhurst as workers planned to establish a whites-only Oak Hill Cemetery on adjacent land. At one point, to protect the remaining headstones in the old Oakhurst Cemetery tract, the owner installed barbed wire to deter vandals who desecrated these graves, which were here first. (Both, author.)

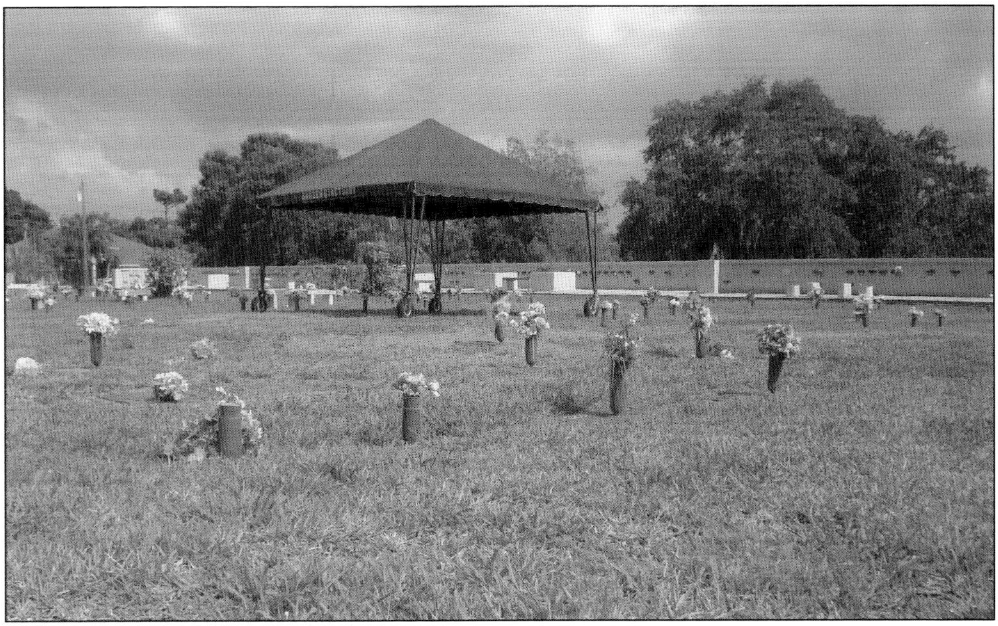

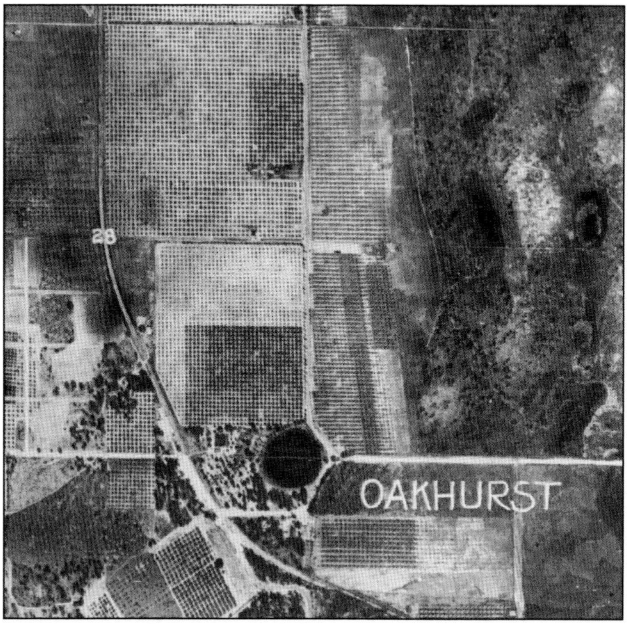

While developers in St. Petersburg leveled groves in neighborhoods such as Bartlett Park, Childs Park, Kenwood, Lakeview, and unincorporated Lealman to build homes during the real estate boom of the 1920s, the groves in Oakhurst and Seminole continued to expand. Lake Meares, now the site of Seminole City Park, appears in the lower center. The future site of Seminole Mall occupies the upper-right corner of this image. (HV.)

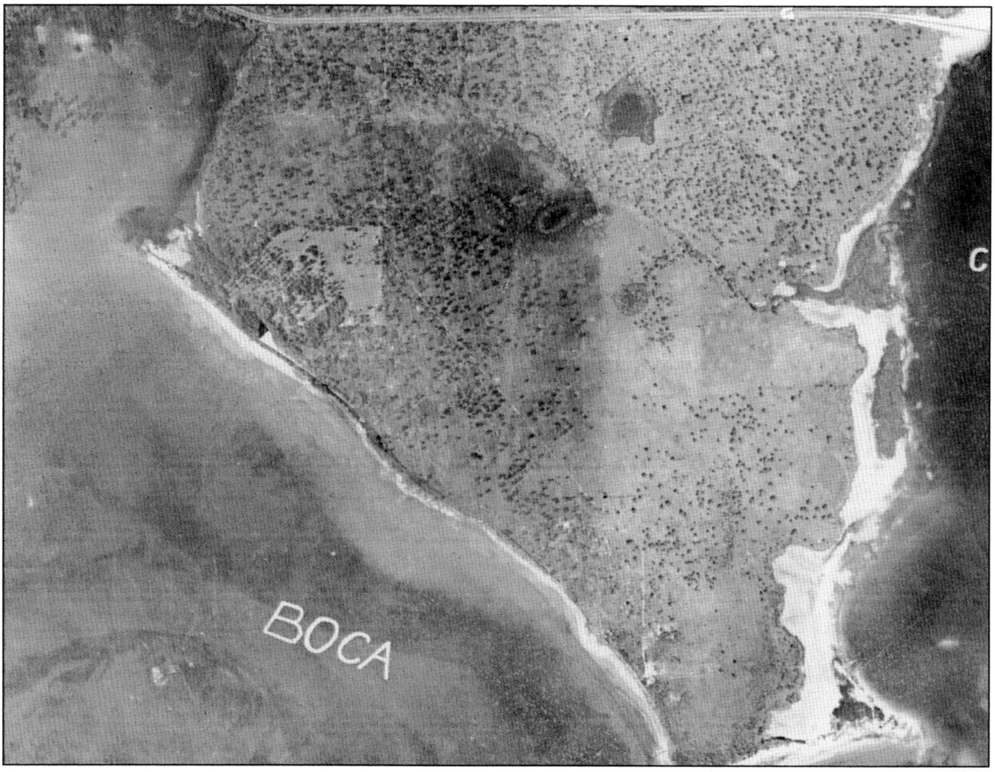

During the 1920s, few people lived on or near Seminole Point, a large tract of land between Hurricane Hole on the upper left, Boca Ciega Bay, and Long Bayou. As plans moved forward to build a federal soldiers' home for recuperating World War I veterans, authorities selected this site in May 1931. Two months later, county commissioners approved a financing plan to acquire the parcel. (HV.)

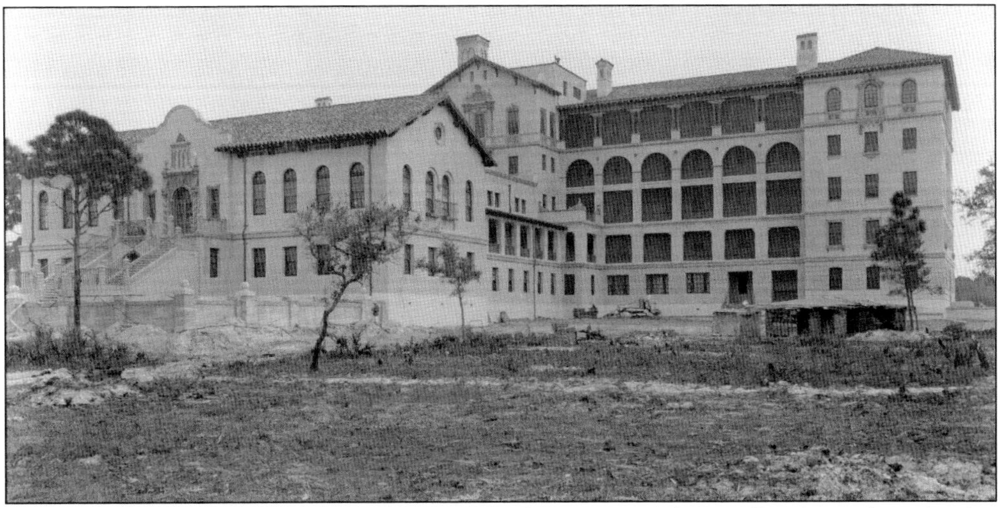

The Great Depression hit Florida hard. Cities such as St. Petersburg suffered significantly after the robust land boom of the 1920s turned into an economic malaise that saddled Florida with the highest per-capita debt in the nation. Soon after the selection of Seminole Point as the location of the National Home for Disabled Volunteer Soldiers in 1931, nearly 800 Pinellas County workers began clearing the land and constructing the first buildings. The images here show Building No. 1, the main hospital structure and one of the first buildings completed in January 1933. The campus included its own well system for freshwater, a power plant, a post office, and public safety facilities. The "Bay Pines" designation came on June 15, 1934, when the soldiers' home became the Bay Pines Veterans Hospital. (Bay Pines VA Collection.)

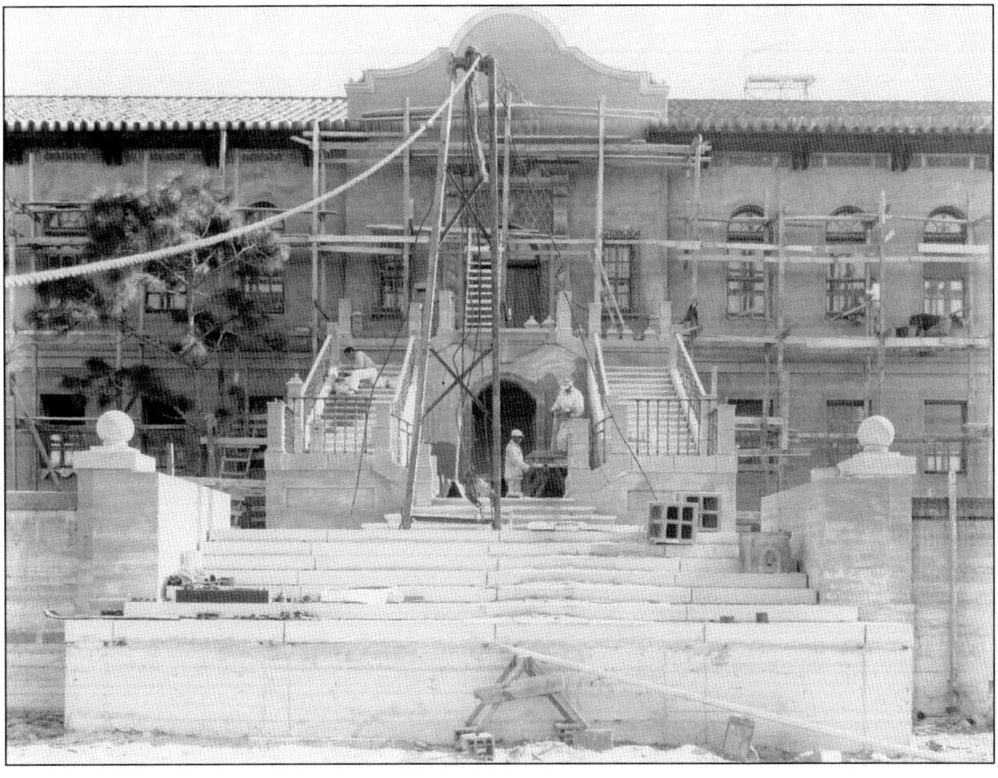

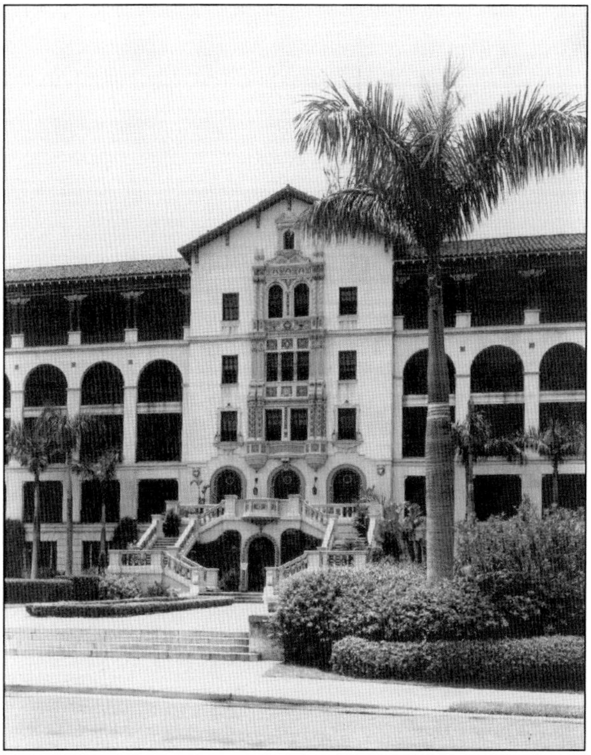

Building No. 1, shown here shortly after its completion, remains in operation more than 80 years after opening for its first patients. Construction continued throughout the 1930s at a steady pace, as new treatment facilities, housing, and medical wings served a growing number of veterans. Although projects stalled out of necessity during World War II, an influx of veterans during the postwar years led to further expansion. (Bay Pines VA Collection.)

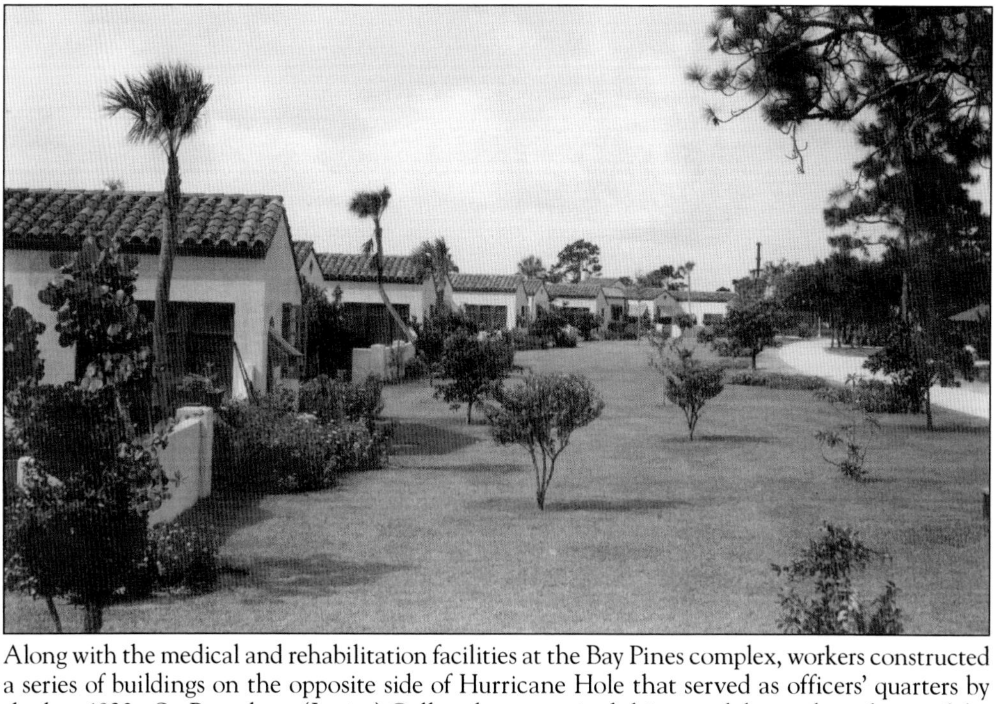

Along with the medical and rehabilitation facilities at the Bay Pines complex, workers constructed a series of buildings on the opposite side of Hurricane Hole that served as officers' quarters by the late 1930s. St. Petersburg (Junior) College later acquired this parcel, located northeast of the elementary school classrooms of Madeira Fundamental School, with plans to develop a marine science facility along the lagoon. (Bay Pines VA Collection.)

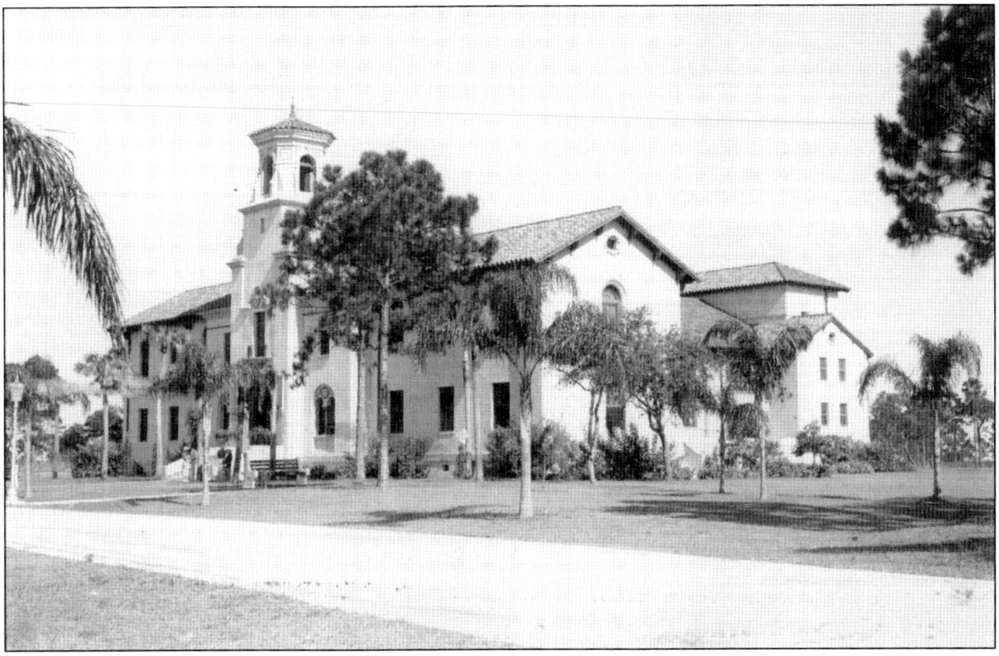

Finished in 1935, this recreation building (known as Building No. 20) offered injured soldiers a site for rehabilitation. In addition, Alex Archibald and David Welch, developers of Madeira Beach, donated a 500-foot stretch of land along the Gulf of Mexico as a private beach for veterans. That site, later known as Archibald Park, is now open to the public. (Bay Pines VA Collection.)

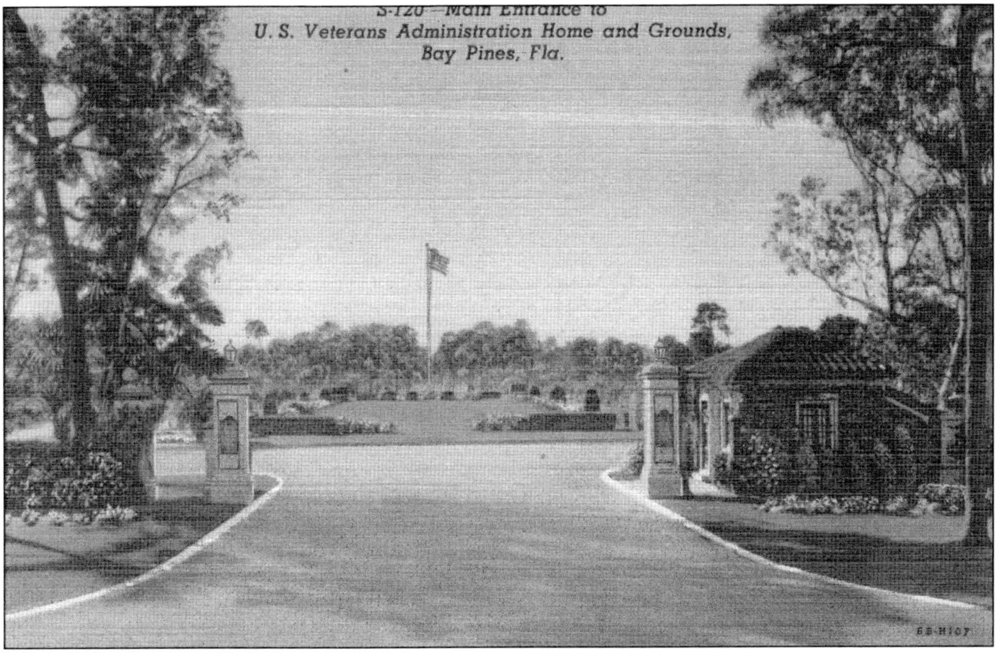

This postcard offers a view of the main entrance to the Bay Pines VA Hospital at the intersection of Bay Pines Boulevard and 100th Way as it would have appeared during the mid-20th century. The guard station remained in place until many years later. By the 1970s, the landscape began to change as new buildings took shape on the site. (HV.)

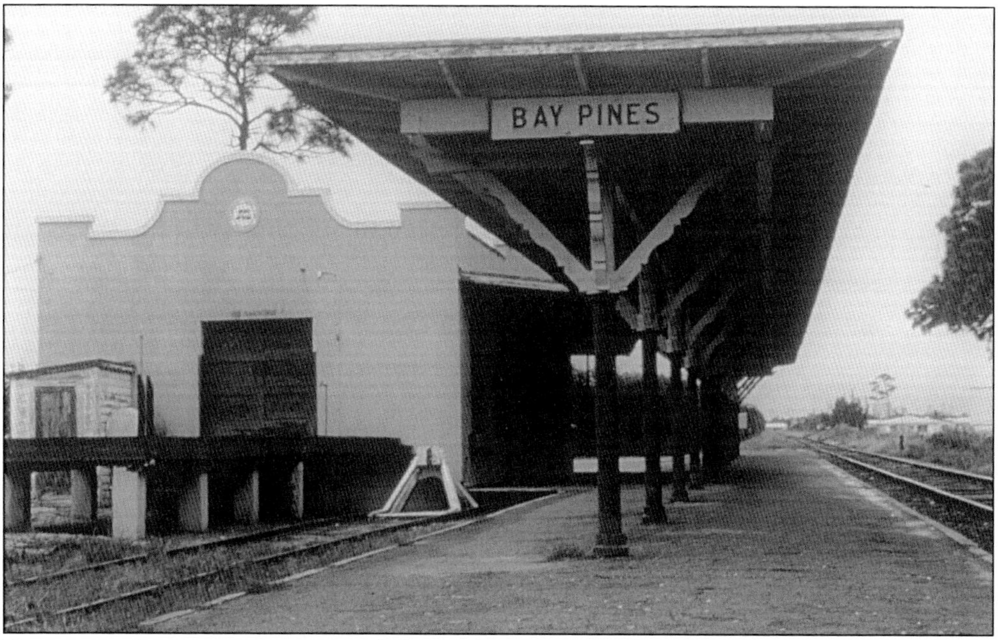

To support the growing campus and those who convalesced at Bay Pines, architects designed a railroad depot at the north end of 100th Way. The structure opened in 1933 for use by those affiliated with the hospital. As time progressed, cargo and fruit shippers brought their commodities to this depot, and the Silver Star and Silver Meteor trains also offered occasional passenger service during the tourist season. The depot closed in the spring of 1968. The photograph above shows the depot shortly before its demolition in the early 1970s, and the image below offers a similar perspective of the same site from the Fred Marquis Pinellas Trial. The depot sat at the site of the private residence on the left. Until 1967, a separate spur of the railroad brought freight directly to Building No. 11 at Bay Pines. (Above, Bay Pines VA Collection; below, author.)

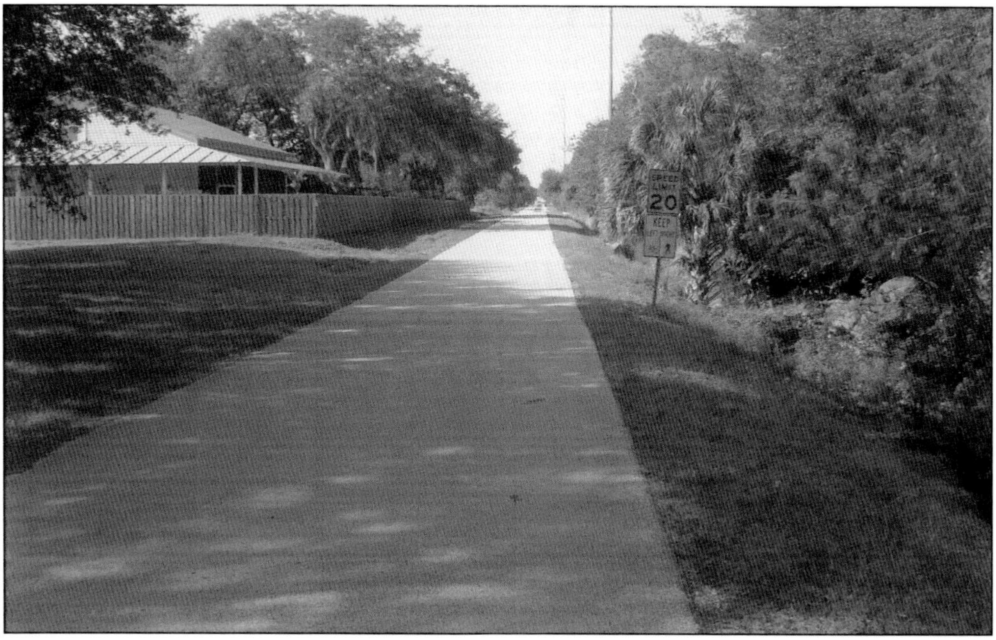

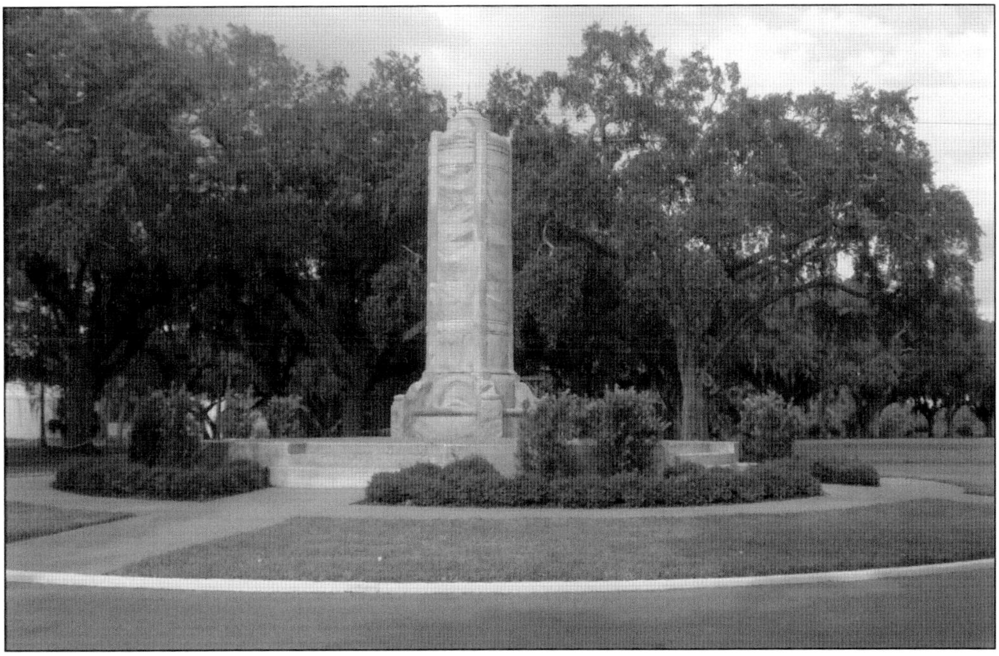

Some who traveled to Bay Pines by rail or motor vehicle made it their final resting place. Officials set aside a 21-acre site at the soldiers' home for use as a cemetery. Dedicated on March 15, 1933, the first burial at the Bay Pines National Cemetery occurred on April 25 of that year. A pink marble monument erected at the entrance to the cemetery in 1937 (above) serves as a reminder of the service those interred on the grounds gave to their country. The cemetery originally filled to capacity in January 1964. Twenty years later, workers removed many hedges between the original 42 sections to provide room for additional burials. The cemetery was listed in the National Register of Historic Places on June 27, 2012. (Both, author.)

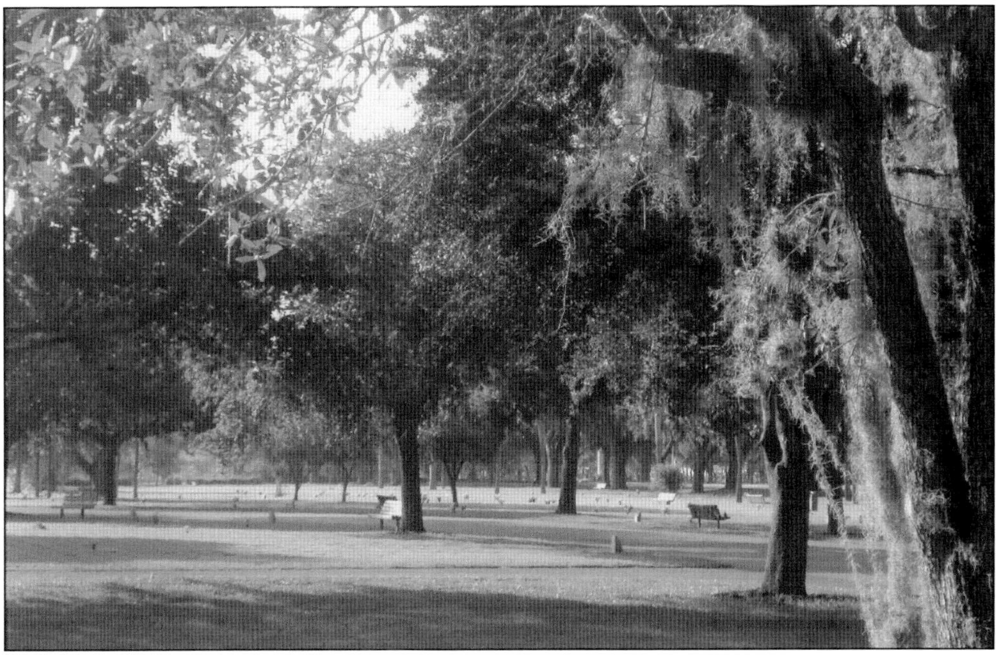

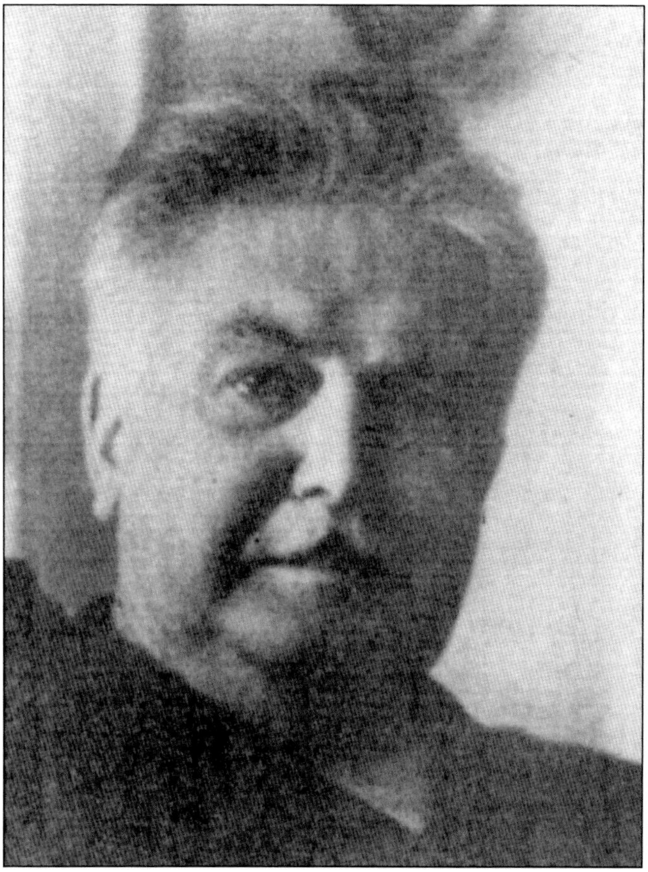

A native of Cincinnati, Frank Duhme came to the Seminole area at the age of 17 in 1910. In time, he acquired approximately 40 acres near where Duhme Road curves between Madeira Beach and Fifty-Fourth Avenue. He constructed a house near the small pond visible along the eastern side of the road and transformed much of his land by planting a variety of exotic species. Proprietor of a fruit packing business, Duhme also uncovered many fossil specimens on his land that he turned over to archaeologists. Duhme claimed that many notable visitors came to his place, often to examine the gardens. The guest list included Calvin Coolidge, Thomas Edison, Harvey Firestone, Henry Ford, and Sir Arthur Conan Doyle. (Both, HV.)

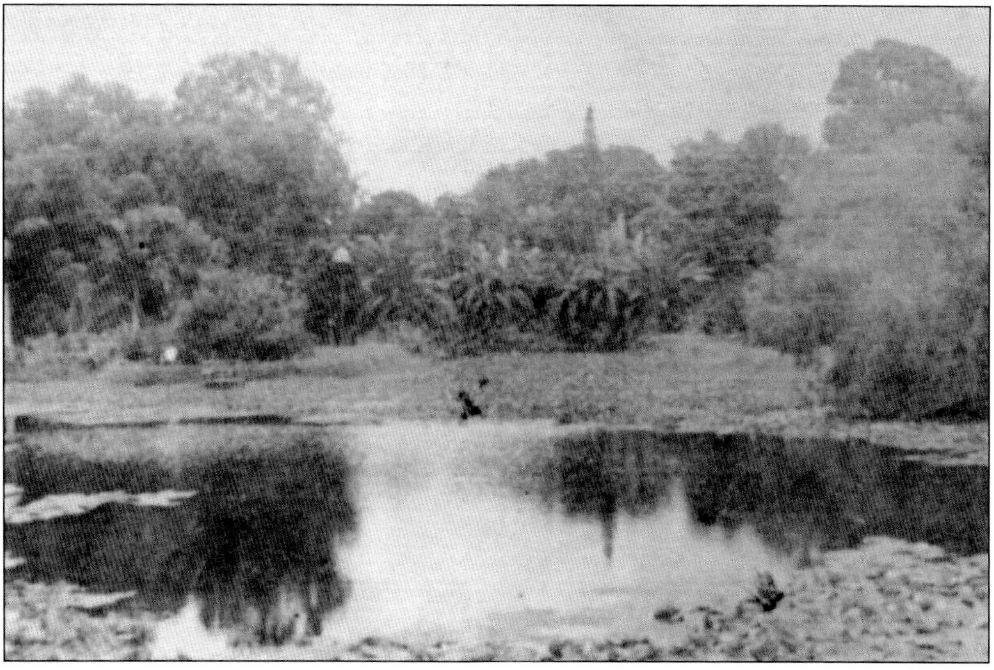

Jesse Wilder Johnson hailed from the pioneer Dieffenwierth and Johnson families of Largo. Born in the Largo area in 1904, he attended the University of Florida, returned with his degree in horticulture, and opened a nursery. He married Sarah Marjorie Campbell, of the Campbell pioneer family in the Seminole area. The Johnsons had four children (Richard, Marilyn, Christine, and Linda), but in reality they became "family" to nearly everyone in Seminole. The family's nursery business and banking interests allowed the economy to expand. A conservationist, Jesse Wilder Johnson realized the value of creating a freshwater lake in the northern section of Long Bayou. Some of his lands became Seminole Mall. Johnson's role in promoting the incorporation of Seminole led to him receiving the title of "Honorary Mayor." The Johnsons are pictured at right in 1966. (Right, HV; below, author.)

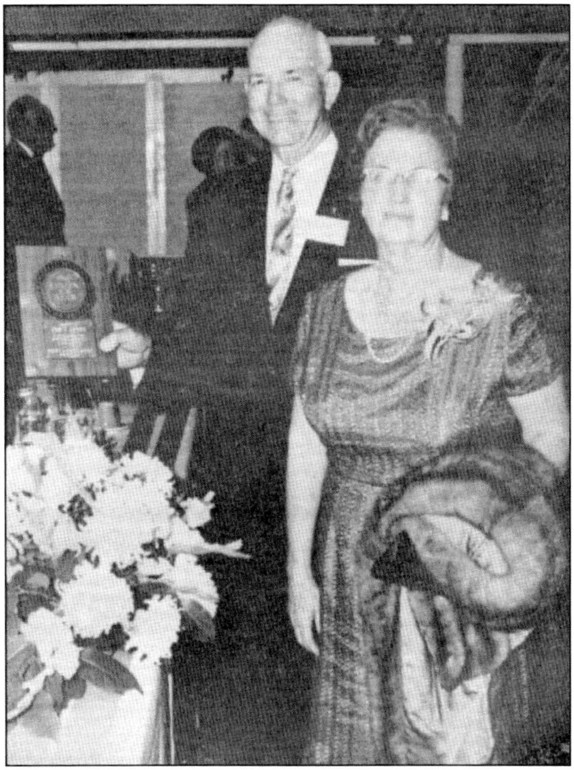

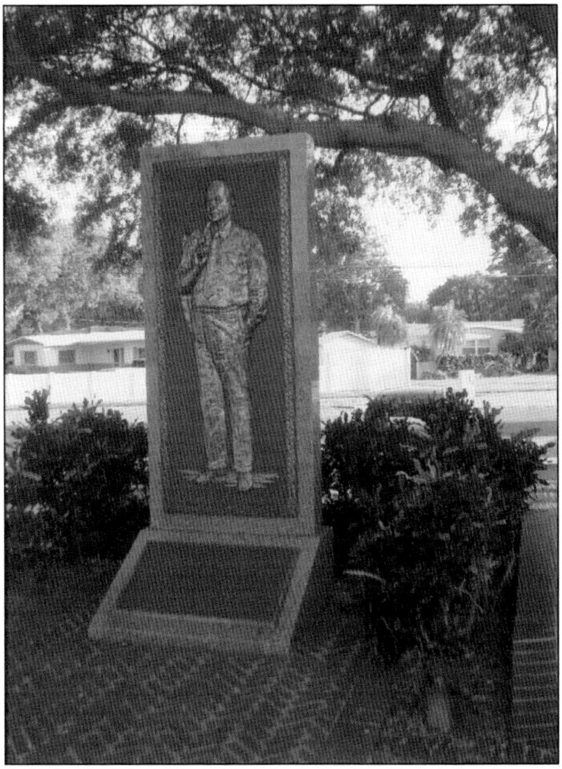

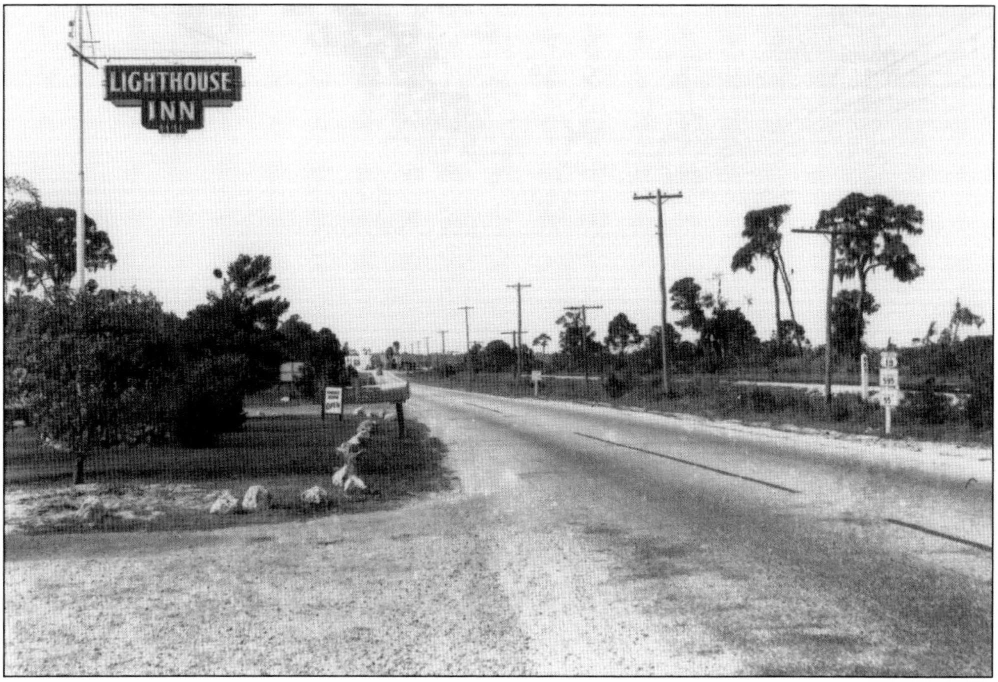

Traveling along this quaint roadway seems much more hectic today. This 1940s view looks northwest from the intersection of Park Street with Bay Pines Boulevard, just beyond Tyrone Boulevard. The Milne-O'Berry packing plant, described on page 35, sits in the distance as the road curves toward the bridge across Long Bayou to Bay Pines. A successful 2000 referendum allowed Seminole to annex land on the right side of the road. (HV.)

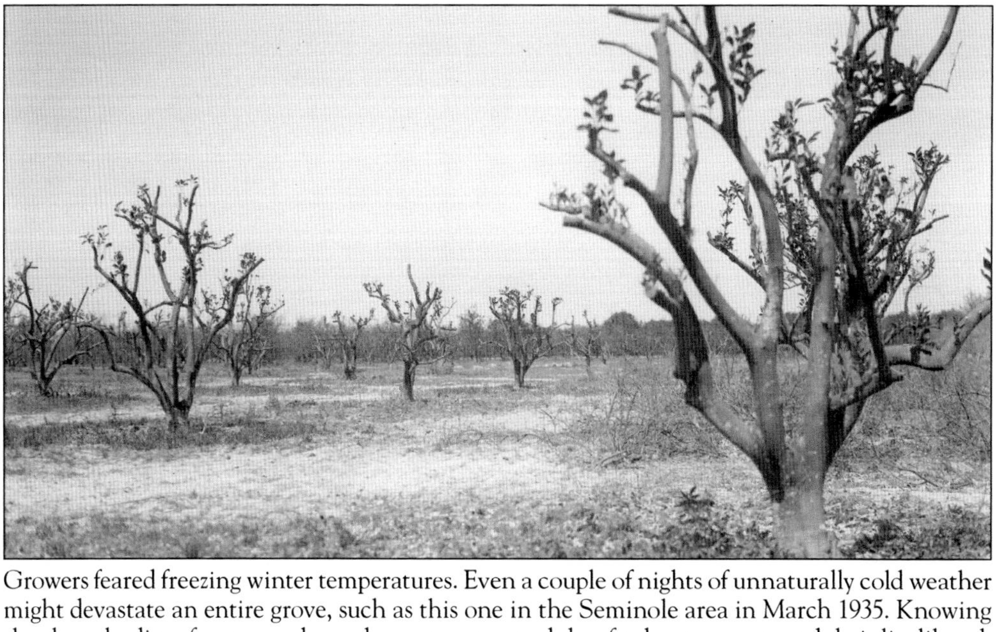

Growers feared freezing winter temperatures. Even a couple of nights of unnaturally cold weather might devastate an entire grove, such as this one in the Seminole area in March 1935. Knowing that large bodies of water moderated temperatures and that freshwater supported their livelihood, farmers along Long Bayou began to advocate the damming of the upper part of the bayou soon after a bitter frost in 1934. (HV.)

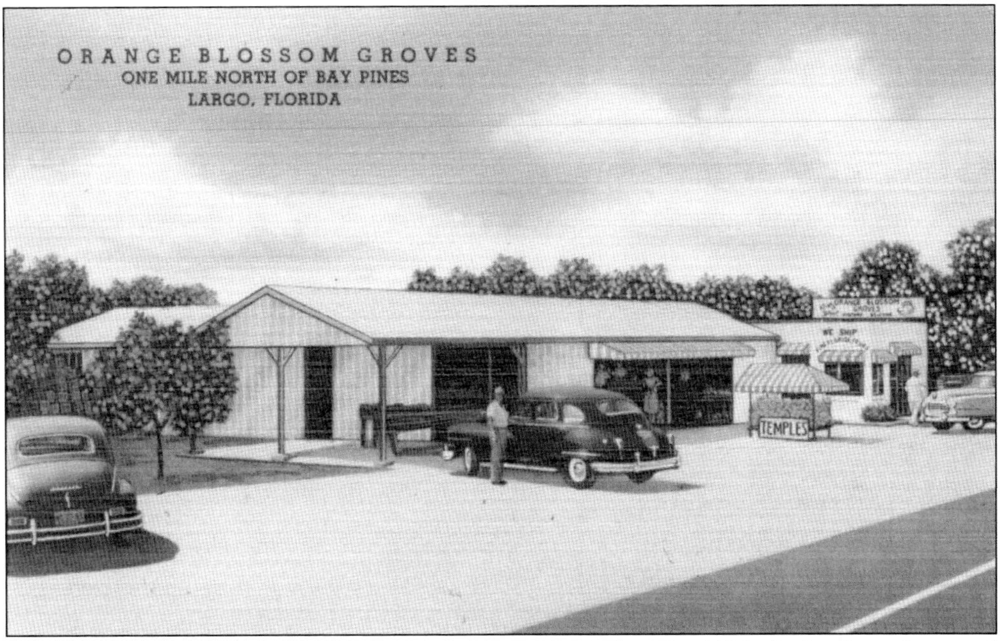

W.M. Cobb came to the Seminole area as a young man before the 1880s, built a log cabin, used lime from oyster shells to fill in the cabin's gaps, grew cotton, and planted many of the original citrus trees in the area along Ridge Road. After World War II, Allison "Al" Repetto capitalized on the potential of the citrus industry when he opened Orange Blossom Groves in 1946. Repetto specialized in navel oranges and the Duncan grapefruit that Pinellas grove operators had perfected, beginning with Arthur Lewis Duncan in the Dunedin area in the 1890s. Overdevelopment harmed the industry, and large groves disappeared from Pinellas. In January 2015, Repetto's estate sold the few remaining groves and buildings on the west side of the 5800 block of Seminole Boulevard for $2.15 million. Bulldozers cleared the site immediately thereafter. (Both, HV.)

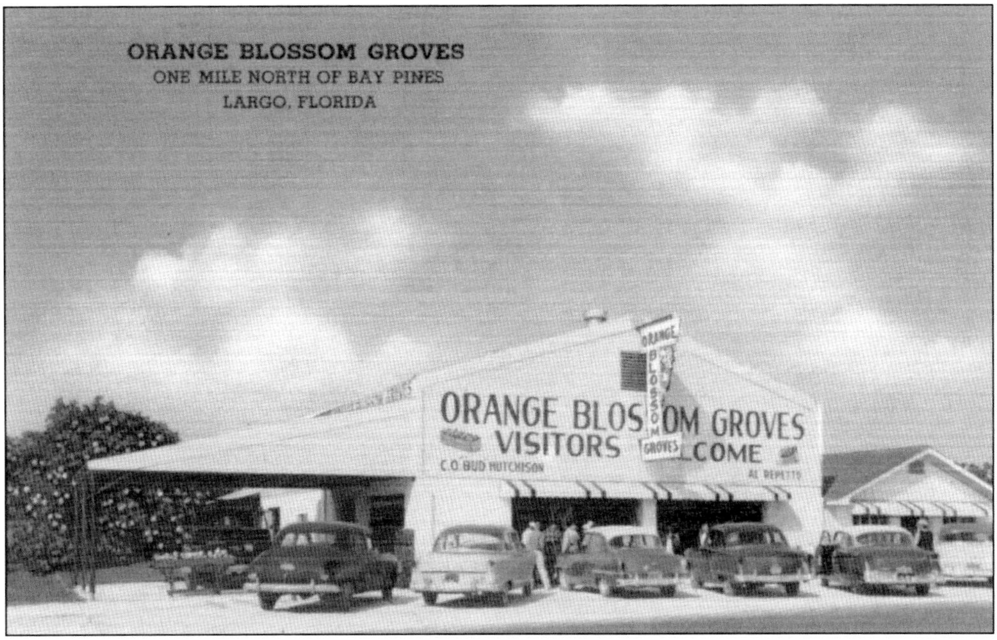

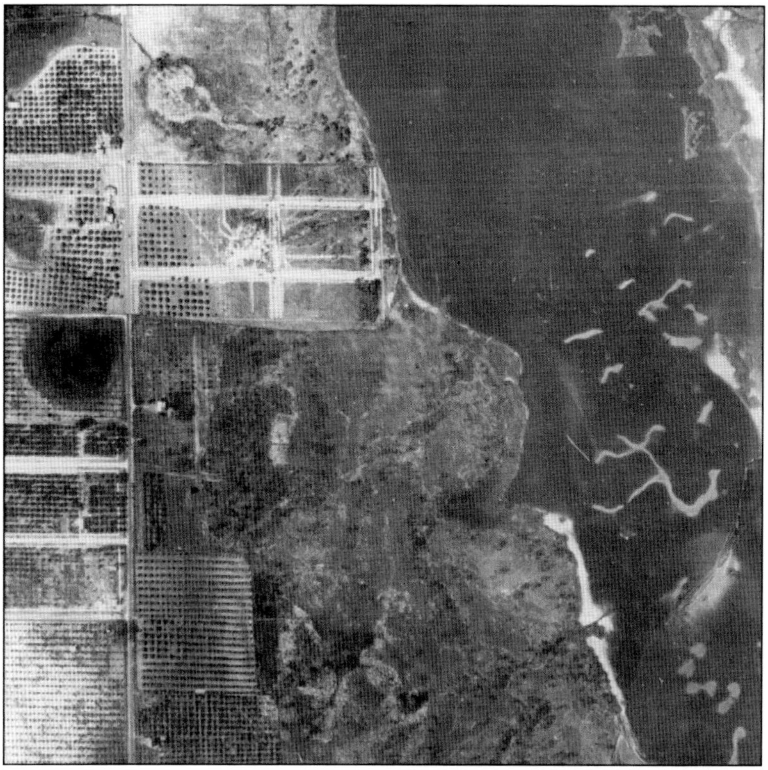

This 1926 aerial photo shows the site where county officials planned to create a dam across Long Bayou in the late 1940s. Jesse W. Johnson and his brother Tim gave many acres to the project for the lake and the roadway approach; they worked diligently with other landowners on the western side of the bayou to support this project. Meetings to discuss the dam took place at the Seminole Cabin. (HV.)

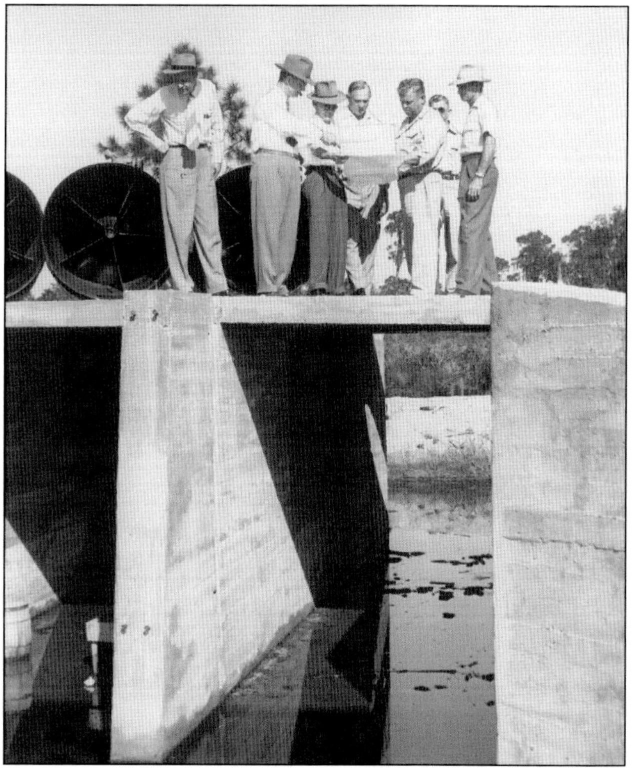

Prior to the construction of the dam and extension of Park Boulevard across Long Bayou to create Lake Seminole, crews also improved the pumping station just south of Ulmerton Road that controlled the flow of freshwater from estuaries and drainage canals at the former Lake Largo site into the bayou. In December 1948, state and county delegates showed conservation officials from Alabama and North Carolina the project's status. (HV.)

Three

Ranch Homes Replace Ranch Lands

1950s–1969

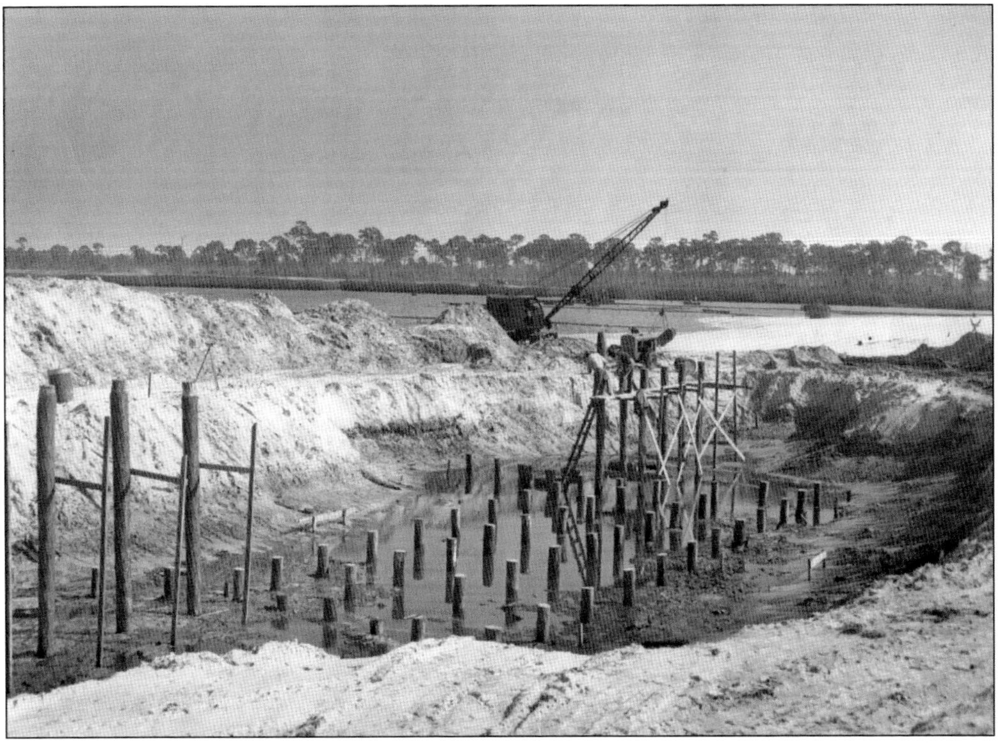

Workers finished construction of a dam along Long Bayou at the present site of Park Boulevard. Built at a cost of approximately $160,000, this dam allowed water north of Park Boulevard to change from a shallow saltwater marsh into the freshwater body of Lake Seminole. The creation of Lake Seminole was hailed as an important development for farmers and cattle ranchers in the area, such as Jay B. Starkey. (HV.)

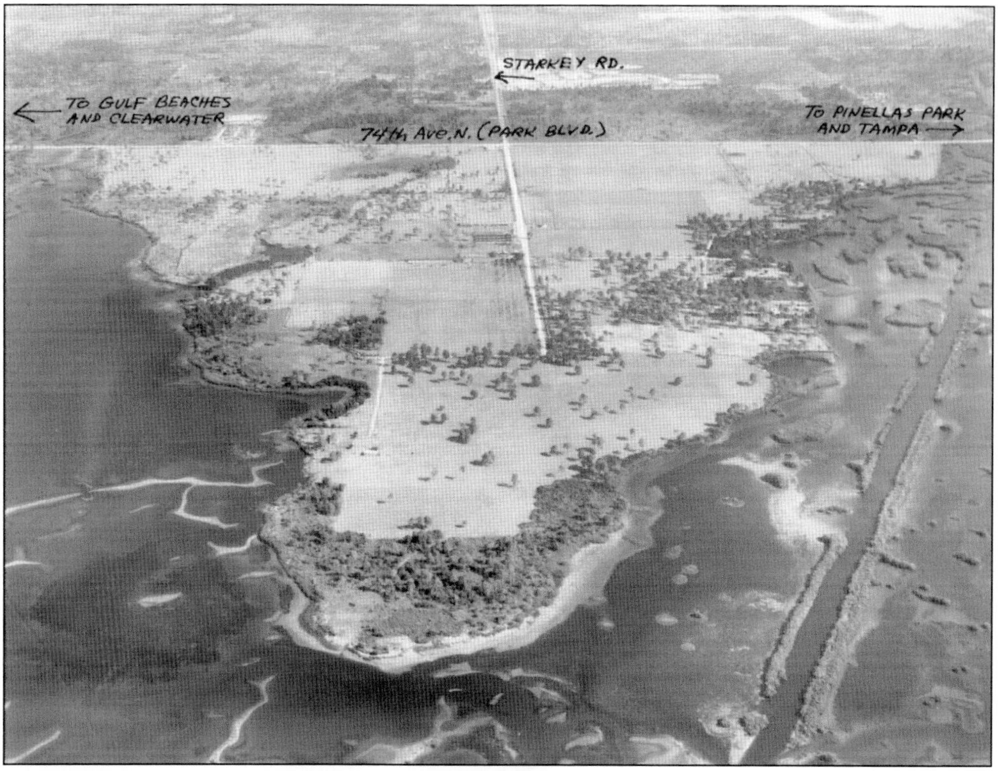

The extension of Park Boulevard over the earthen dam connected the Seminole area directly with Pinellas Park. Along the eastern shore of the new freshwater lake, cattle and agricultural enterprises continued during the early 1950s near Starkey Road, then a narrow country roadway connecting Jay Starkey's farming interests with Ulmerton Road and Park Boulevard. Change came quickly as Starkey and others sold their holdings later that decade. (HV.)

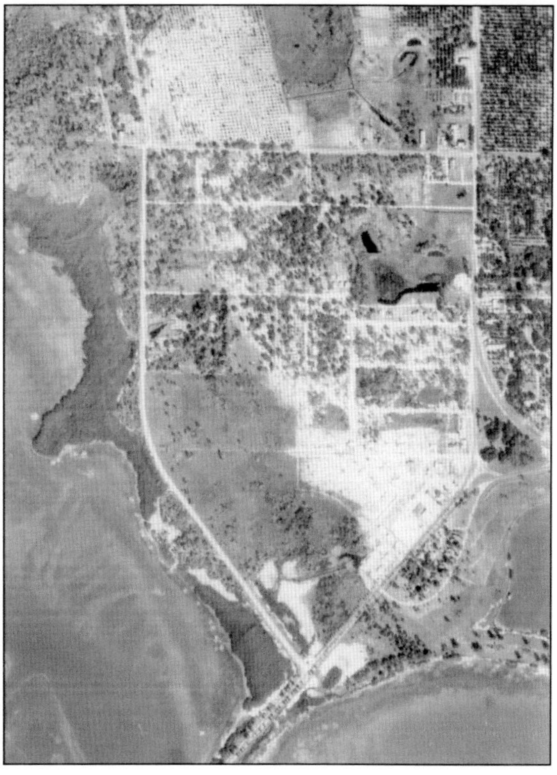

Citrus trees and agricultural tracts greatly outnumbered residential and commercial developments in this November 1951 aerial view. A sparsely traveled Seminole Boulevard and Bay Pines Triangle anchor the right side of the photograph. The Seminole Cemetery occupies the center of the image, and a few houses surround it. By 1960, homes appeared throughout this area, as well as newly constructed school facilities and shopping centers on soon-to-be dredged land. (HV.)

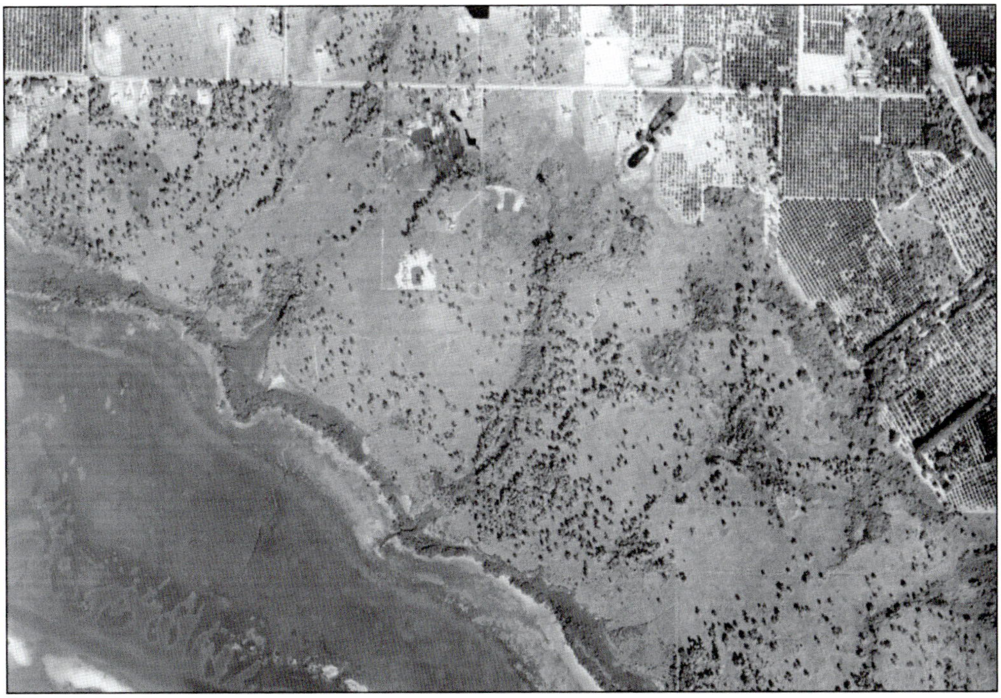

Two other views from November 1951 illustrate the presence of groves on sites that would soon develop into residential subdivisions. Few homes appear along or south of Old Oakhurst Road (Seventy-Fourth Avenue), shown here. During and after the 1960s, sections of these areas once platted as Pinellas Groves took on new names, such as Harbor View, Oakhurst Gardens, Kapka Groves, Drew Oaks Estates, and Rosetree Place, to name a few. (HV.)

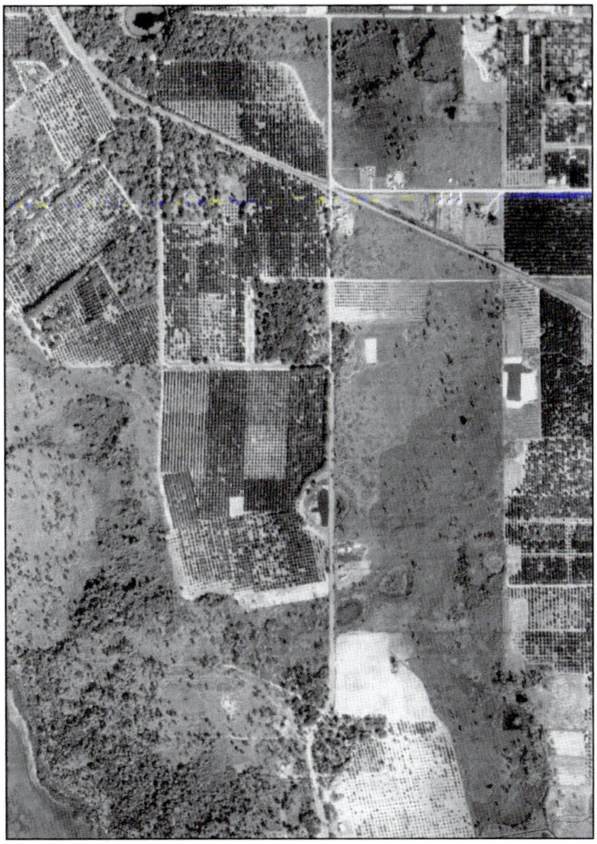

Lush groves appeared along either side of the southern extension of Ridge Road, a stretch now known as 113th Street. On some maps and for obvious reasons, this section north of Fifty-Fourth Avenue was also called Grove Road. In 1958, developers launched Bay Ridge Terrace in the left-center groves, with ranch homes selling on lots for $11,790–$14,000. The groves of C.E. "Bill" Williams, lower right, became Williamsdale Square in 1966. (HV.)

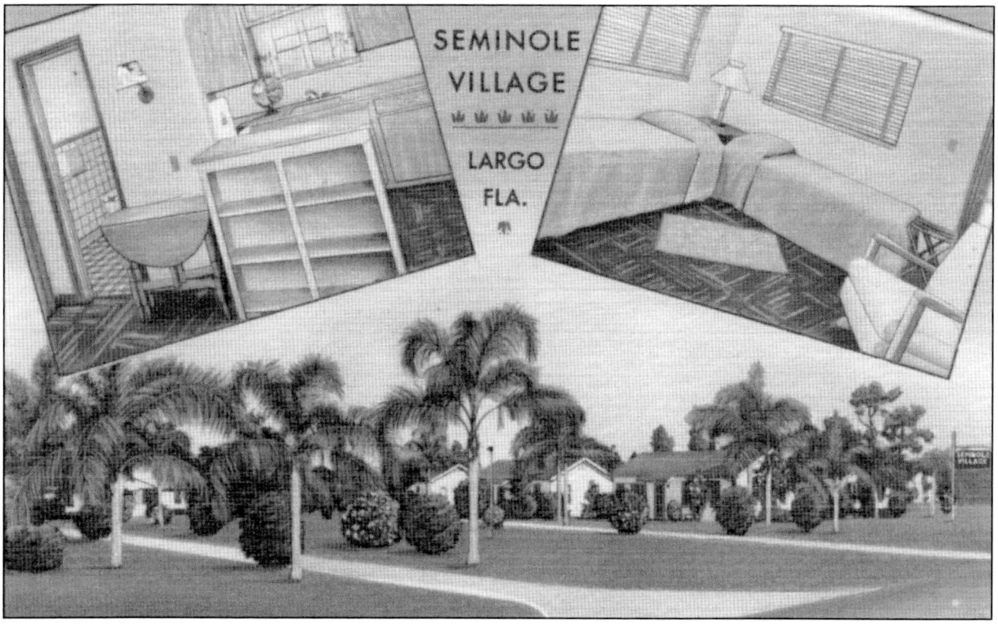

Developments such as Seminole Village enticed short-term and seasonal visitors during the postwar years. Located along Seminole Boulevard and Lake Seminole a short distance north of Park Boulevard, the completely furnished apartments, cottages, and duplexes included utilities and linen service as part of the rent. Air-conditioning remained optional, though all residents could enjoy a private dock and shuffleboard court. The Mohney family owned Seminole Village at this time. (HV.)

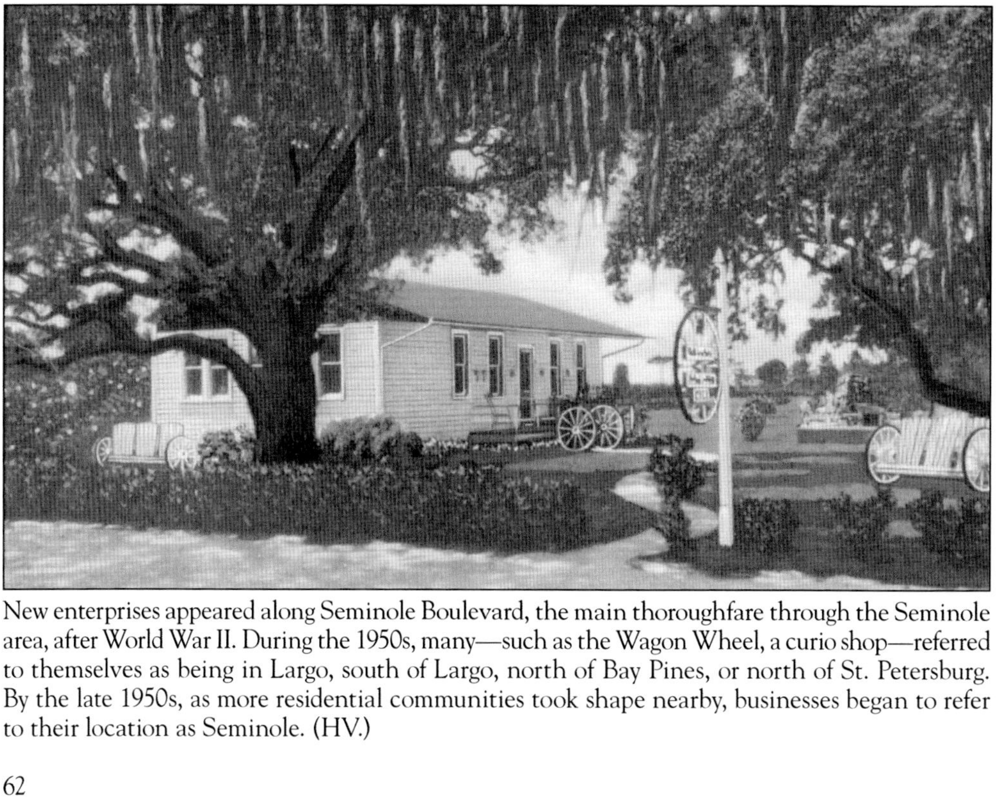

New enterprises appeared along Seminole Boulevard, the main thoroughfare through the Seminole area, after World War II. During the 1950s, many—such as the Wagon Wheel, a curio shop—referred to themselves as being in Largo, south of Largo, north of Bay Pines, or north of St. Petersburg. By the late 1950s, as more residential communities took shape nearby, businesses began to refer to their location as Seminole. (HV.)

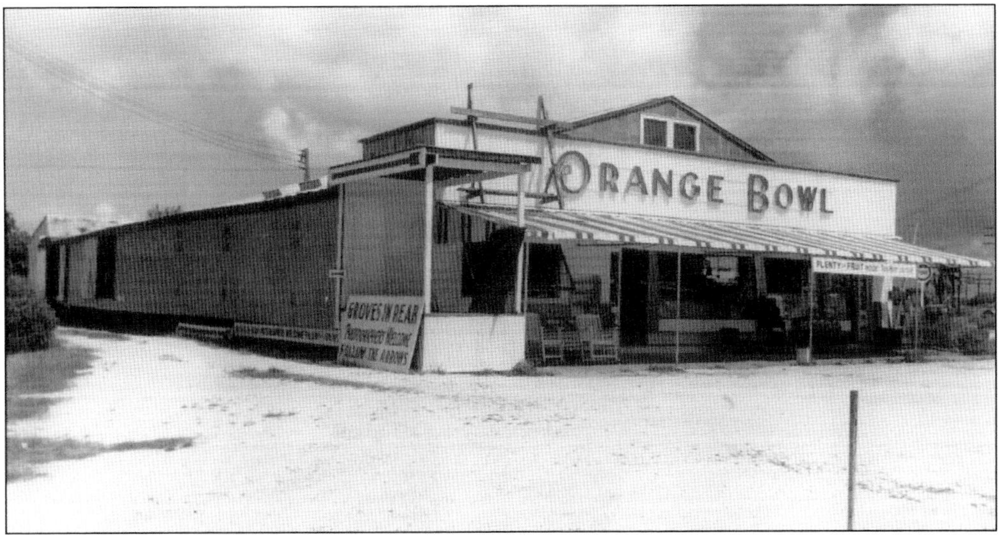

Large packinghouses often sat alongside strategic transportation routes. The Orange Bowl, shown here before 1950, occupied a prominent location just south of the 6600 block on the eastern side of Seminole Boulevard. The railroad lines, originally part of the Tampa & Gulf Coast and then owned by the Seaboard Air Line, allowed for convenient shipping of fruits to distant areas. The tiny Seminole railroad depot erected in the 1910s once occupied a space directly west of the Orange Bowl (at lower right below) but had disappeared by the 1940s as customers preferred the larger Bay Pines depot. The area east of the Orange Bowl (top portion of image below) later became the Long Bayou Acres and Gem Village subdivisions. As citrus trees disappeared from the area, Orange Grove Elementary opened in 1961. (Both, HV.)

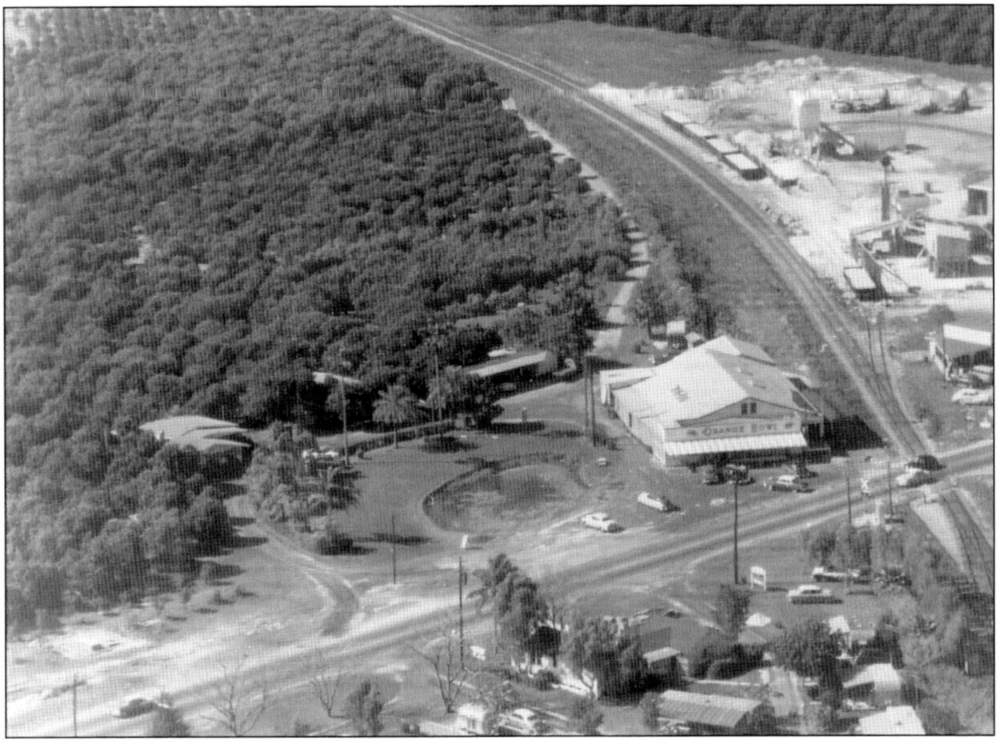

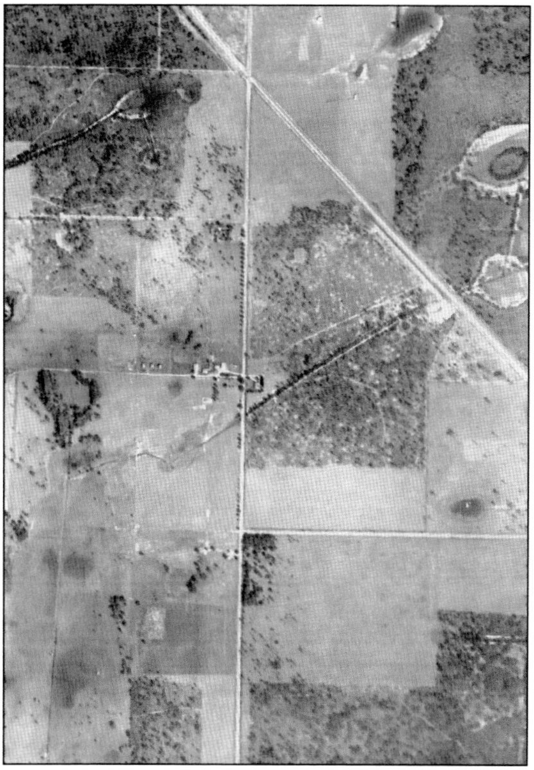

A March 1957 flight above Starkey Road captured this view of pastureland just before great changes occurred. Jay Starkey's ranch holdings soon transformed into new developments along the eastern shore of Lake Seminole between Park Boulevard and Ulmerton Road. The railroad, still heavily used, intersects with Starkey Road near the top. The intersection at bottom center with Bryan Dairy Road soon experienced increased traffic. (USFSP.)

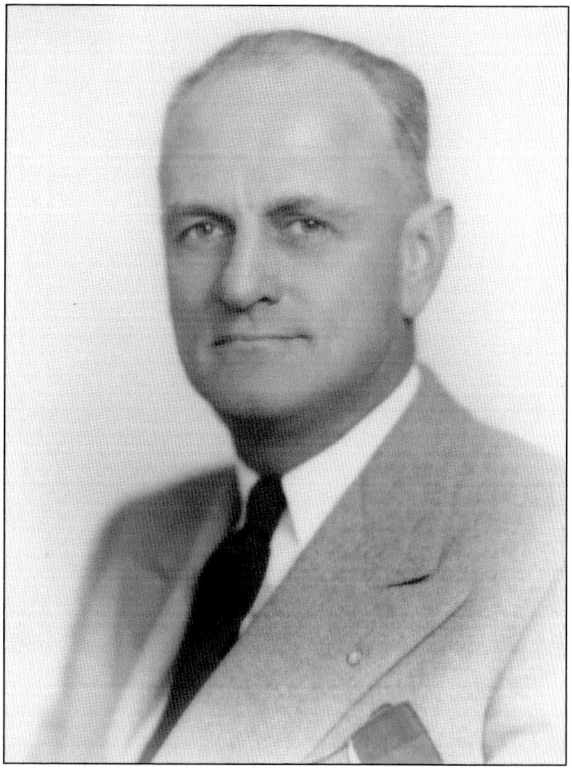

Jay Starkey, shown here in the 1950s, heard from Pansy Bryan—the owner of Bryan Dairy—that an unknown buyer wanted to purchase some of her family's acreage east of the railroad tracks during the spring of 1956 but needed a quick decision. After talking with Starkey, Bryan sold this land and it soon became the General Electric plant at Belcher Road. Starkey began selling his lands soon thereafter. (HV.)

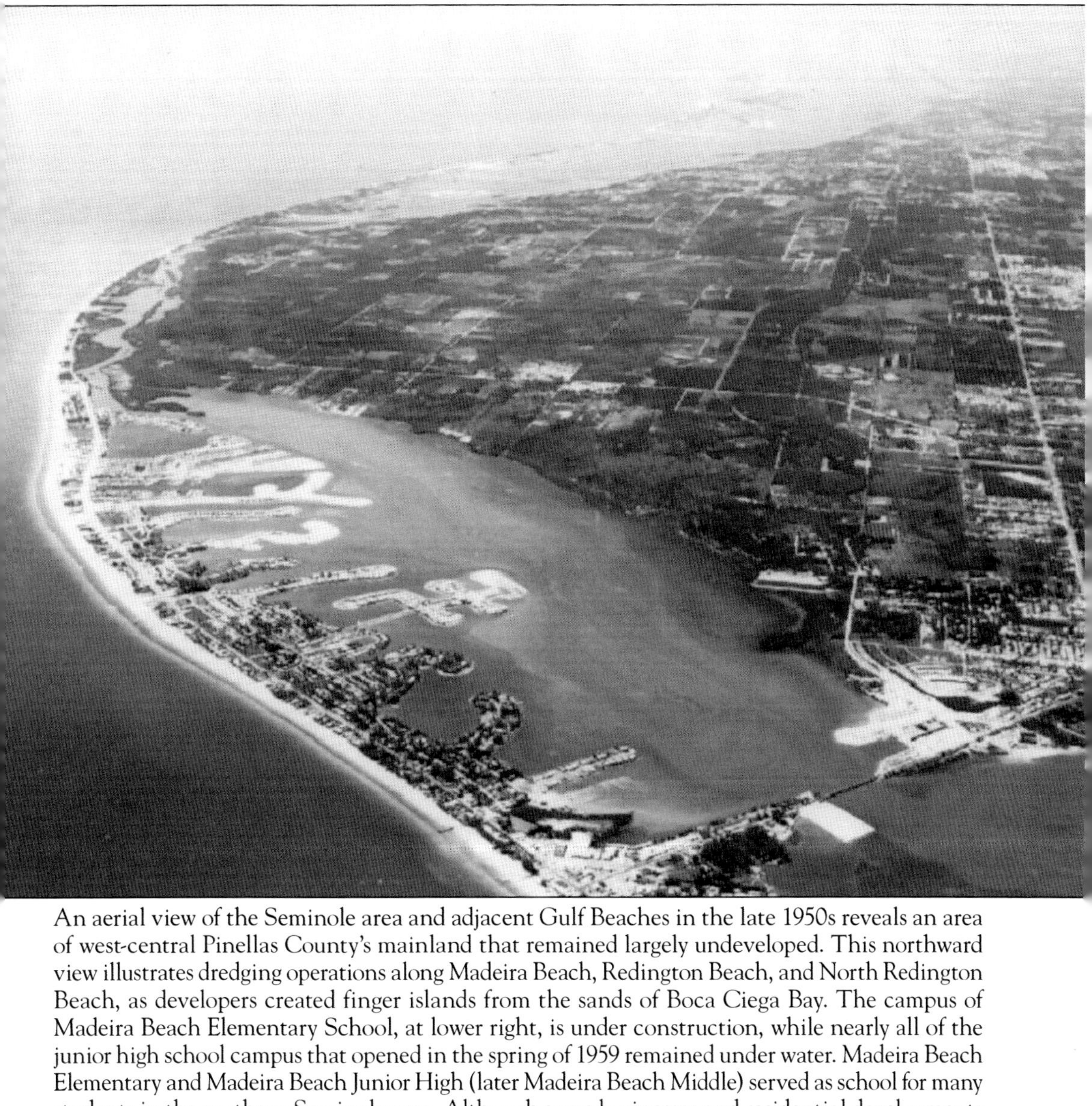

An aerial view of the Seminole area and adjacent Gulf Beaches in the late 1950s reveals an area of west-central Pinellas County's mainland that remained largely undeveloped. This northward view illustrates dredging operations along Madeira Beach, Redington Beach, and North Redington Beach, as developers created finger islands from the sands of Boca Ciega Bay. The campus of Madeira Beach Elementary School, at lower right, is under construction, while nearly all of the junior high school campus that opened in the spring of 1959 remained under water. Madeira Beach Elementary and Madeira Beach Junior High (later Madeira Beach Middle) served as school for many students in the southern Seminole area. Although some businesses and residential developments started to take shape along Seminole Boulevard, shown along the right side, most of the acreage west of Ridge Road remained in use for agricultural purposes or undeveloped. (HV.)

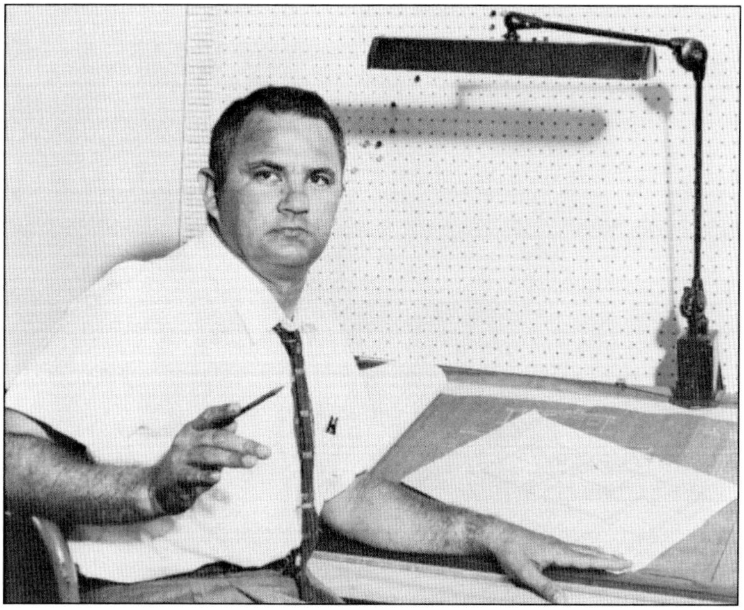

By the 1950s, successful developers of mid-Pinellas County understood the value of balancing flashy marketing with established reputation. Charles K. Cheezem, above, began developing residential communities in the St. Petersburg area in the early 1950s and soon discovered the untapped potential of transforming groves to homes in unincorporated Seminole. He successfully built and marketed Ridgewood Groves and Ridgewood Mountain Village by hiring a team that understood the proper balance between offering amenities families—often retirees—wanted, while also keeping enough of the fruit-bearing trees so that the community maintained a distinctive flair. By the early 1960s, he had won national recognition from groups in the construction industry, including the Citation for Building Excellence from the American Standard Plumbing Division. During the late 1960s, he oversaw the development of the Sea Towers condominium development along Duhme Road. (Both, Swenningsen Collection.)

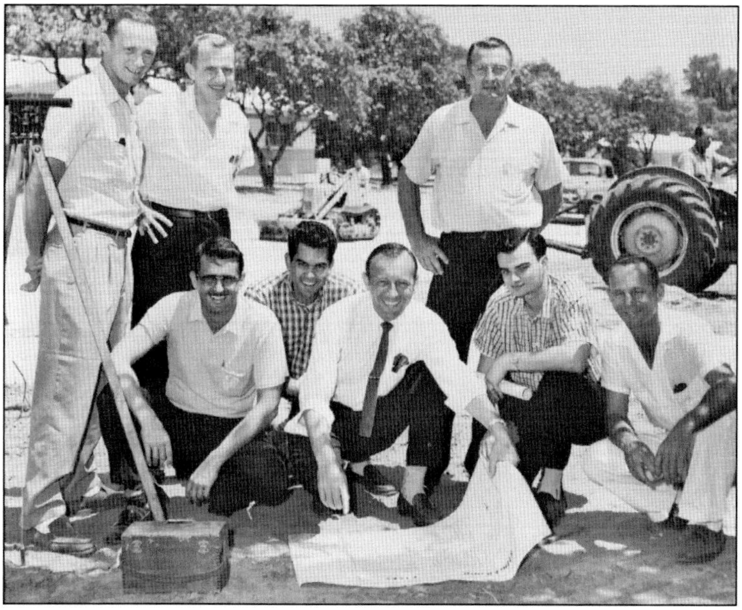

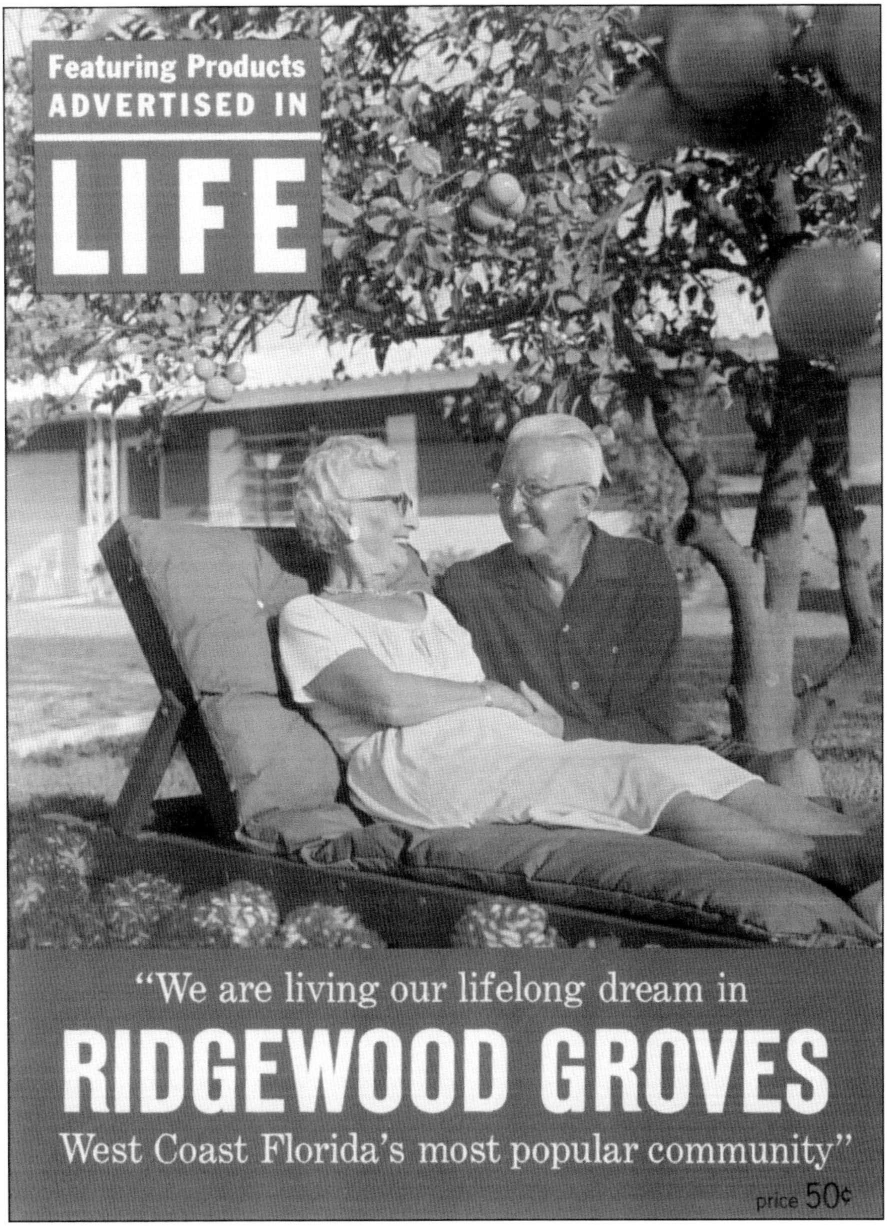

Promotional literature, such as a colorful booklet selling the beauty of the Ridgewood Groves subdivision north of Park Boulevard and west of present-day Duhme Road, targeted newcomers by the early 1960s. The cover shown here has an interesting if somewhat deceptive pedigree. This idyllic image of a retired couple relaxing outside their dream home was contrived by a photographer who worked for the developer. The man and woman saw Jack Swenningsen, the photographer, in front of the empty model home while taking a walk and asked what he was doing. After a short conversation, they went home, "dressed the part," and returned to serve as models. The photo shoot took place in late summer, long before the oranges had ripened. Swenningsen had a solution for that as well; he painted one side of the green fruits orange, giving the impression of a ripe harvest. Swenningsen's imagery and marketing strategy proved fruitful as sales accelerated. (Swenningsen Collection.)

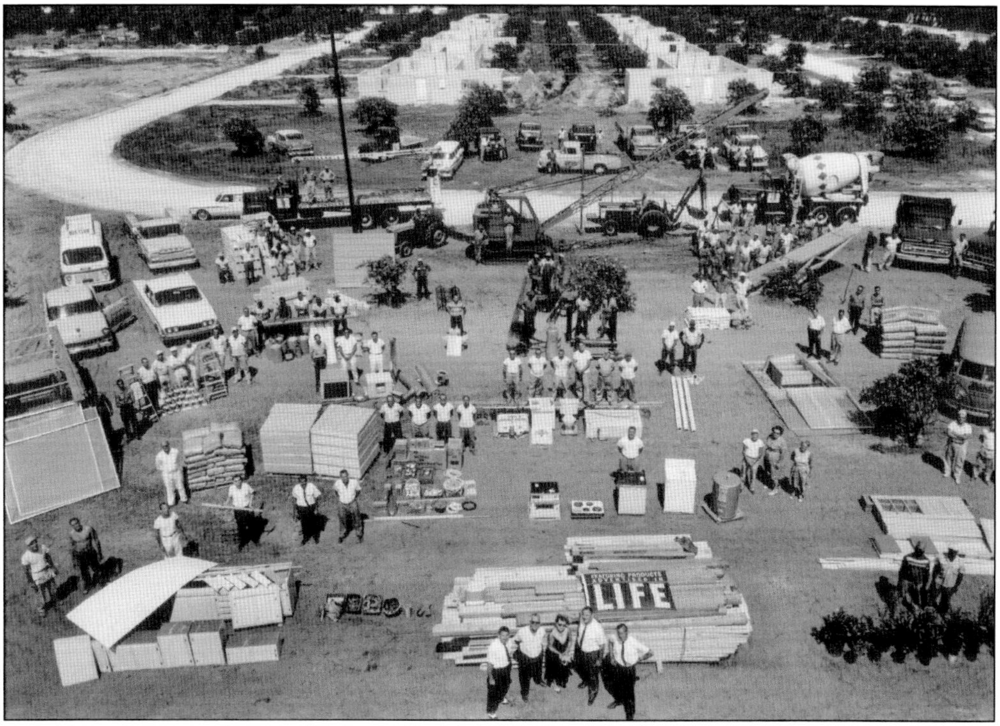

Jack Swenningsen's talents with a camera took him to new heights as sales of the properties offered by his employer, Charles K. Cheezem, soared. This photograph taken from a high ladder allowed Swenningsen to capture every item within a future home at Ridgewood Groves, right down to the kitchen sink. Note the homes under construction in the background as rows of manicured dwellings replaced groves of citrus trees. (Swenningsen Collection.)

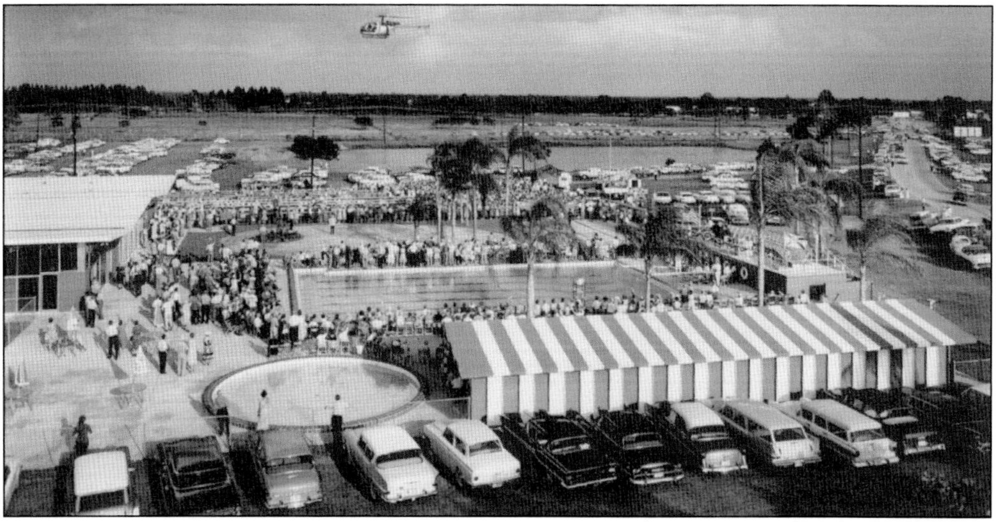

Crowds gather at the dedication ceremonies for the Ridgewood Groves subdivision. Automobiles jammed the easements of Park Boulevard, then a narrow two-lane road. In 1977, the lake visible beyond the festivities later became the location of the Albertsons (more recently, Publix) grocery store at the intersection of Park Boulevard and 113th Street. Vacant land beyond the lake became the home of Seminole Mall in the mid-1960s. (Swenningsen Collection.)

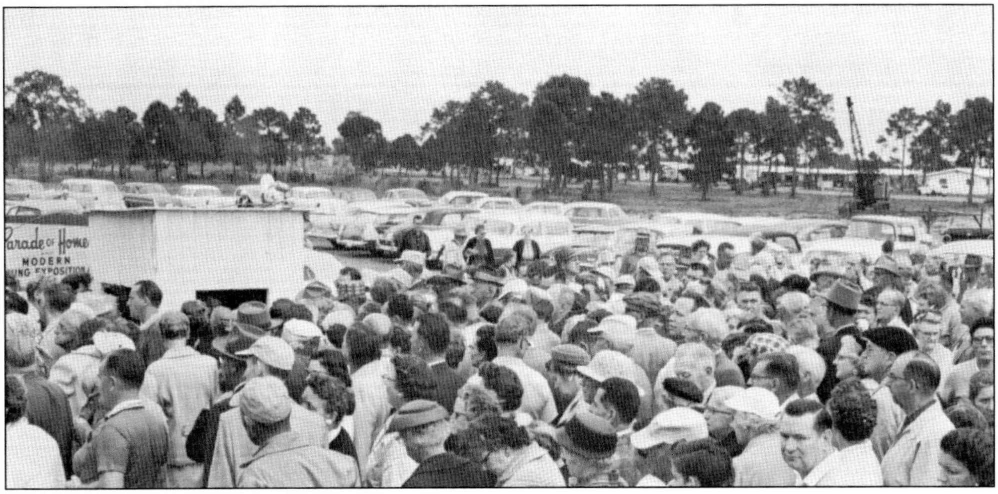

Cheezem developed Ridgewood Mountain Village as a retirement-themed section of Ridgewood Groves that catered to the senior lifestyle. He created special advertising sections as inserts in issues of *Life*, a popular magazine at that time. His sales team advertised during expositions such as the "Parade of Homes," drawing large crowds who had an interest in the area. Promotional literature claimed that retirees who bought a home in Ridgewood Mountain Village would enjoy "that Florida feeling" with elevations that soared to "55 feet above sea level," not to mention the presence of sanitary sewers and a "grove with every home." One or two trees spared from the chainsaw often constituted the "grove." Advertisements telling buyers to "be young again" in homes costing under $11,000 with tiles roofs and terrazzo floors certainly attracted significant interest in 1961! (Above, Swenningsen Collection; below, author.)

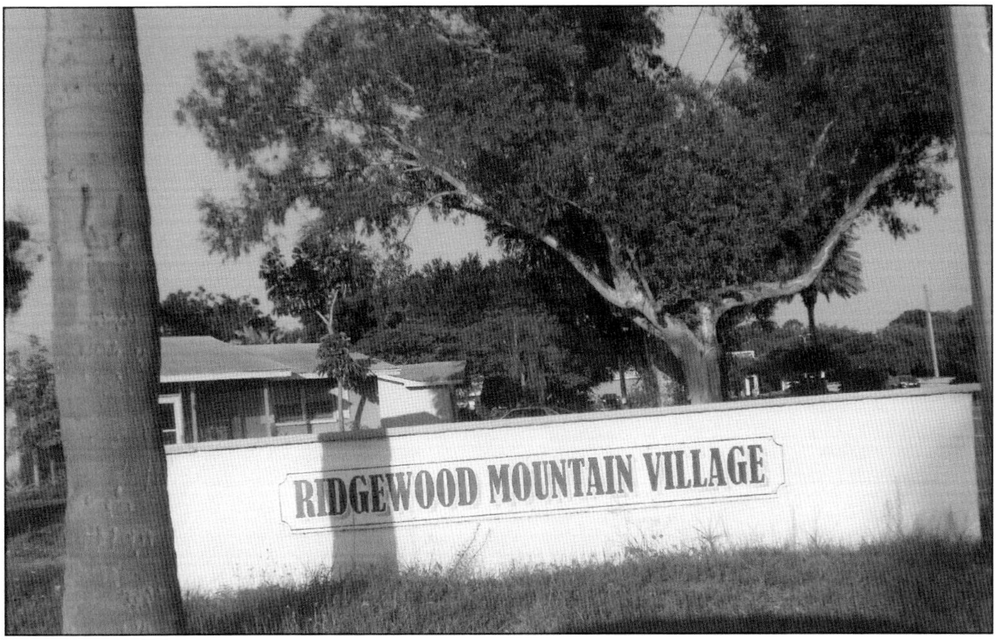

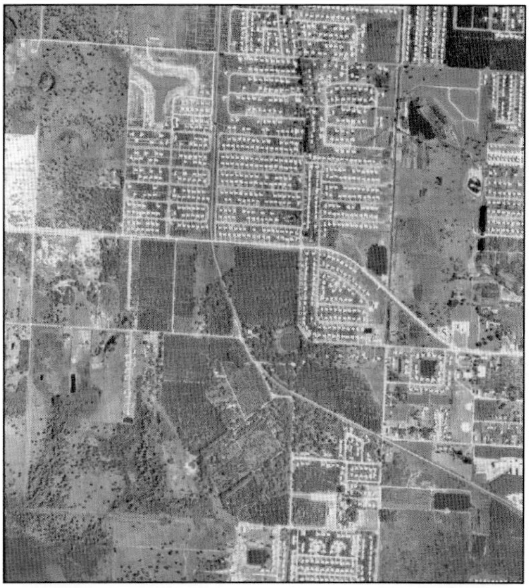

The July 1961 aerial photo at left shows Cheezem's Ridgewood Mountain Groves at upper center. Near Meares Lake, Col. Martin C. Rhodes had established a handful of elegant homes on large parcels for his High Oaks development during the 1950s. Rhodes, a veteran of World War I and World War II in the Quartermaster Corps of the US Army, had participated in the June 1944 Normandy invasion. He moved to the area in the early 1950s, where he became a successful banker and developer until his death in December 1967. The image below, also from July 1961, illustrates patterns of growth with the intersection of Park Boulevard and Seminole Boulevard at center. Meares Lake appears at center left, and the site of present-day Seminole Mall remained undeveloped. (Both, HV.)

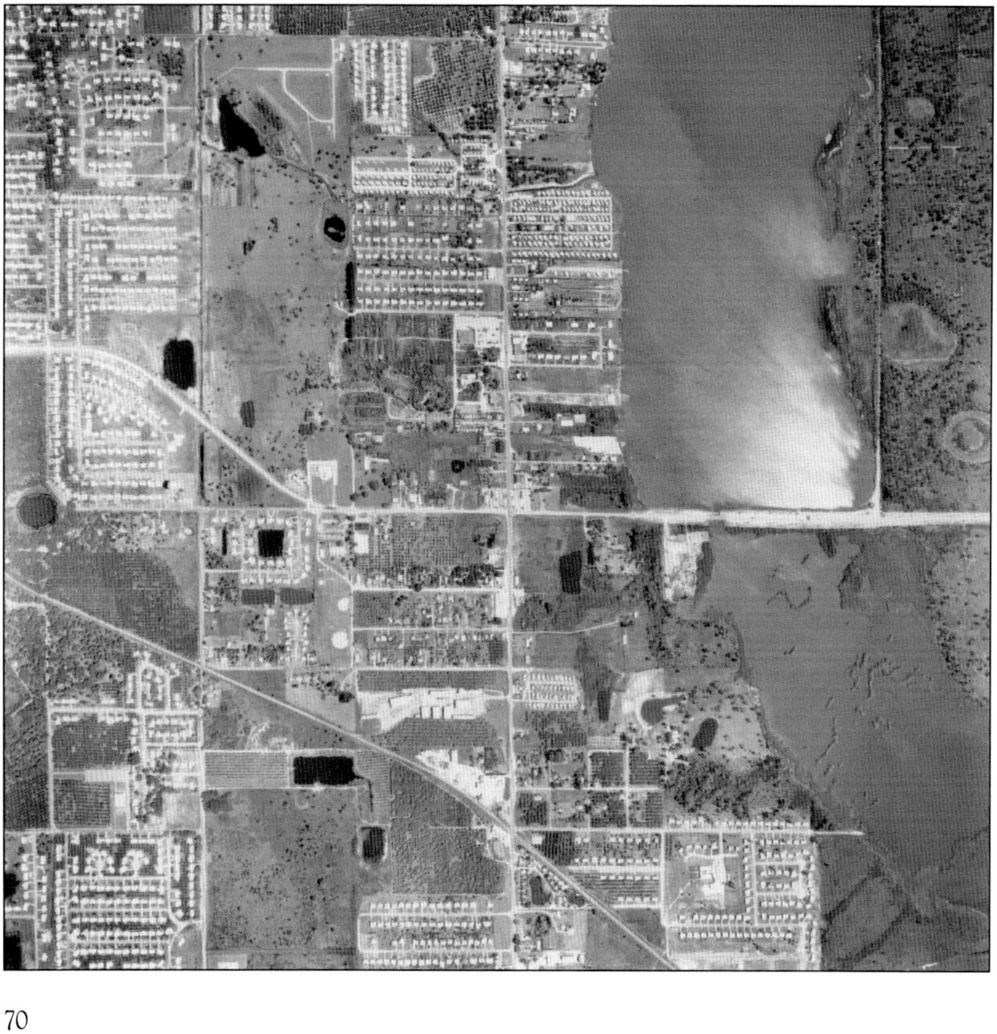

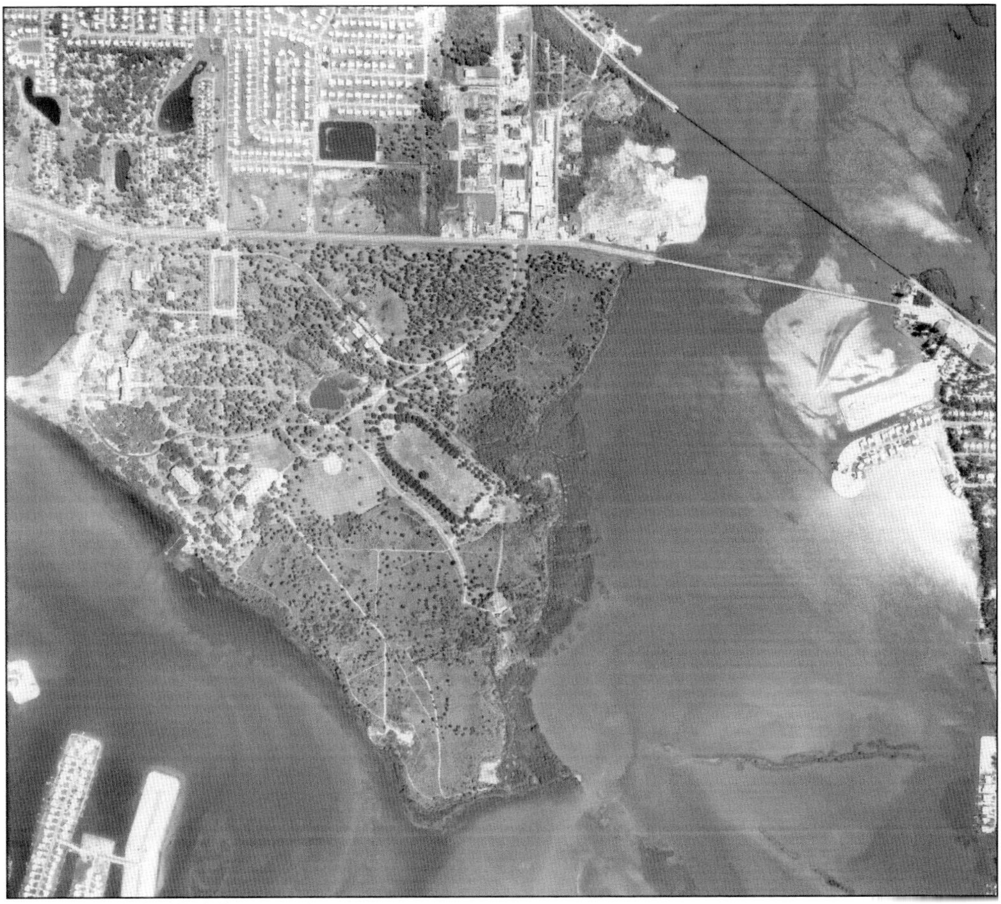

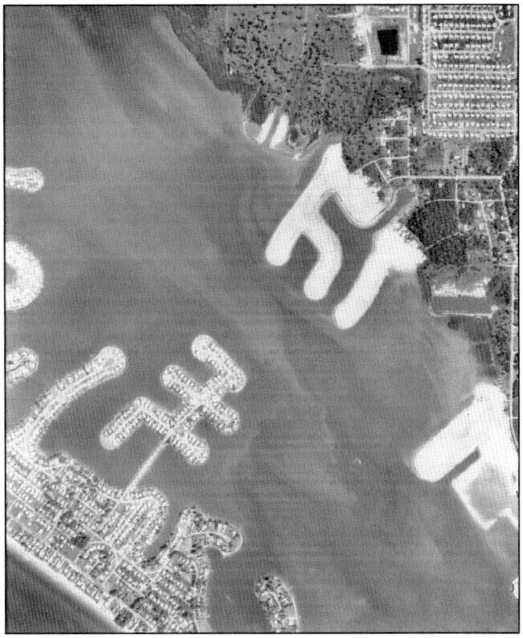

Two other July 1961 images show substantial developments that had appeared north of the Bay Pines complex (above) and along the Intracoastal Waterway of Boca Ciega Bay (right). The new residential communities of Orange Estates and Bay Pines Estates sat upon lands north of Bay Pines Boulevard, above. The Bay Pines hospital area and cemetery occupied much of Seminole Point, though federal authorities would soon dispose of 122 acres of the eastern portion near Long Bayou in 1963 that later opened in 1974 as War Veterans' Memorial Park. At right, dredge-and-fill operations prepared the earthen foundation for Cheezem's Sea Towers and the Ridgewood Riviera homes (lower right), as well as the Oakhurst Shores subdivisions (center) located just west of the original Seminole Estates development mentioned on page 36. (Both, HV.)

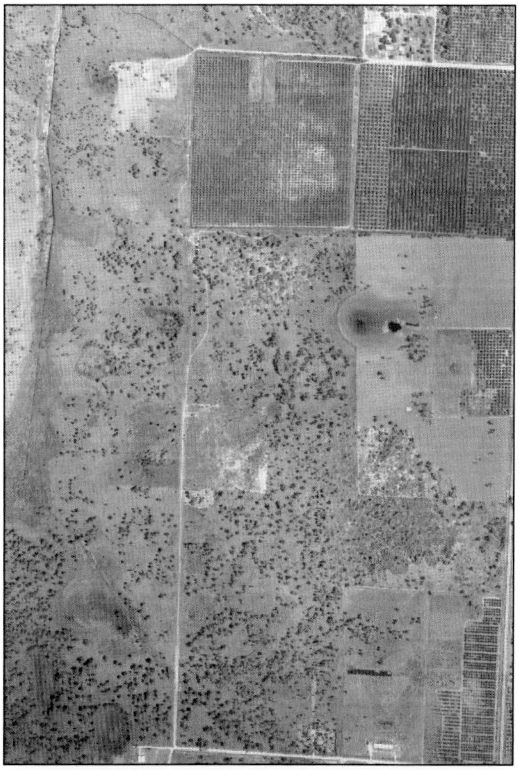

At left, a 1961 aerial view of the area west of the railroad tracks between Eighty-Sixth Avenue and Walsingham Road shows a rural area that remained quite remote. Shortly after a photographer captured this image, construction started on the campus for Seminole High School near the lower-left corner. The original campus, shown below, opened in September 1962 with an initial faculty of 24 teachers instructing approximately 700 students. When Stanley Moore, the school's first principal, drove to the area in search of the construction site before the school opened, he actually had difficulty locating the campus on the bluff. Finally, he came to a narrow shell path that served as a southern extension of Vonn Road (131st Street). Atop the hill, he discovered the site of the school he would soon lead. (HV.)

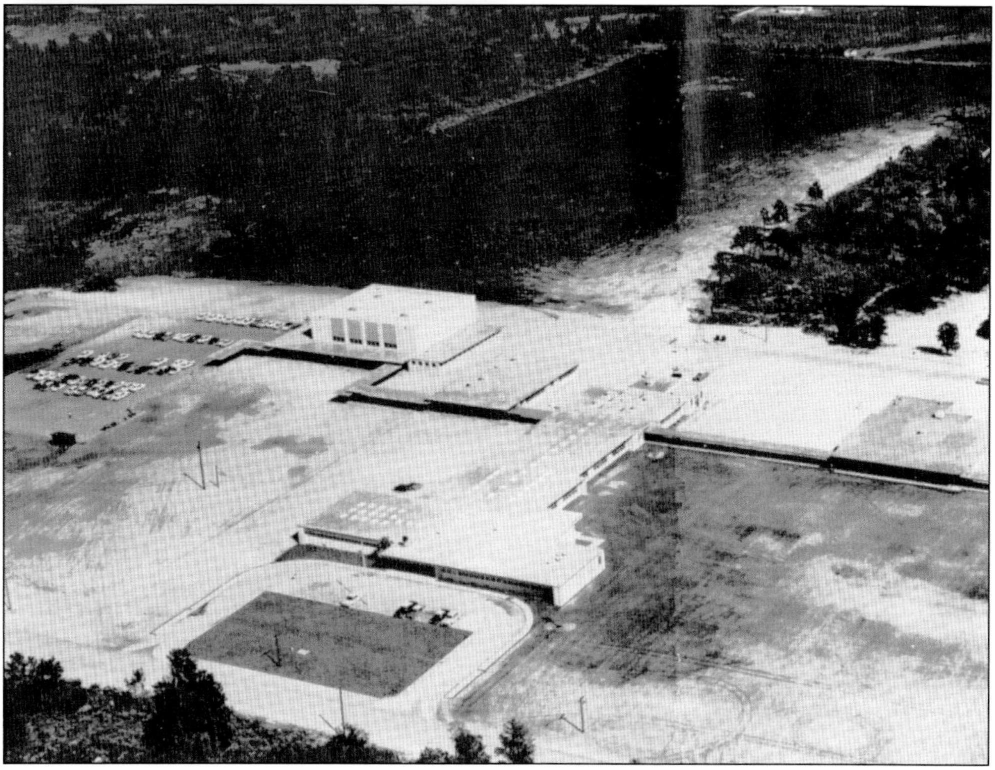

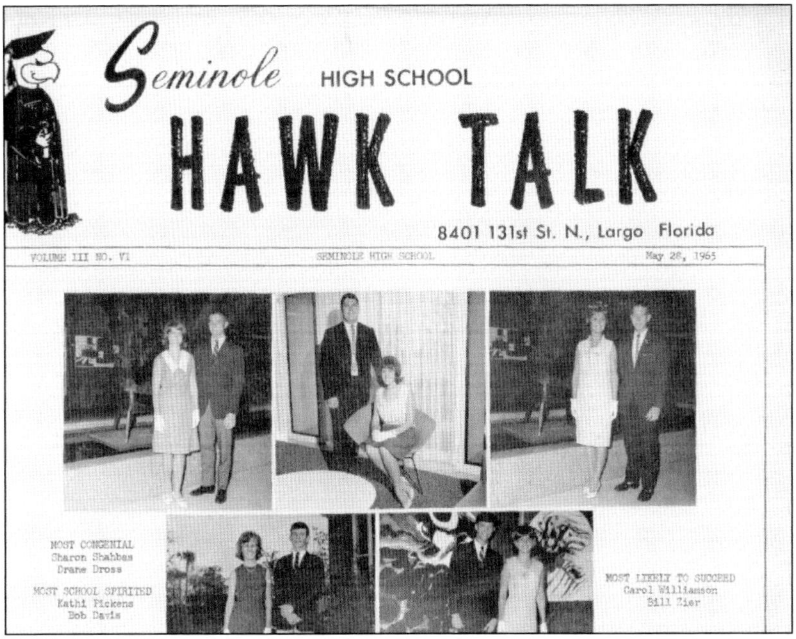

Seminole HIGH SCHOOL

HAWK TALK

8401 131st St. N., Largo Florida

VOLUME III NO. VI SEMINOLE HIGH SCHOOL May 28, 1965

MOST CONGENIAL
Sharon Shahbas
Drane Dross

MOST SCHOOL SPIRITED
Kathi Pickens
Bob Davis

MOST LIKELY TO SUCCEED
Carol Williamson
Bill Zier

At the time the school opened, the site of the present-day football field and athletic facilities along Eighty-Sixth Avenue hosted snakes, alligators, and other swampland wildlife, rather than Warhawks in orange and green uniforms. Members of the student body established their traditions and soon engaged in fierce athletic rivalries with Largo High School, the high school that many in the area formerly attended. The annual Seminole Pow Wow festival began in 1967 as a way to raise funds for lights at the football stadium. School boosters, volunteer firefighters, and other community leaders planned a large barbecue and parade. Cat Mangum suggested the name Pow Wow, and bright lights soon rose above the football field, shown below in the late 1960s. The Pow Wow included carnival rides beginning in 1970. (Both, HV.)

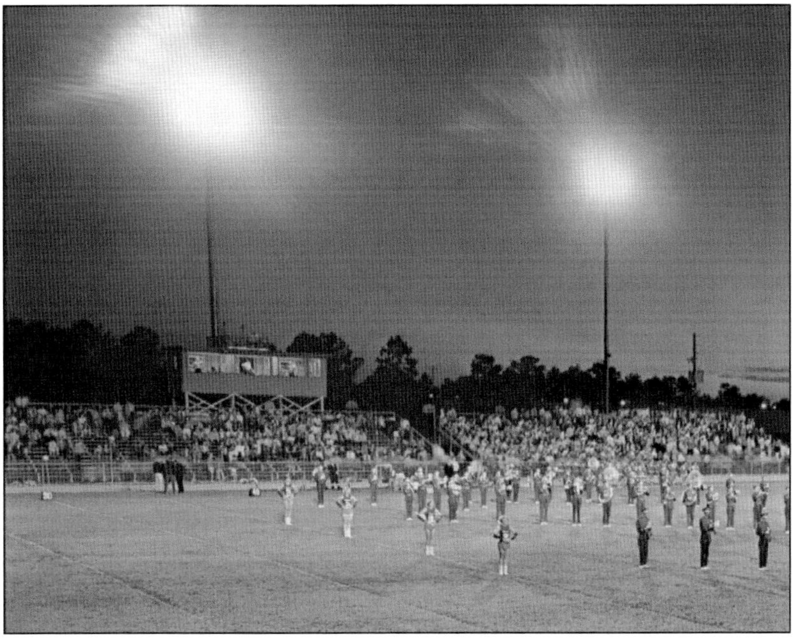

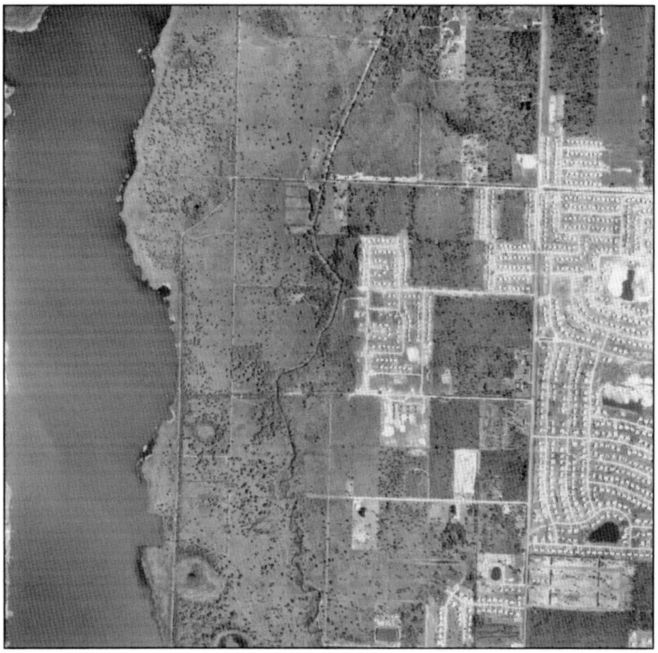

An aerial view from the summer of 1961 offers evidence of the transitions that had occurred on the eastern side of Lake Seminole about five years after Jay Starkey sold his lands in the area south of Ninety-Fourth Avenue. Starkey Elementary School appears in the lower center, just south of the Clearwood subdivision. Homes in Clearwood, Crestridge, and Cross Bayou Estates had also sprouted in subdivisions east of Starkey Road. (HV.)

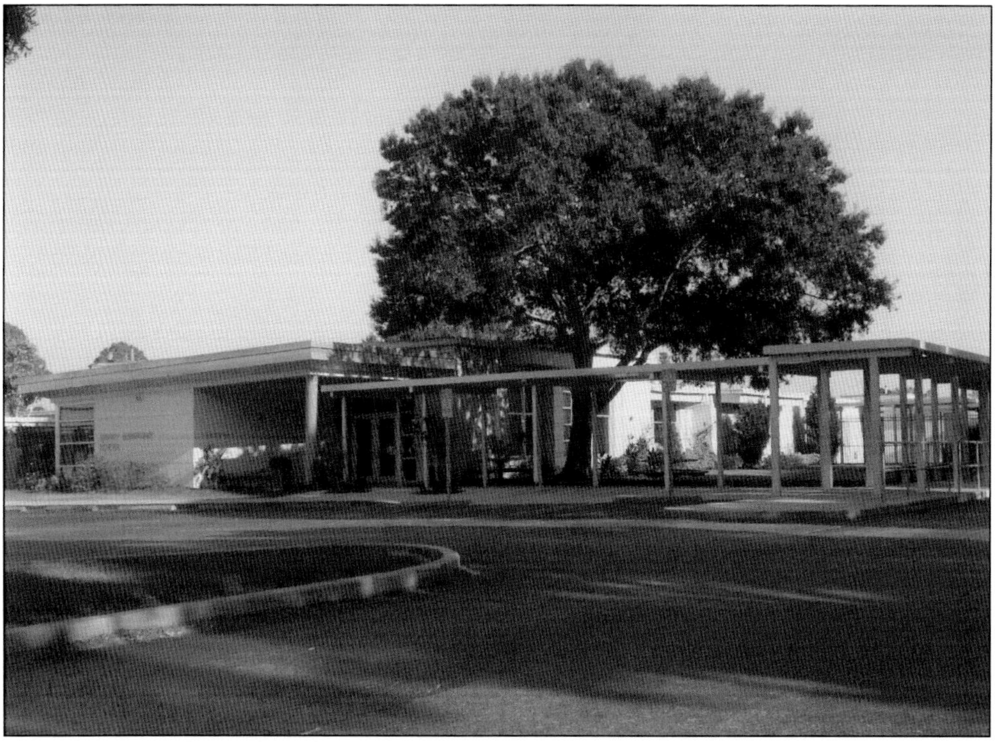

Classes began on the Starkey Elementary School campus in September 1960, after a year of double sessions at Cross Bayou. Located on 10 acres that once formed part of Jay Starkey's vast ranch holdings, the original campus included 12 classrooms, 15 teachers, and 396 students. At the time, Eighty-Sixth Avenue was only a dirt road, with a single telephone on a utility pole providing communication to the outside world. (Author.)

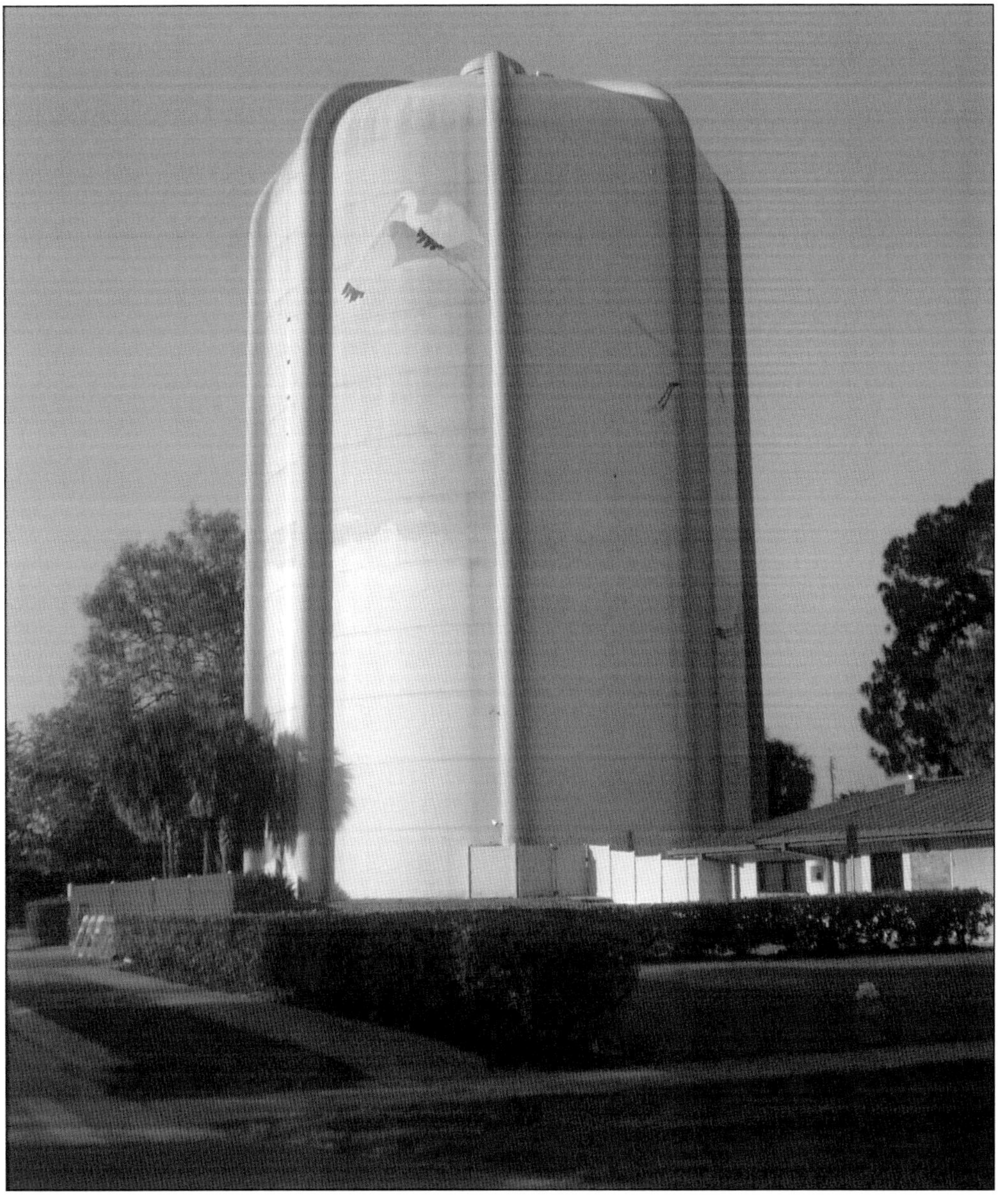

Construction of one of Seminole's most notable landmarks, the Oakhurst Water Tower, began in August 1958. A long convoy of concrete trucks drove along Bay Pines and Seminole Boulevards toward the site at 11323 Seventy-Fourth Avenue that month, pouring more than 6.4 million pounds of concrete in one day alone as workers created the base for the three-million-gallon water tower, then the largest in Florida. Pinellas County had received the land in the Ridgewood Groves area from St. Petersburg developer George R. Davis. The 140-foot Oakhurst tank went into service on February 20, 1959, providing water to the Seminole area and adjacent communities of the Gulf Beaches and serving as a navigational beacon for many years before condominiums lined the coast. Pinellas County officials paid Tom Stovall, an artist from St. Petersburg, $25,000 to paint the bird murals on the water tower in 2000. One of his original plans was to paint the tower more colorfully, so it would appear as a large gumball machine. This image captures part of the mural in December 2014. (Author.)

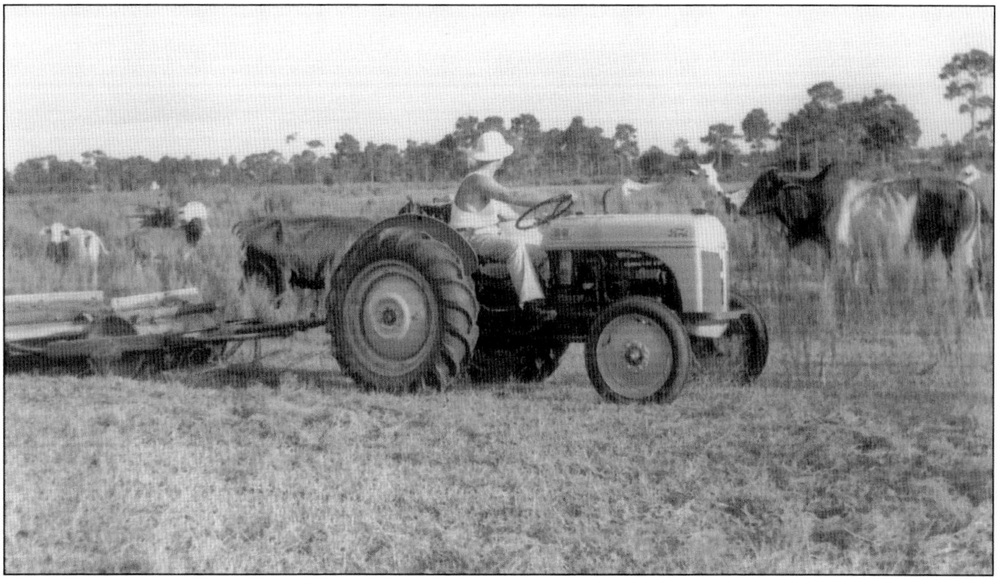

This photograph from the mid-20th century captures Jesse W. Johnson riding a tractor on his farmlands near Seminole Elementary School. Johnson's rural pastureland near the family's Seminole Nursery and other enterprises had substantially increased in value as developers marketed new subdivisions, such as the Ridgewood Groves community to the west. By the mid-1960s, Johnson had decided that this land should have a new commercial purpose. (SHS.)

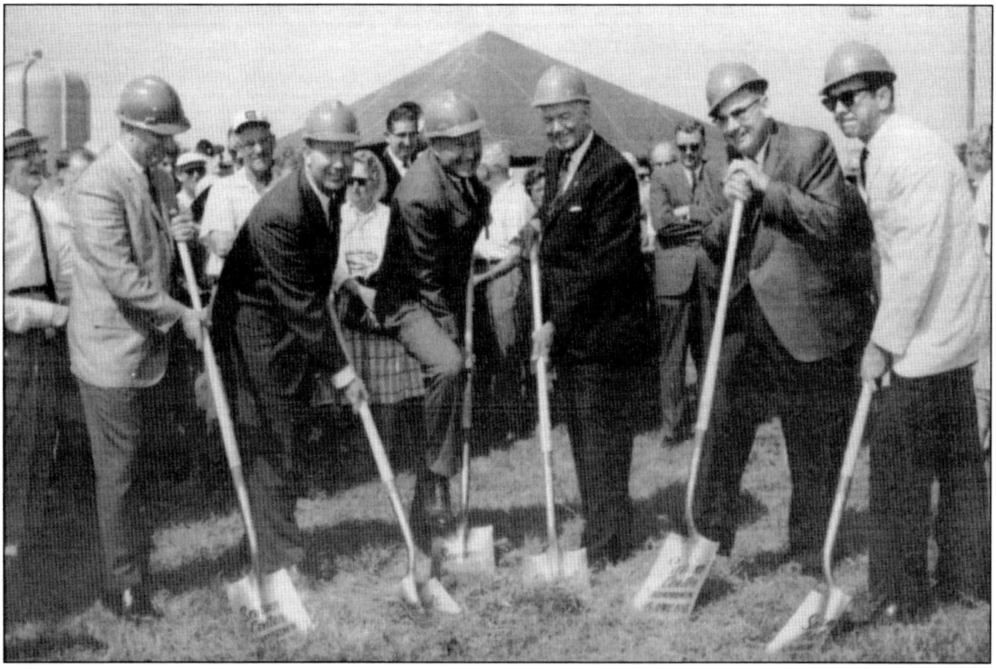

Crowds came to Jesse Johnson's former pasture in April 1965 to witness the ground-breaking ceremony for the Seminole Center, a shopping center designed by Frank Mudano, a noted Pinellas County architect. Johnson, third from right, wisely realized that new commercial enterprises would attract widespread interest, especially since many residents had to travel to Largo, western St. Petersburg, or the beach areas for consumer goods. (HV.)

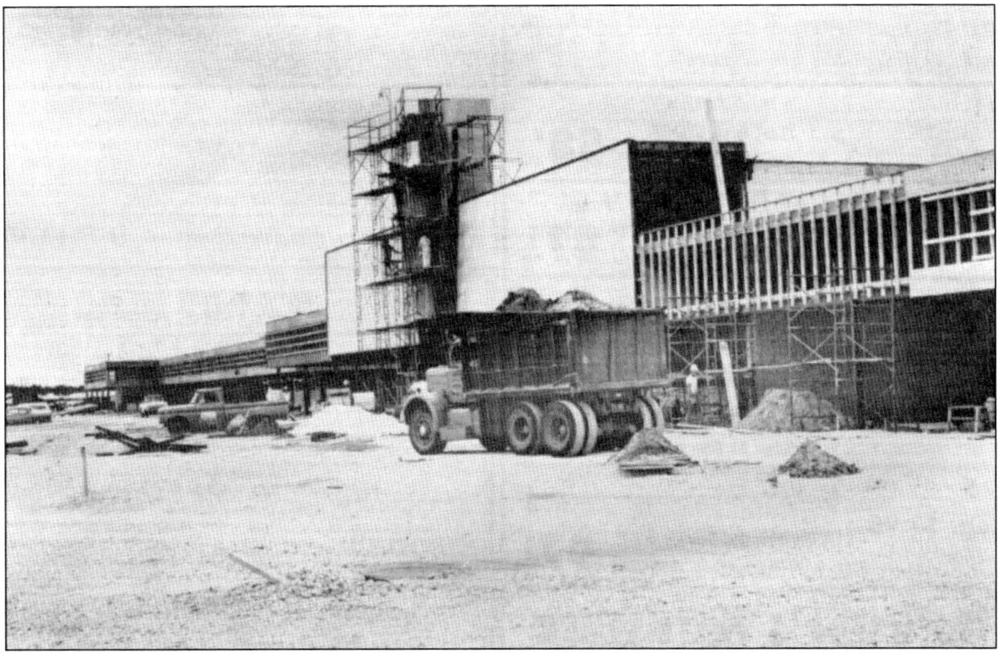

Construction ensued at a rapid pace. Cows soon disappeared from the landscape, and the framework for a Publix grocery store, visible above, took shape at Seminole Center along Park Boulevard. This July 1965 image illustrates the storefronts by looking westward toward 113th Street. Crews hoped to complete the Seminole Center by November 4, 1965. Below, three seniors from Seminole High School appear in a posed mid-October photograph, which shows final preparations at the south entrance to Seminole Center. A few years after this shopping center opened, larger and fully enclosed and air-conditioned malls such as Sunshine Mall in Clearwater and Tyrone Mall in St. Petersburg increased the competition among merchants. By the 1970s, the original Seminole Center had expanded into a full fledged mall. (Both, HV.)

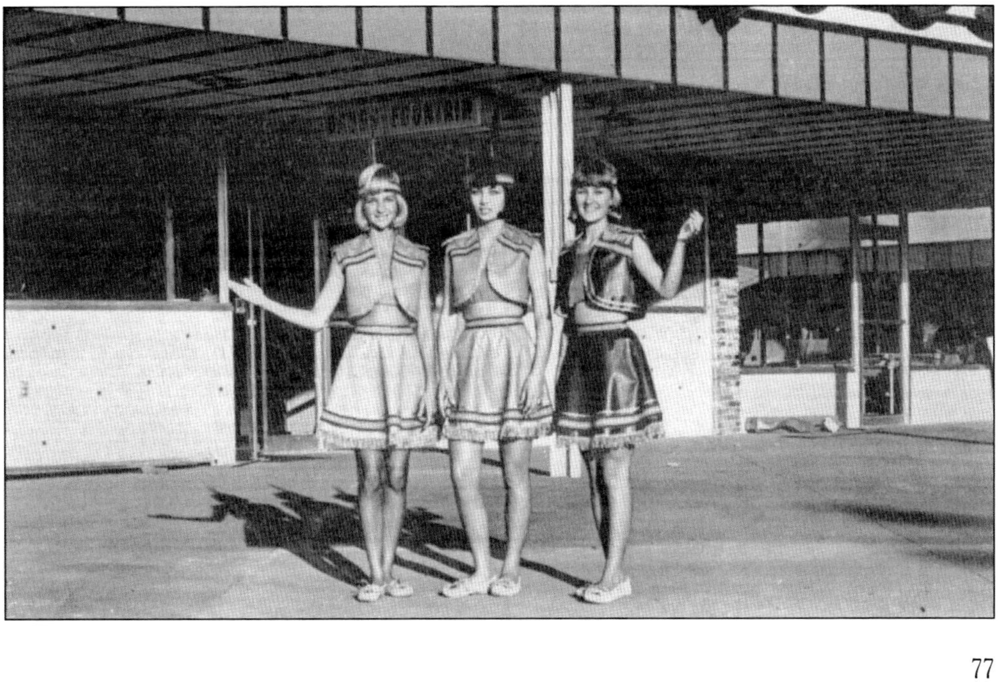

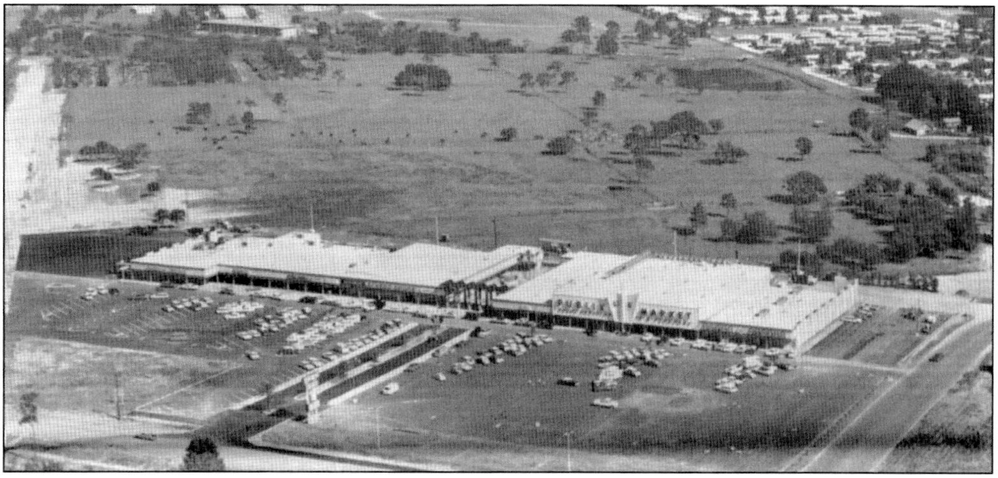

Businesses at the new Seminole Center opened in November 1965. This view looks north from Park Boulevard, with an unpaved extension of 113th Street on the left serving as a western boundary for the original 13-acre development. Johnson Boulevard, a privately owned road, borders the property on the right. Jesse W. Johnson announced plans to expand the shopping center into a 350,000-square-foot shopping mall in February 1969. (HV.)

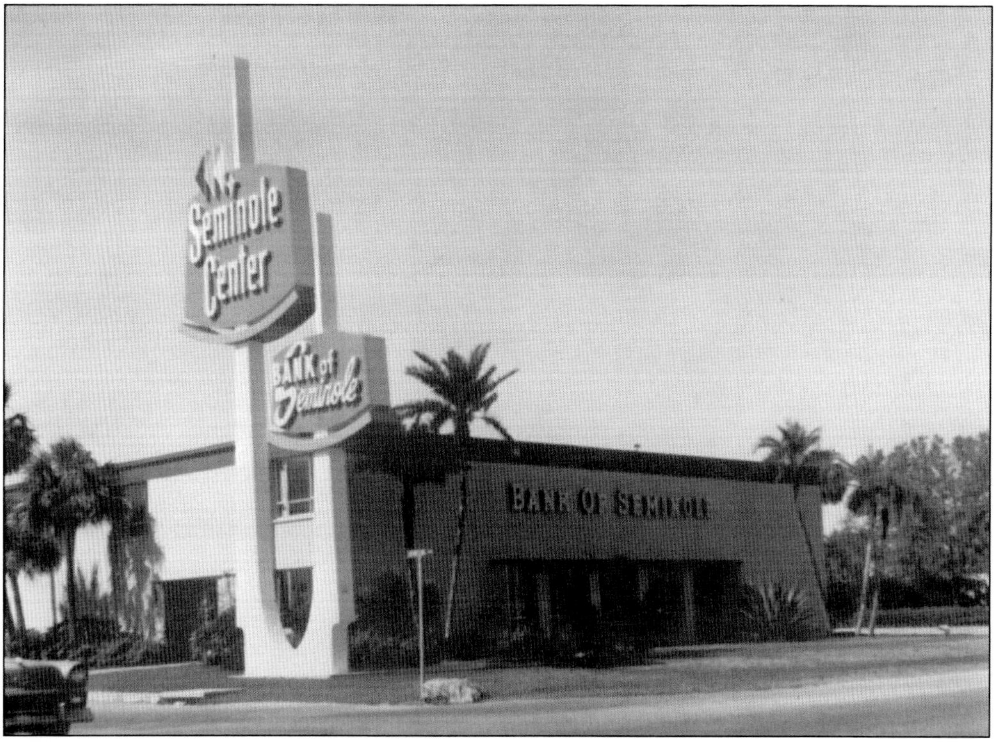

The Johnson family led efforts to establish the Bank of Seminole in December 1960. Jesse W. Johnson served as an early chair of the bank's board of directors, and his son Richard also participated. In 1960, the Bank of Seminole had assets of $1.53 million, an amount that soared to nearly $24.75 million nine years later. This November 1965 image shows the bank and sign for the new Seminole Center. (HV.)

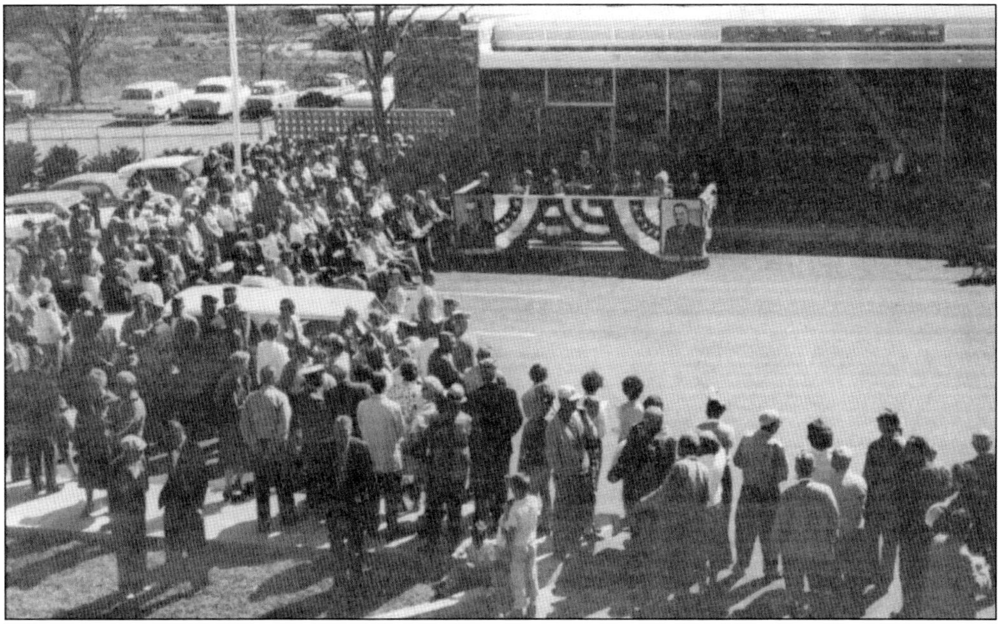

Nearly 1,000 people gathered along Johnson Boulevard for the dedication of the first Seminole Post Office on February 27, 1965. The facility's opening marked the first time that residents officially received mail addressed to "Seminole" instead of "Largo," though the building remained a branch of Largo. In April 1985, the city bought nearly 10 acres east of 113th Street as the site for an expanded post office. (HV.)

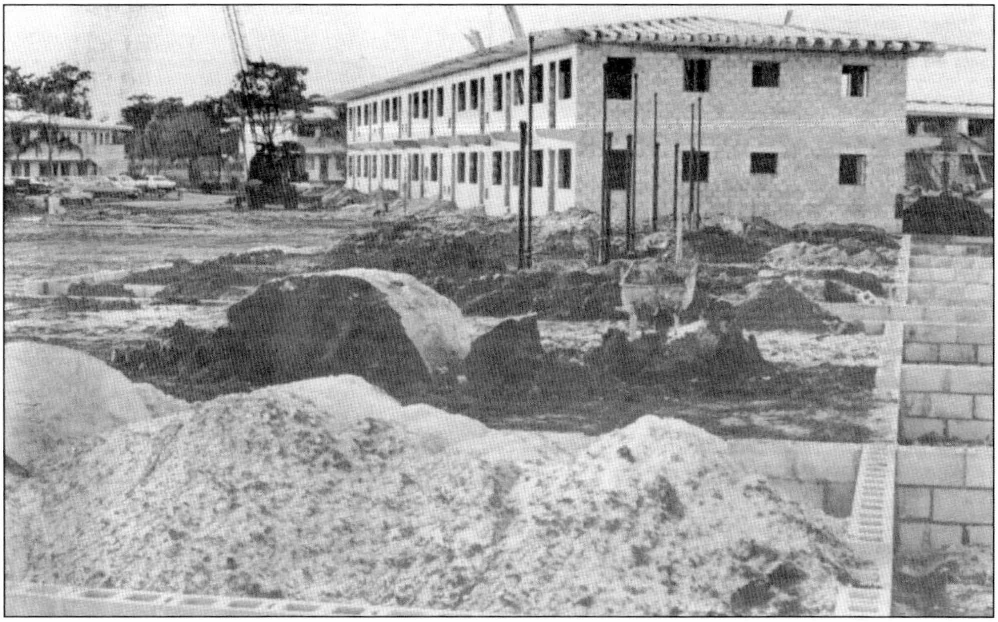

The new post office facility certainly handled a lot of mail from the Seminole Garden Apartments, located between Eightieth and Eighty-Sixth Avenues north of the present-day mall complex. The first units opened for occupancy in February 1965, two months before construction of the first phase of the Seminole Center (later Seminole Mall) started. The Seminole Garden Apartments remain a vibrant community for retirees a half century later. (HV.)

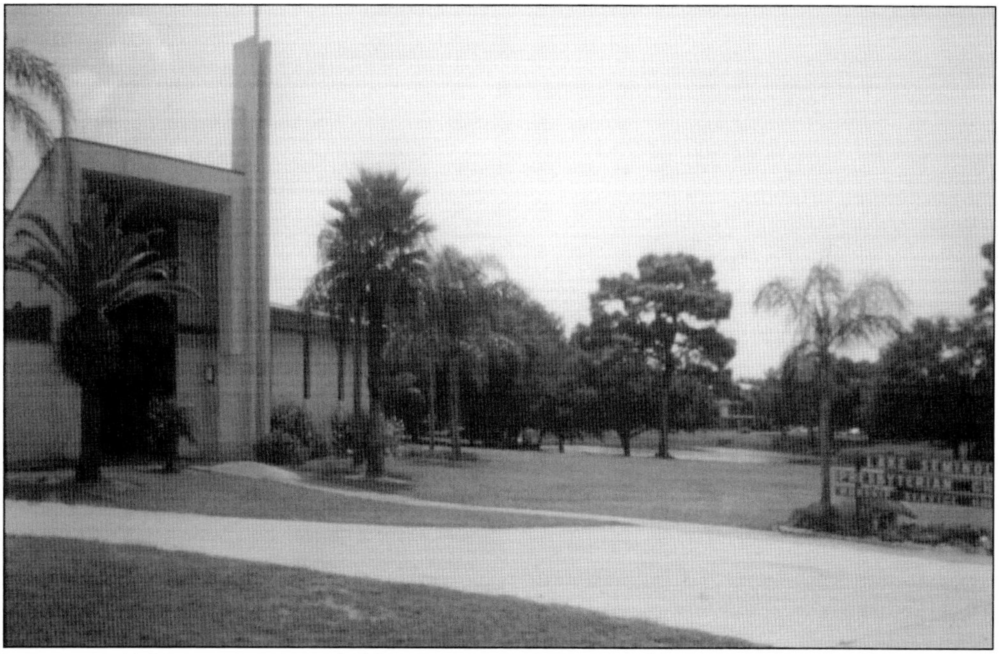

In January 1964, some residents held a meeting at Seminole Elementary School to worship and discuss the possibility of establishing a church near the heart of the community. They selected land at the southeast corner of Eighty-Sixth Avenue and 113th Street for their sanctuary. Services officially began at Lake Seminole Presbyterian Church in the spring of 1965. (SHS.)

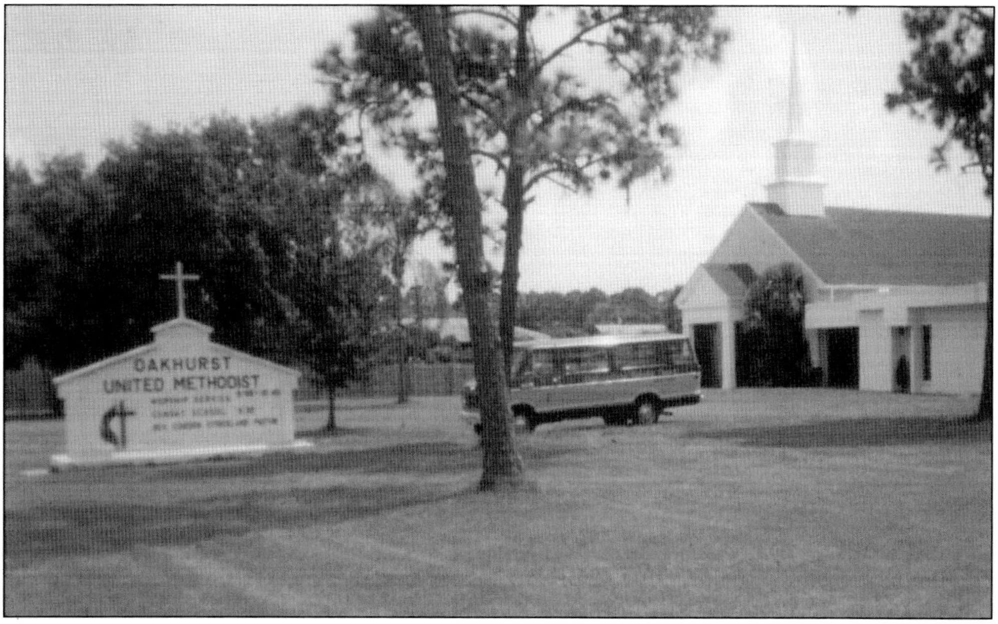

As residential subdivisions spread into former farmlands, new churches and other religious institutions followed them. Oakhurst United Methodist, located at 13400 Park Boulevard, also celebrated its first half-century in 2015. Religious institutions for a variety of faiths appeared throughout the area during the latter 20th century, with a notable surge between the mid-1960s and early 1980s. (SHS.)

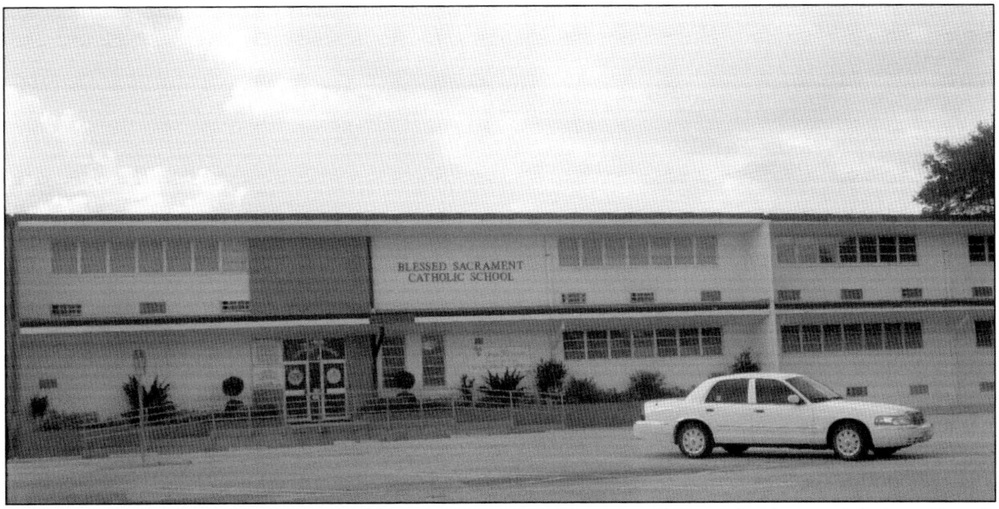

Blessed Sacrament Catholic Church traces its origins to a Mass that took place in Madeira Beach on May 17, 1959. Services then moved to a structure in a former citrus grove at 11501 Sixty-Sixth Avenue in January 1960. Ground breaking for the parish school, shown above in a 2015 springtime image, took place in May 1962, with the first class enrolling in September 1962. Popular springtime carnivals served as fundraisers for many years, allowing the church to expand its services under the Diocese of St. Petersburg. Families in the parish celebrated the growth of the church with a new sanctuary at the corner of Sixty-Sixth Avenue and 116th Street in the late 1970s. A view of this structure from the southwest corner of the church property in the early 1980s appears below. (Above, author; below, SHS.)

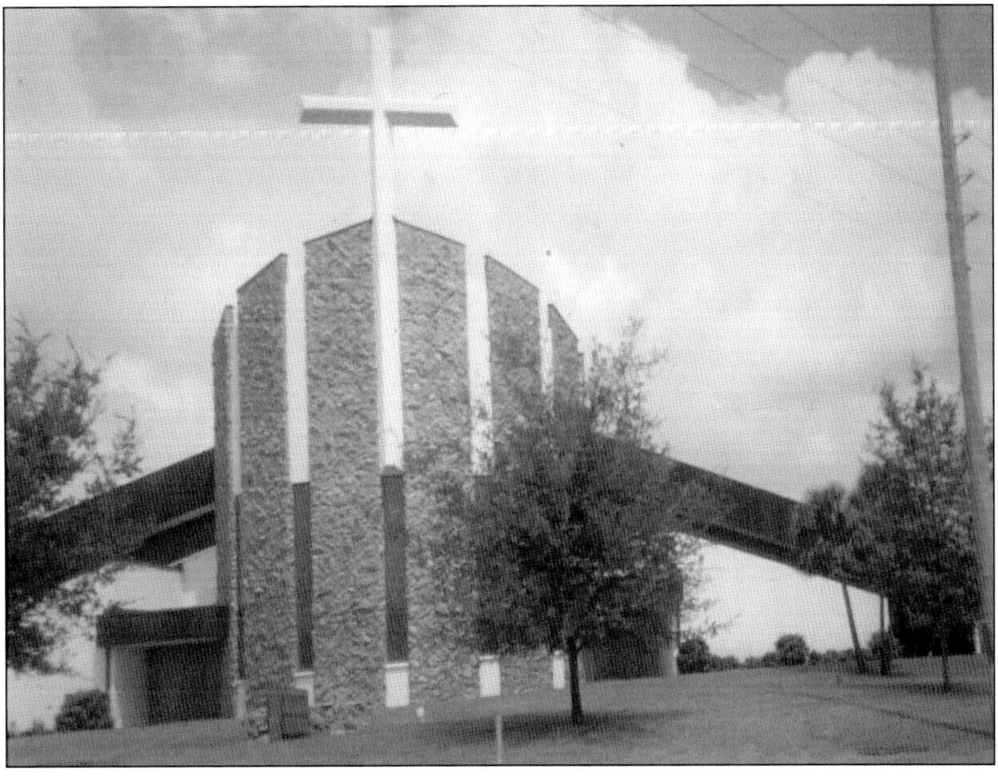

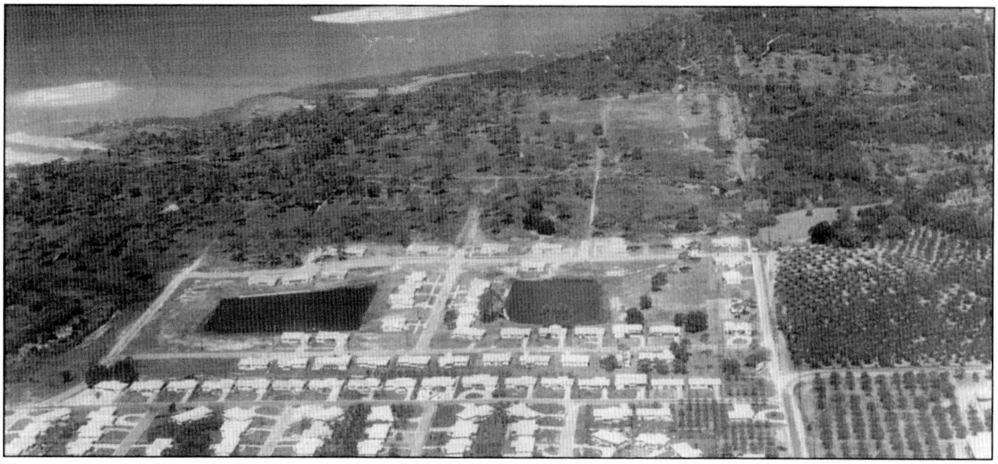

The groves at Blessed Sacrament appear in the lower-right corner of this 1963 aerial photo. The westward view shows the Bay Ridge subdivision (at bottom) and the 120-acre Sheraton Shores development. A decade later, in 1973, the Tides Golf Club opened on lands in the center of this image. By that time, the Canterbury Chase subdivision had replaced the groves at right center. (Courtesy of Kaye Davies.)

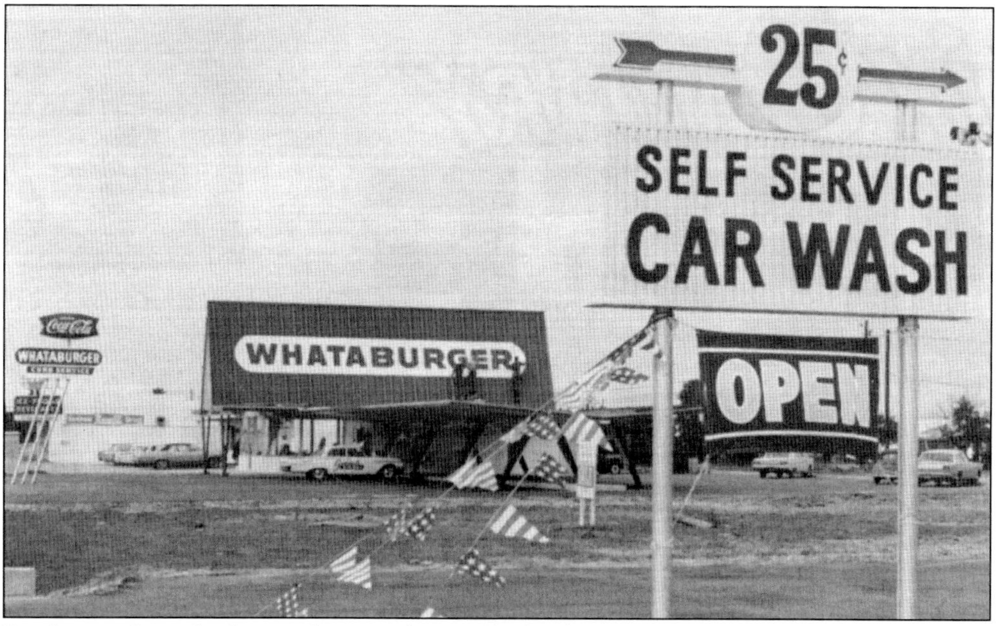

Similar to other suburban enclaves in the rapidly developing Tampa Bay region, new businesses sprouted up along formerly vacant lands and groves throughout the Seminole region. In January 1966, a popular hamburger fast food chain added a local restaurant near a new car wash on the eastern side of Seminole Boulevard, just north of Pineapple Road. The restaurant later closed, but the structure remains in use 50 years later. (HV.)

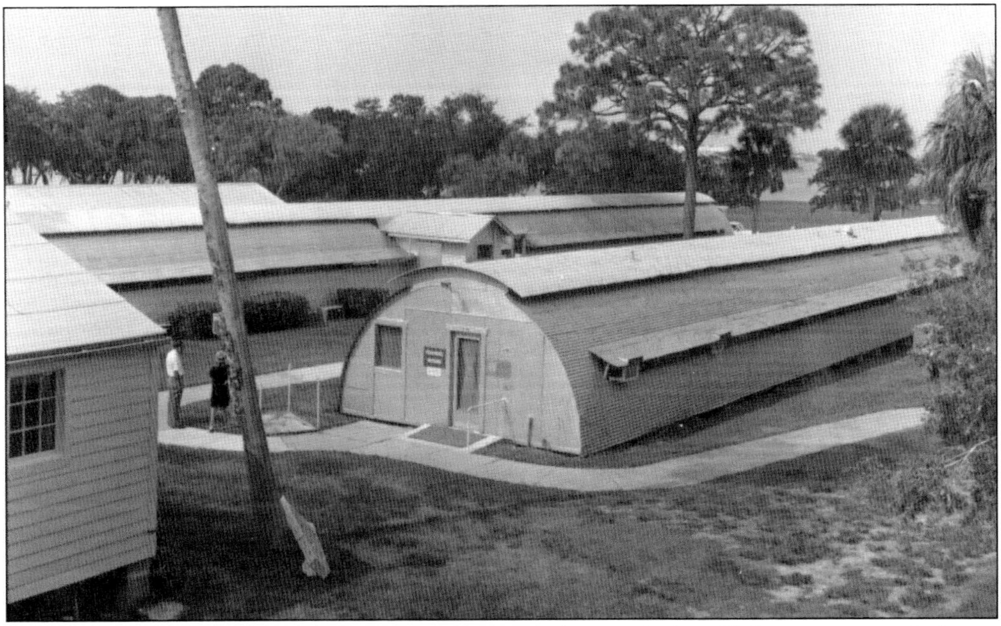

The influx of new residents to the Tampa Bay area during the late 20th century—including a substantial number of military veterans—stretched the resources of the Veterans Administration, including medical services at Bay Pines. Quonset-type structures first appeared on the campus in the 1940s and many remained until the larger hospital structure, Building No. 100, opened in the early 1980s. (Bay Pines VA Collection.)

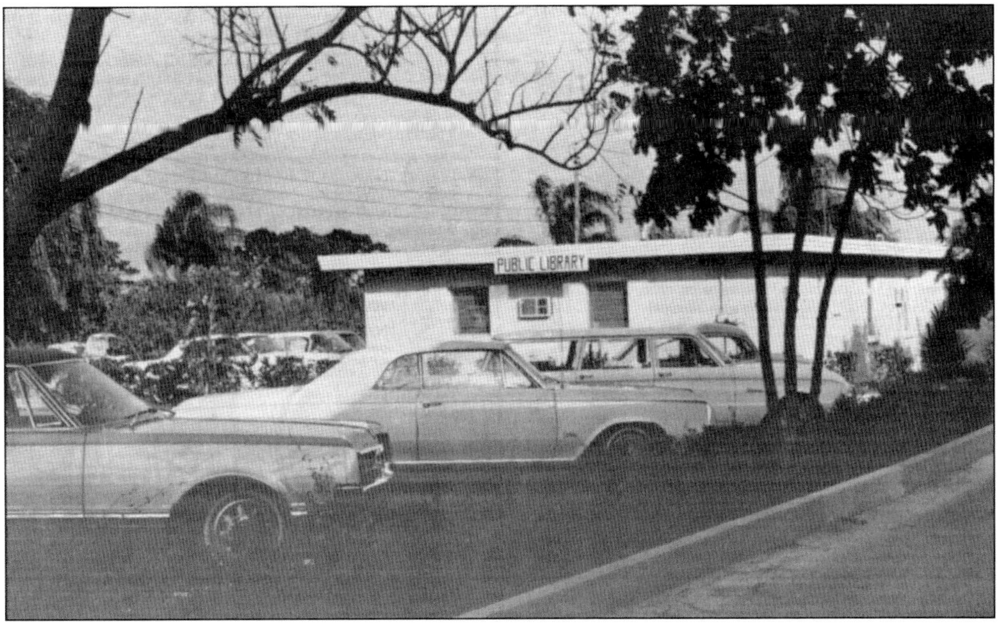

Residents of the unincorporated area supported an expansion of library facilities for the community. By 1965, the Seminole-Ridge Community Library had outgrown its small facility. With support from Russell Stewart and the Home Federal Savings and Loan Association, staff members and volunteers moved the 6,000-volume collection on November 10, 1965, to the structure pictured here at 7415 Seminole Boulevard, just north of Home Federal. (HV.)

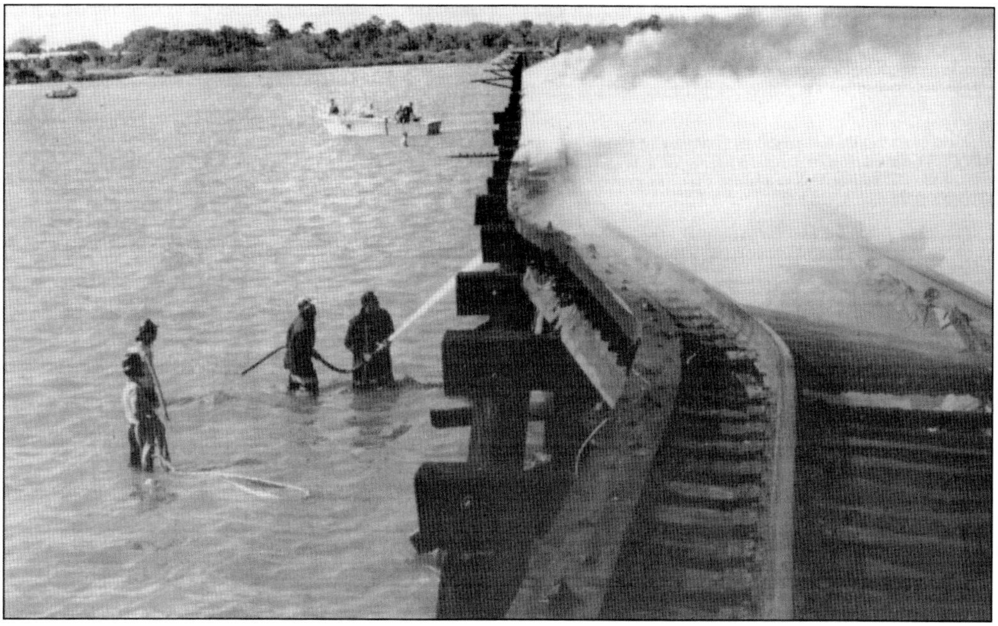

Constructed as part of the Tampa & Gulf Coast Railway in 1914, a railroad trestle spanning Long Bayou connected Seminole to St. Petersburg. The original trestle suffered damage during the devastating October 1921 hurricane. Rebuilt soon after with log pillars and railroad ties soaked in creosote, a section of the half-mile trestle caught fire on November 20, 1947. The image above shows volunteer firefighters in Seminole joining other agencies in a battle to put out a noontime fire on February 17, 1965, which destroyed 500 feet of track. Another devastating trestle fire during the summer of 1979 led to the abandonment of this rail route, now part of the Pinellas Trail. The image below offers a similar perspective of the spot of the 1965 fire a half century later, as part of the recreation trail. (Above, HV; below, author.)

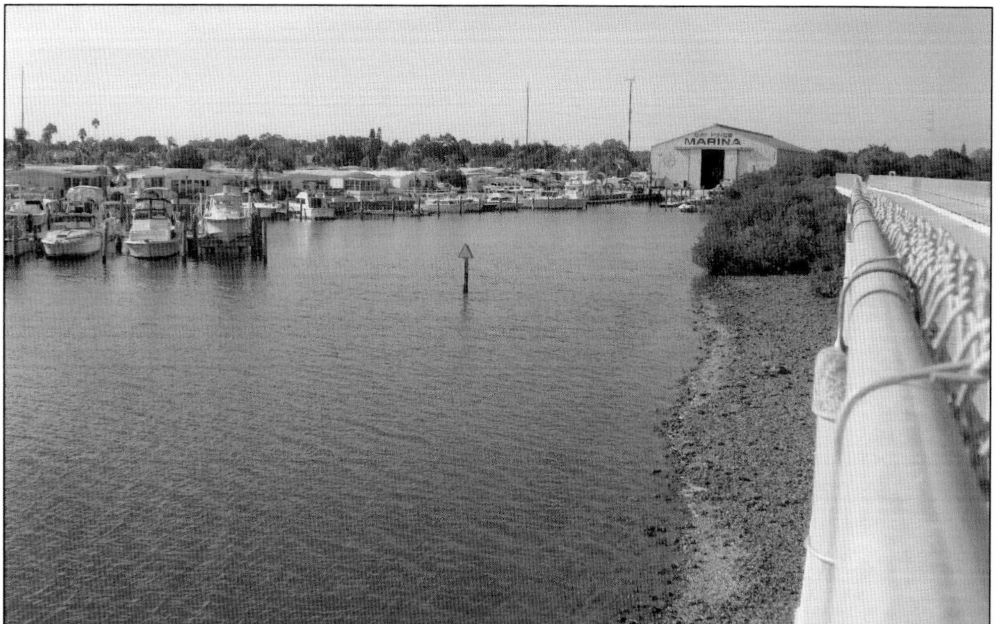

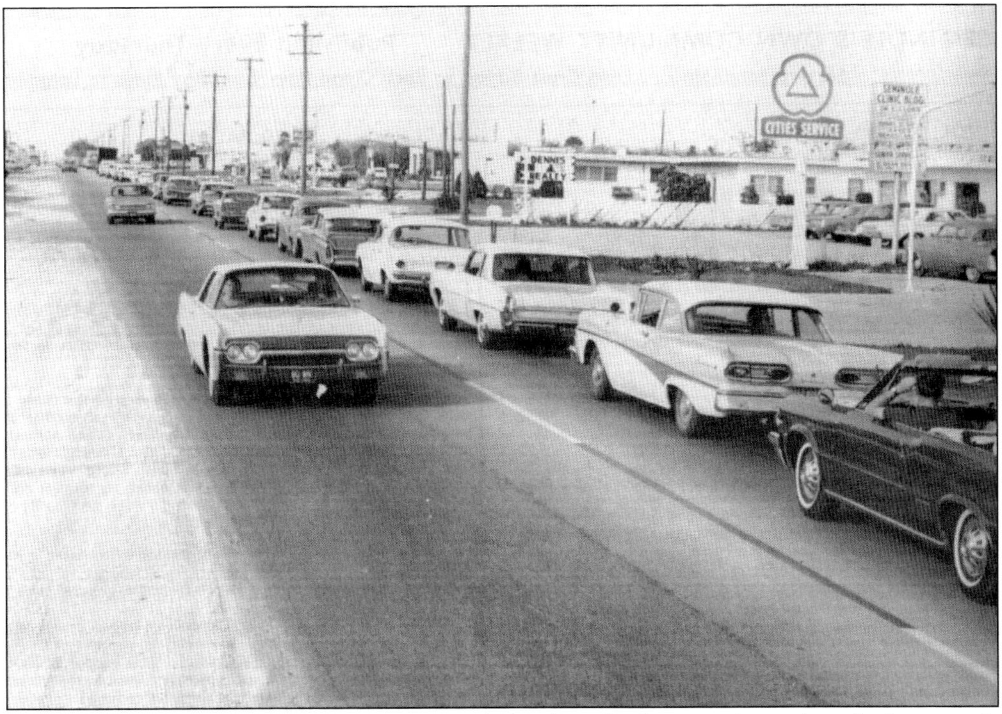

The February 1965 trestle fire at Long Bayou led to long backups, as shown here looking north along a two-lane Seminole Boulevard just north of Fifty-Fourth Avenue. However, by the mid-1960s, traffic jams became more commonplace even without exceptional events such as trestle fires or automobile accidents. The narrow, outdated span of the Bay Pines Bridge across Long Bayou and the Bay Pines Triangle became areas of immediate concern. (HV.)

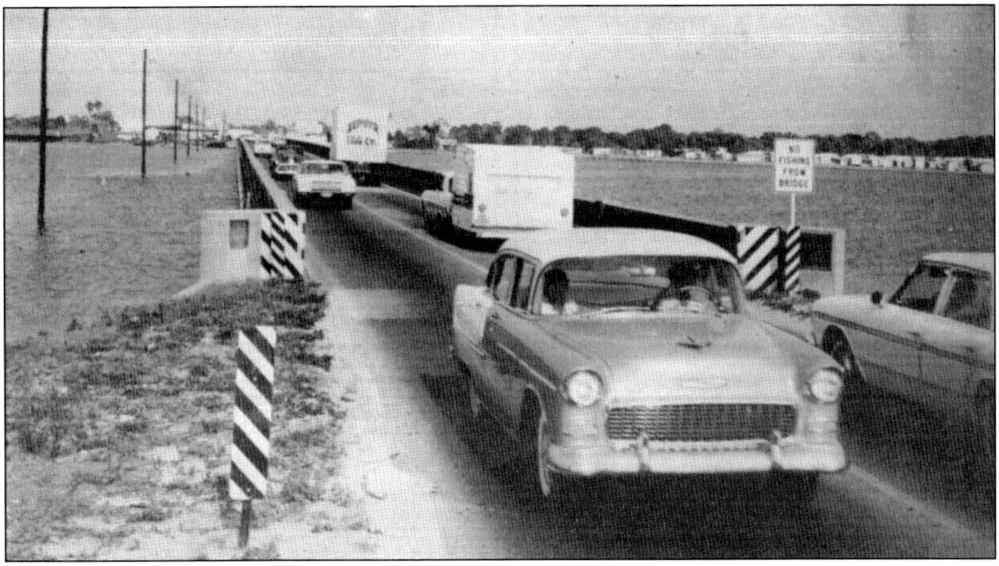

Compared to the image of an isolated causeway in the mid-1920s shown on page 34, the Seminole Bridge across Long Bayou had transformed into a narrow, hazardous roadway as it passed its 40th anniversary in service. This eastward view from Bay Pines toward St. Petersburg in May 1965 reveals the perils that drivers faced trying to cross the span. (HV.)

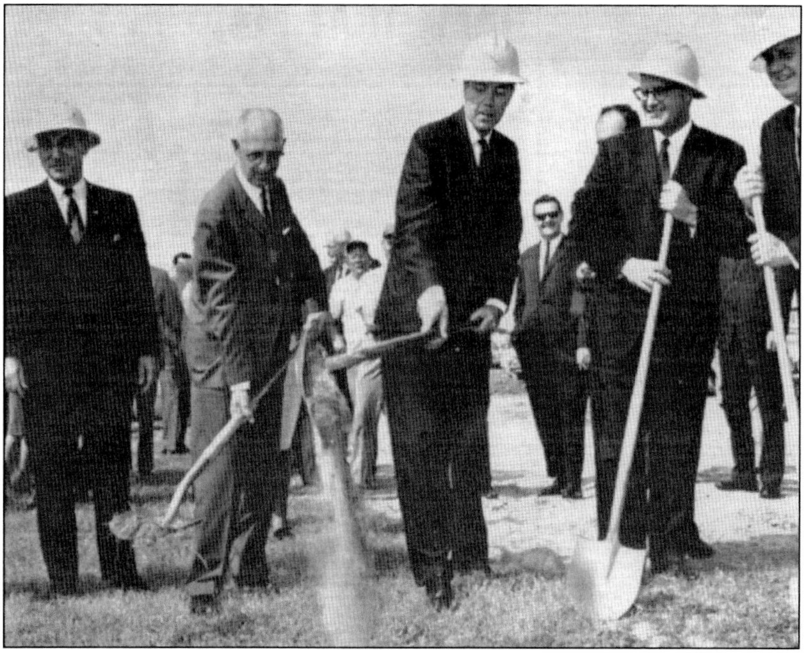

A concerted effort to replace the outdated 1924 span began in the late 1950s. Momentum increased in the mid-1960s, when the Greater Seminole Community Council gathered approximately 22,000 signatures in support of the cause. County commissioners unanimously approved funds for right-of-way acquisition in June 1965. Gov. Harden Burns, turning dirt above on October 21, 1965, participated in the long-awaited ground-breaking ceremonies that took place at the baseball field on the Bay Pines VA facility. In his remarks, Burns called on the removal of "two-lane death traps" like the old Seminole span as part of a statewide $300-million road bond initiative. Improvements also led to the removal of a railroad spur across Bay Pines Boulevard between Ninety-Fourth and Ninety-Fifth Streets, near the eastern entrance to Bay Pines, in the area shown in the January 16, 1966, image below. (Both, HV.)

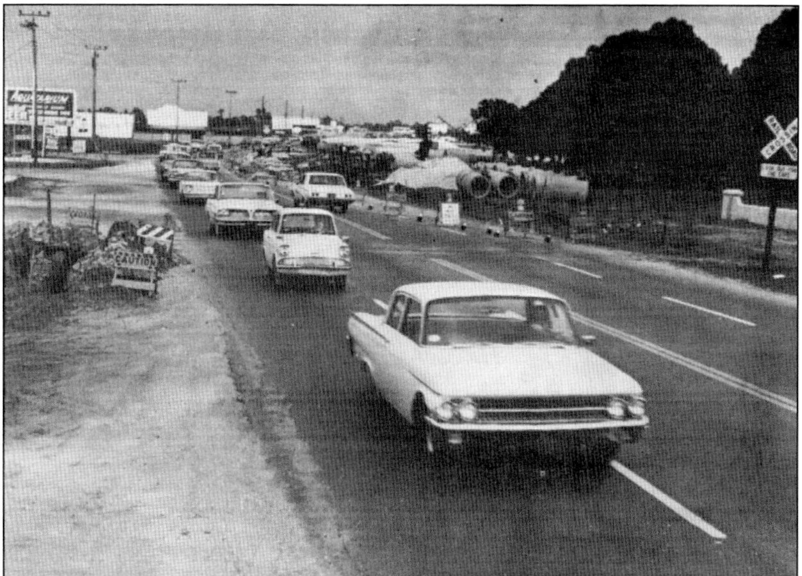

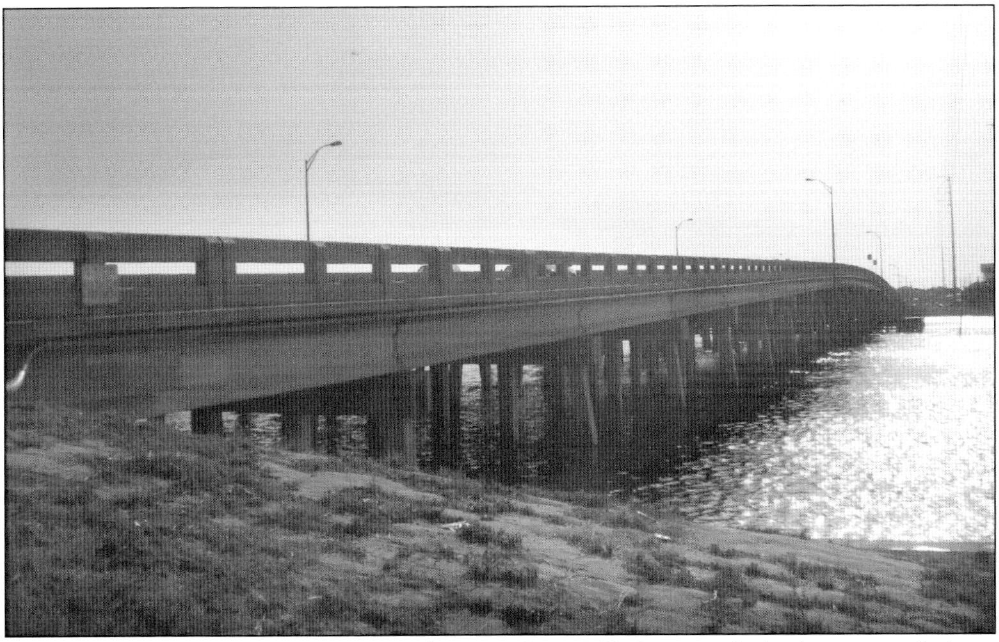

Site preparations for the new twin spans began in late 1965. Crews sank the first series of pilings into Long Bayou in February 1966, and construction moved forward at a rapid pace to replace a bridge that many called the worst bottleneck in Pinellas County. Marvin Bradshaw, president of the Seminole Chamber of Commerce, hoped that the construction of the dual spans would allow Seminole to become "the retail outlet of Pinellas County." The Seminole and St. Petersburg Chambers of Commerce participated in dedication ceremonies for the new bridge on May 3, 1967. Frank Byers, the proprietor of the Polynesian-themed Tiki Gardens roadside attraction in Indian Shores, provided a rickshaw as the first vehicle across the new bridge. The view above looks west toward Bay Pines, while the image below shows the eastbound bridge approach. (Both, author.)

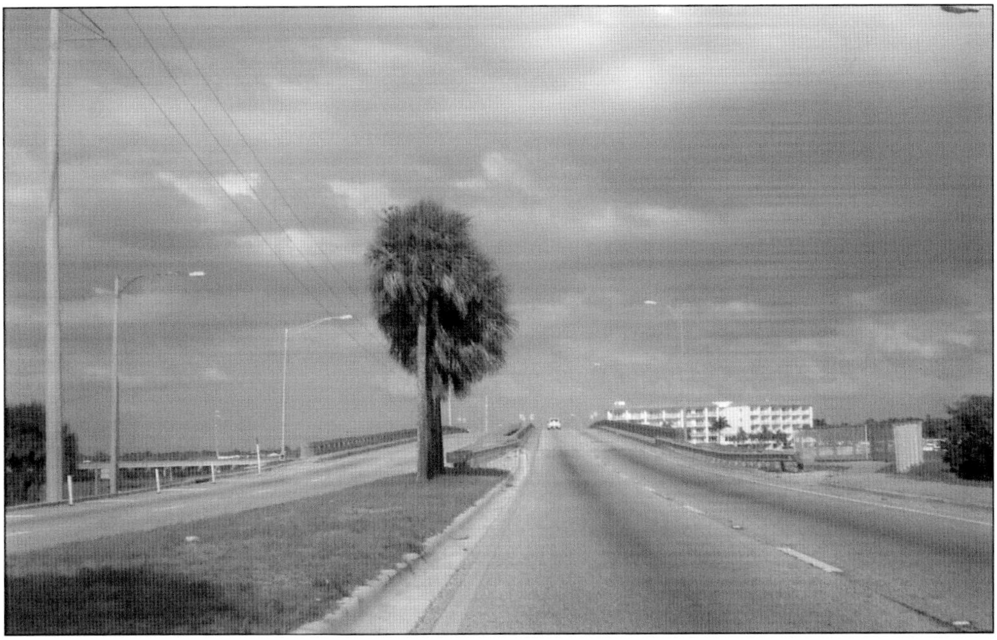

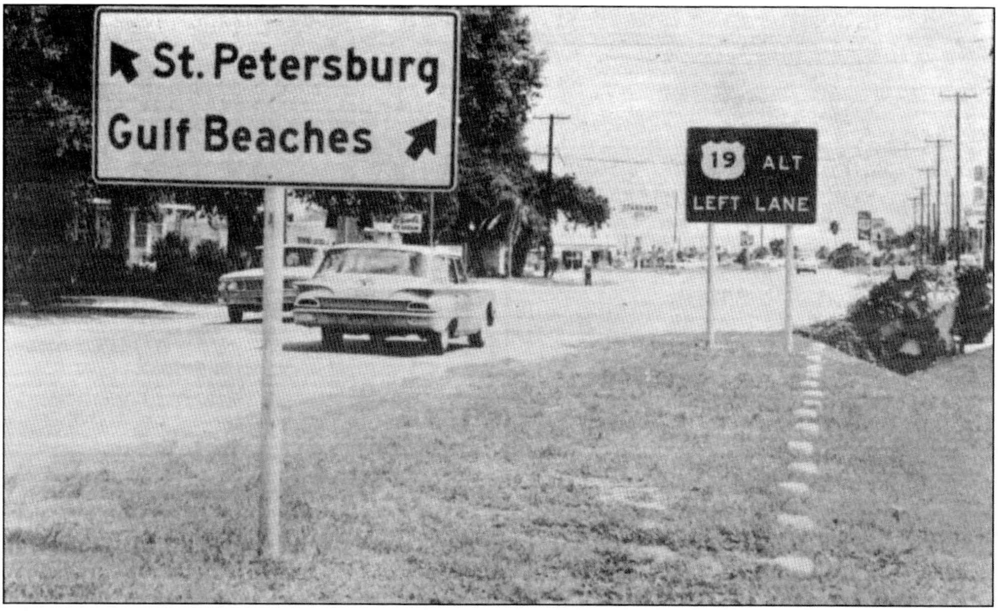

The opening of the new bridges across Long Bayou moved the traffic bottleneck west to the Bay Pines Triangle. This contorted maze of turnoffs dating to the 1920s connected Bay Pines Boulevard, Seminole Boulevard, and the road leading to Welch Causeway and Madeira Beach. Lax development laws further complicated navigation at the Bay Pines Triangle after a variety of businesses—including gas stations, a liquor store, restaurants, and even a Towne Club soda distribution store—occupied space within the center of the triangle. The mid-1960s view above looks south along Seminole Boulevard at the approach to the Bay Pines Triangle. Attempts to modify the Triangle in the early 1970s stalled. However, by the early 1980s, overpasses had replaced the abrupt curves and traffic lights. The view below shows a similar perspective in April 2015. (Above, SHS; below, author.)

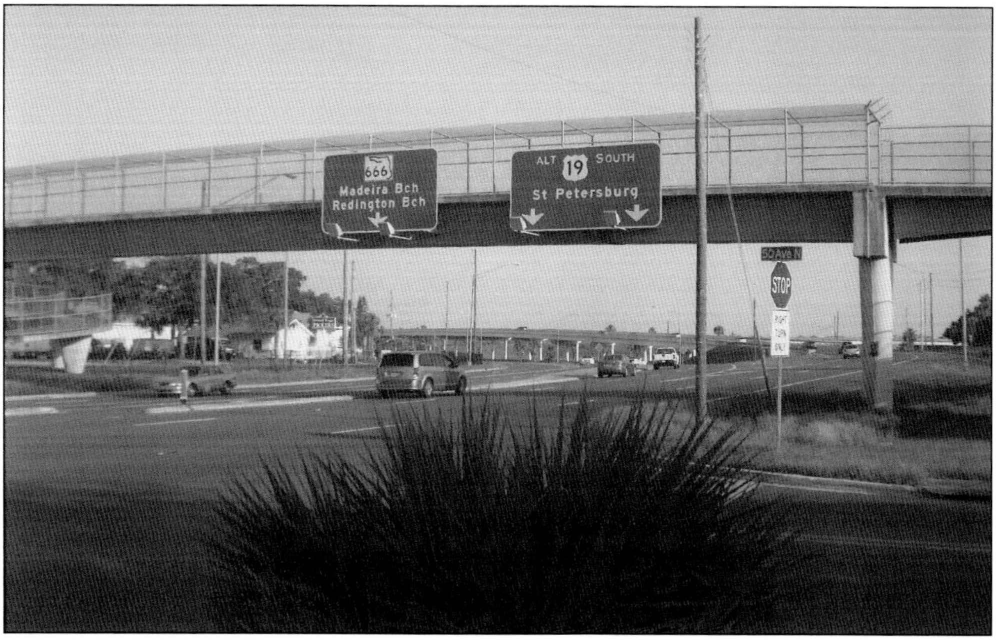

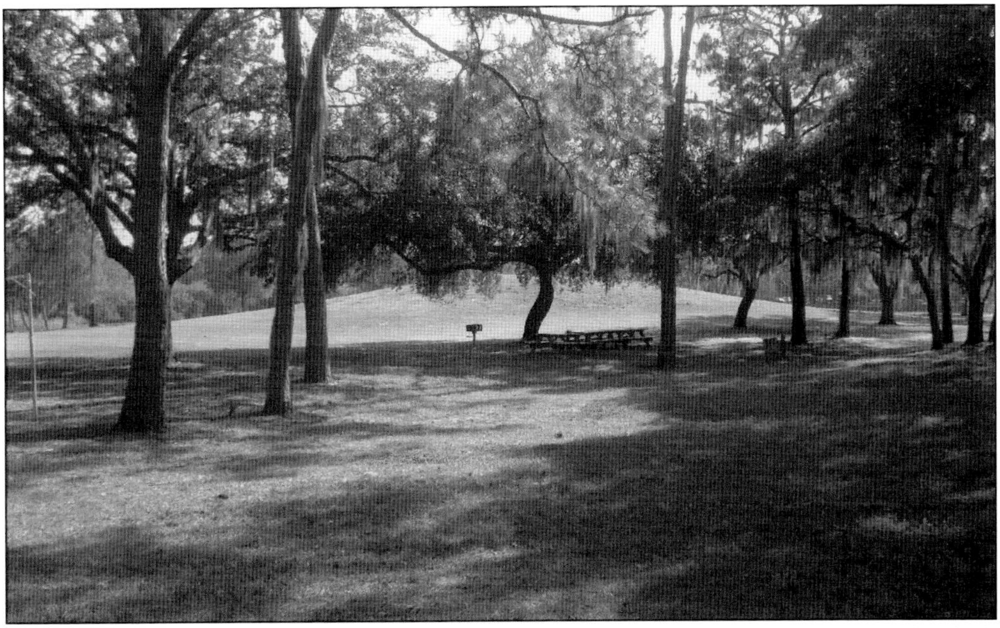

In 1961, a little more than a decade after the transformation of part of Long Bayou from a brackish saltwater estuary into the freshwater Lake Seminole, county officials discussed plans to create a new park along the southeastern corner of the lake. Opened in February 1968 and officially dedicated on May 18 of that year, Lake Seminole Park originally had 60 acres developed for public access, including picnic areas along the lakeshore and a smaller lake near the popular "hill" that has attracted generations of families. Subsequent additions have expanded the park to include more than 260 acres, new picnic and recreational facilities, and a two-mile trail through the pinelands and hammocks where joggers and bicyclists often see a variety of wildlife. (Both, author.)

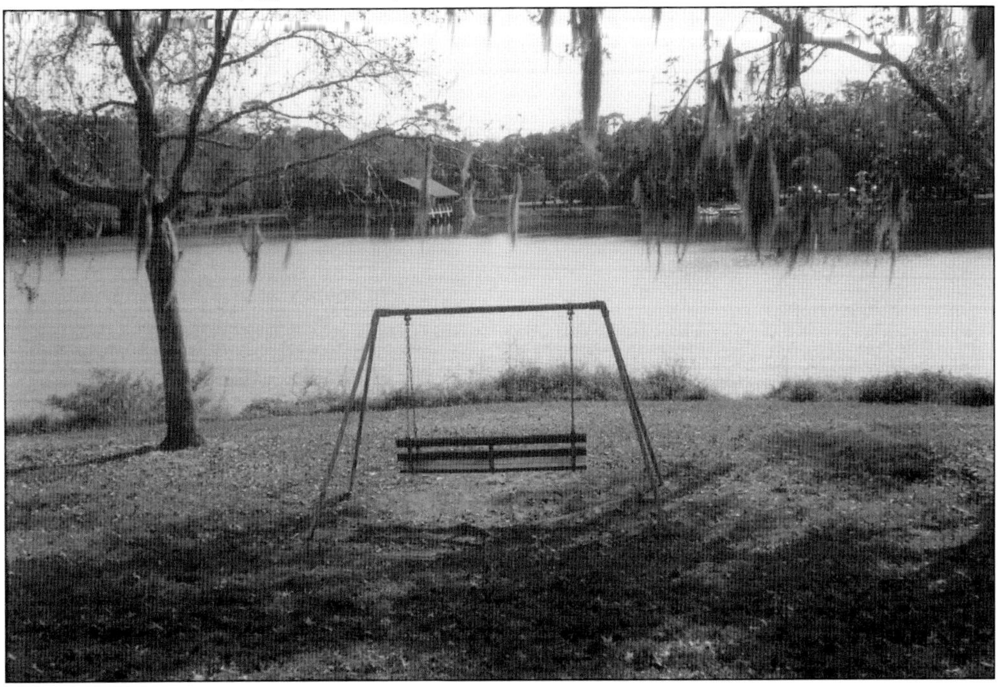

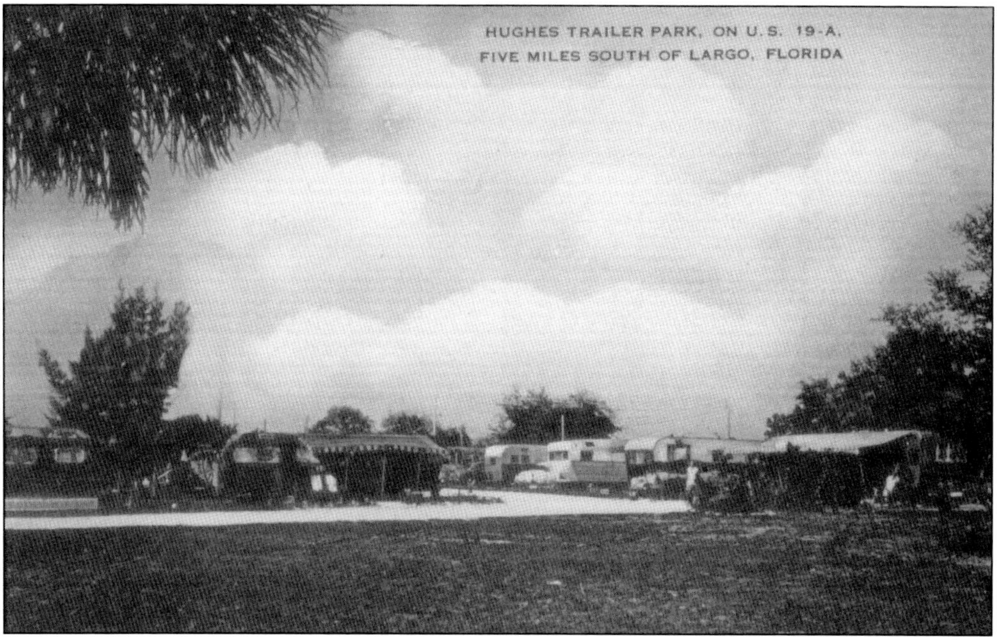

During the two decades immediately following World War II, trailer parks and mobile home communities replaced many tracts of undeveloped or agricultural land. Some parks remain to this day, though many have themselves become subdivisions, planned communities, or shopping centers. Hughes Trailer Park, above, represents the parks of the early 1950s. Operated by James William Hughes along Seminole Boulevard in the early 1950s, this site included a gas station and basic facilities. Holiday Campground, below, a 101-acre park at 10000 Park Boulevard south of Lake Seminole Park along Long Bayou, opened in 1969 when the proprietors allowed trailers to stay for $3 per night plus 50¢ daily for electricity and free sewer hookups. The Baynard family sold Holiday Campground in July 2003 for $14 million to a developer who built the Seminole Isle condominium community. (Both, HV.)

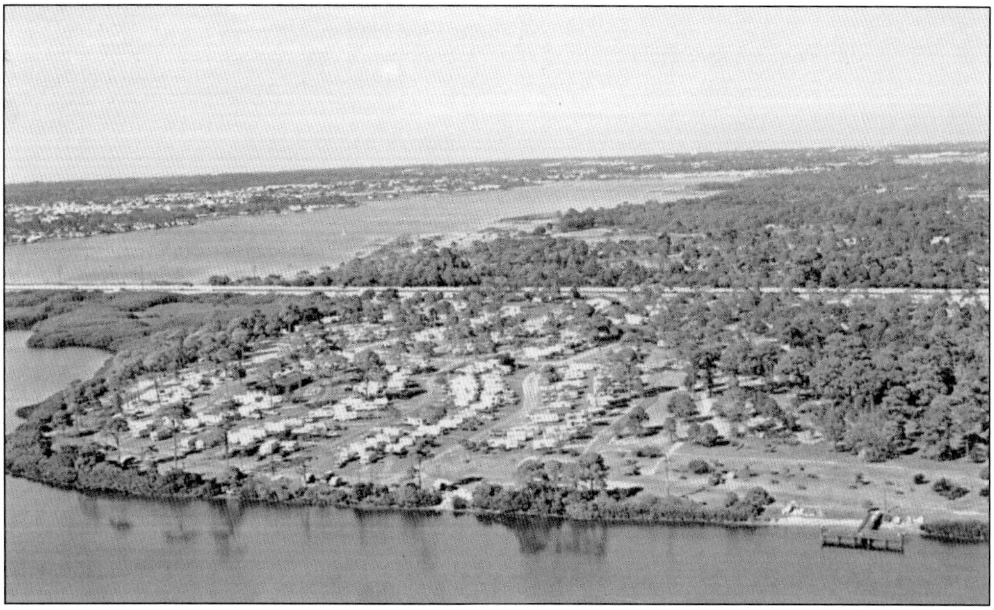

Four

Incorporation and Expansion 1970–2000

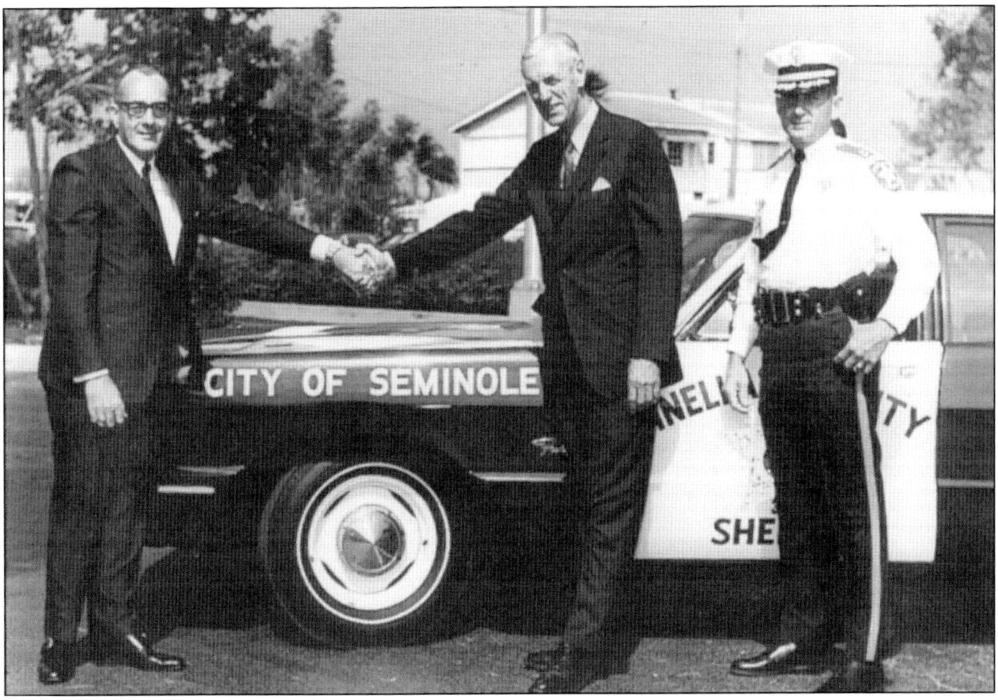

The City of Seminole came into existence on November 15, 1970. Pictured shortly after the city's inception, Mayor Russell L. Stewart (left), Pinellas County Sheriff Don Genung (center), and Carl McMullen (right), a leading officer in the department and grandson of "Uncle" Dan McMullen from one of the county's pioneer families, stand in front of a 1970 Plymouth Fury adorned with "City of Seminole." (Penny Cooke Collection.)

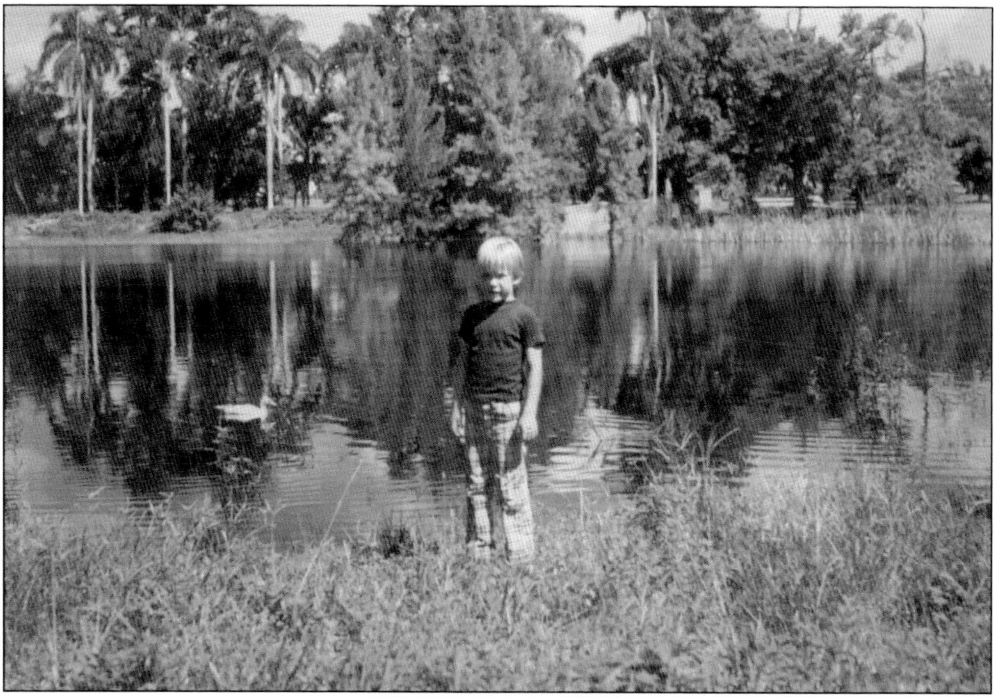

In early 1974, the City of Seminole acquired the 10.8-acre Meares Lake tract for $200,000. The city provided $50,000 in cash and financed $150,000 with a 20-year mortgage after Vance K. Meares and his daughter June Kirkland agreed to the terms of the sale. The image above illustrates the undeveloped condition of the site, with a young Kevin Holloway standing near the edge of the 2.8-acre pond. Safety concerns led to the placement of a fence on this site once given the new name Seminole City Park in June 1974. A $75,000 grant from the Florida Department of Natural Resources, now the Department of Environmental Protection, allowed for the construction of a small pier over part of the lake by 1976. Turtles, birds, alligators—and even an occasional peacock—congregate at the park. (Both, Sandy Holloway Collection.)

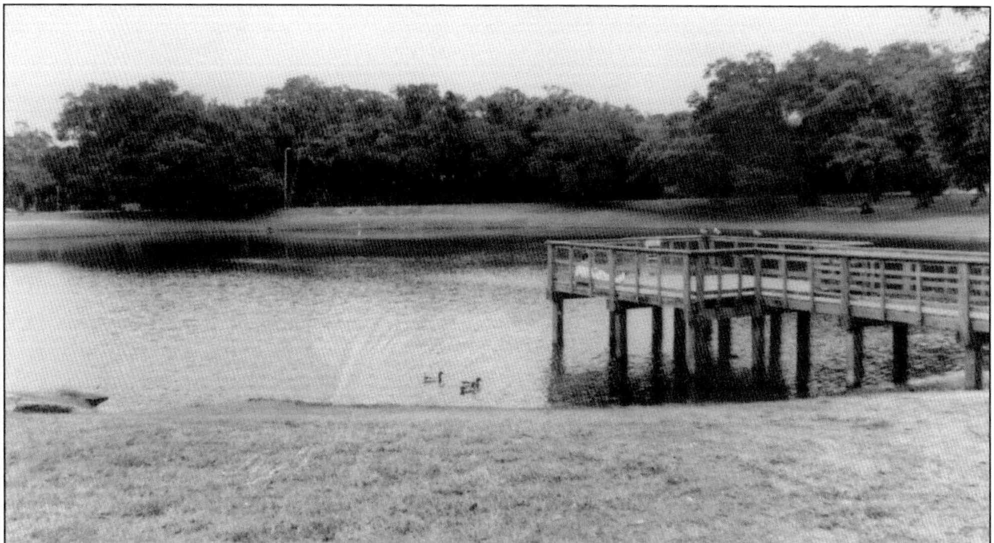

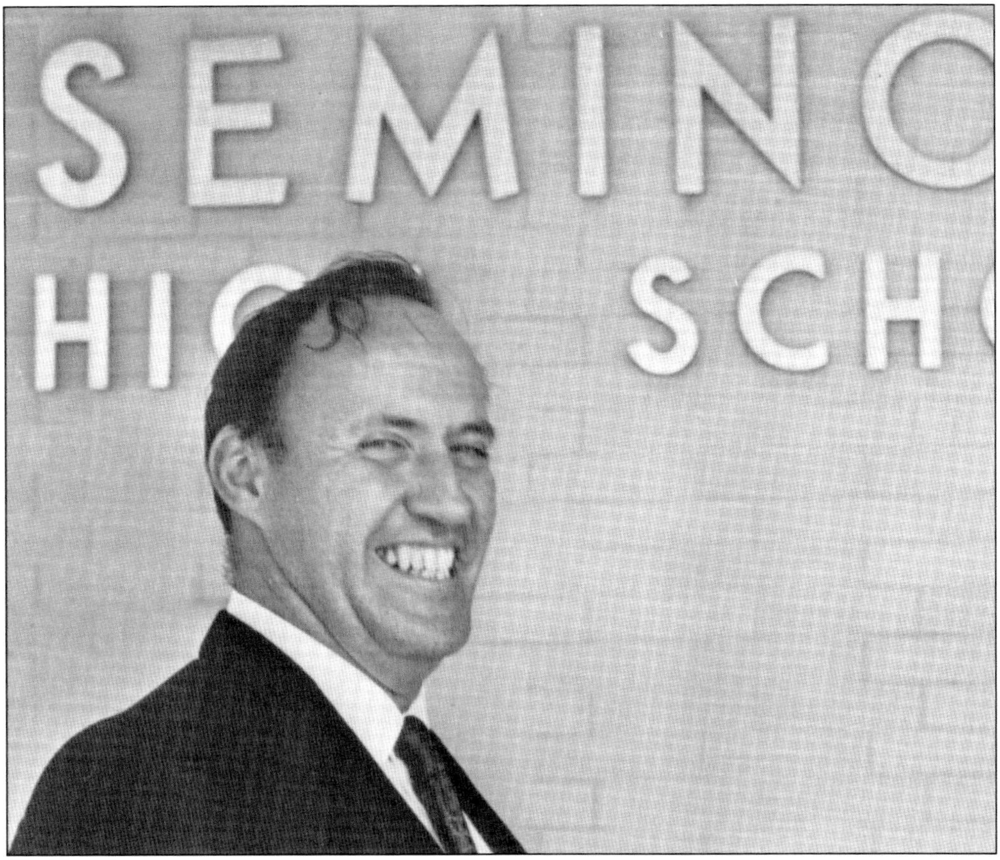

Scott Rose, later the superintendent of the Pinellas County School District, served as a popular principal of Seminole High School between 1965 and 1970, a period when enrollment doubled to 1,800 students. Major expansions to the campus took place in the late 1960s and 1970s, coinciding with the substantial residential development of the greater Seminole area. A neighborhood school until federal court orders required cross-district busing for racial desegregation beginning in 1971–1972, the expanding campus never lost its neighborly touch. As school officials planned for a major expansion of the campus that was completed in the 1977–1978 academic year, they also had to place the nearly 3,500 students on a schedule with double sessions that lasted from 1973–1974 until the 1980–1981 school year. (Both. HV.)

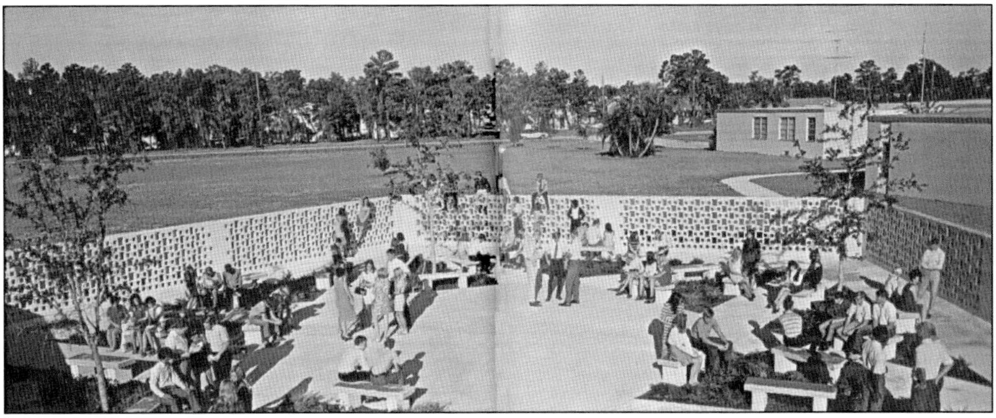

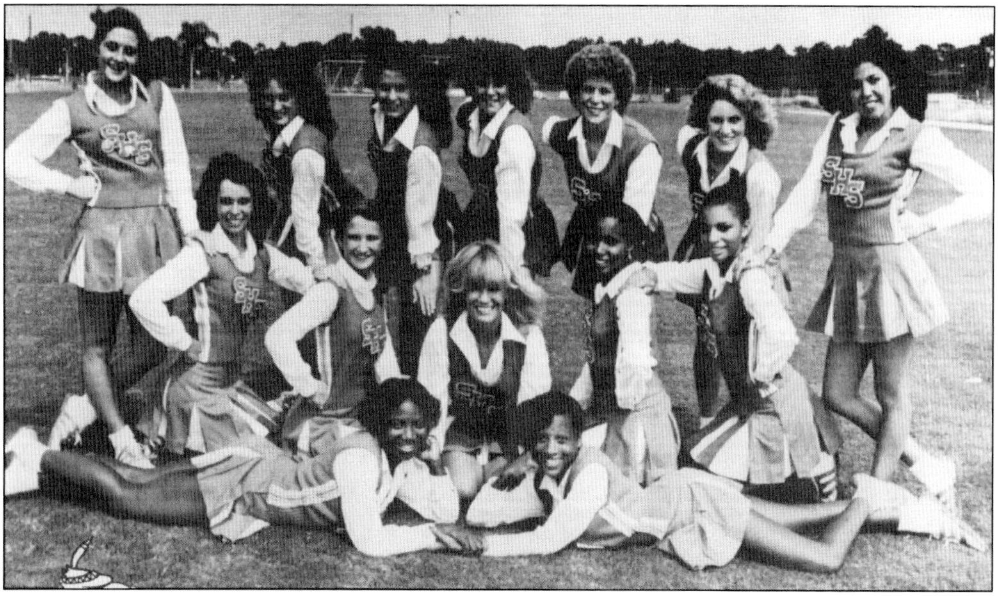

Overcrowding at Seminole High came to an end as a new campus arose on the eastern side of Lake Seminole. Beginning in the 1981–1982 academic year, some Warhawks became Warriors at the newly opened campus of Osceola High School. Others became Pirates at Boca Ciega High School, a Gulfport school that had experienced a decline in enrollment. Warhawk pride remained strong in the Seminole area, however. (Author.)

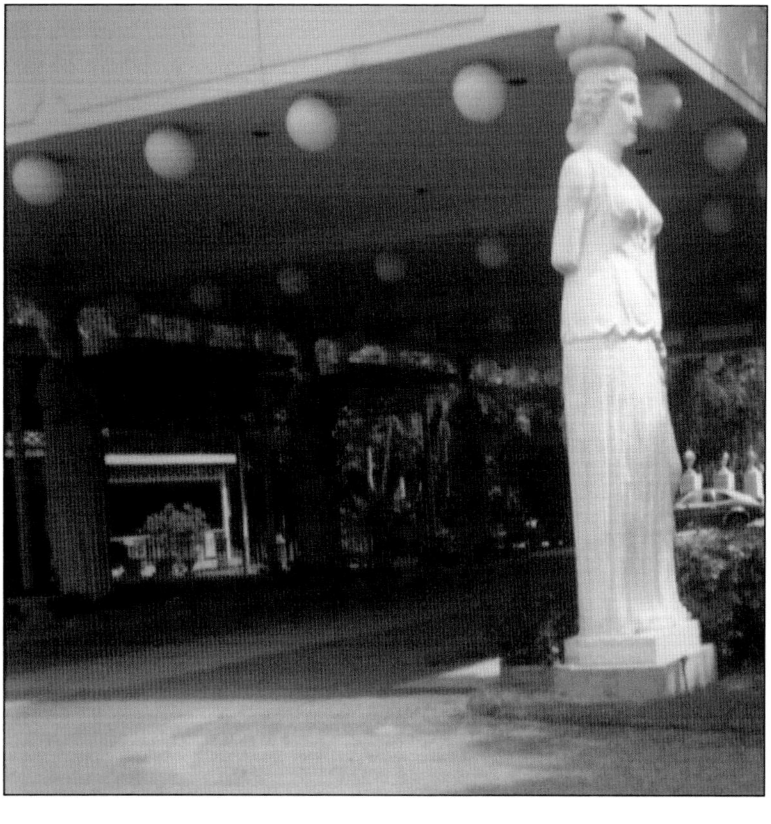

Richard B. Baumgardner acquired the former Duhme parcel. During the late 1960s, he owned and operated the Kapok Tree Inn, a unique and exotic restaurant along McMullen-Booth Road a little south of Alligator Creek. After gaining approval to develop the 10-acre site along Duhme Road between Seminole and Madeira Beach, this second Kapok Tree Inn opened with an elaborate covered entryway. (SHS.)

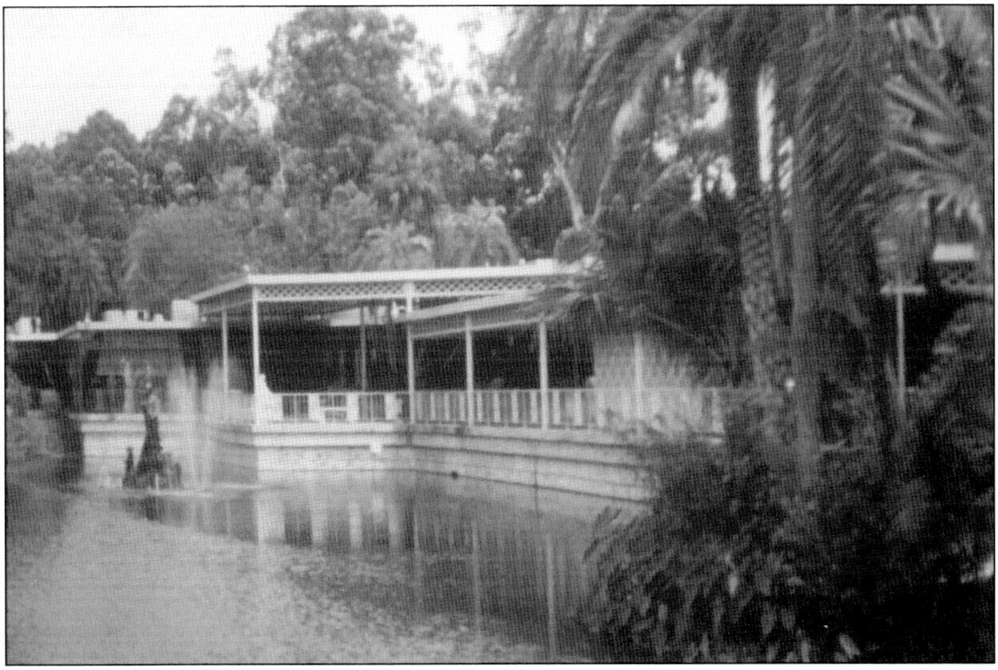

The Kapok Tree Inn of Madeira Beach offered an over-the-top dining experience during its early years, complete with its signature apple butter and unlimited refills of the relish tray. The northern part of the restaurant sat alongside the pond where the Duhme family once planted ornamental gardens (above). The Kapok Tree's exaggerated decor certainly turned a few heads, but almost everyone enjoyed the after-dinner strolls in the restaurant's gardens near the pond. Briefly known as Richard's Restaurant in the early 1980s, shown below with the Sea Towers condos in the distance, the restaurant closed later that decade. After briefly serving as the Jewish Community Center of Pinellas County and a temporary home for the predecessor of the Florida Holocaust Museum now in downtown St. Petersburg, the restaurant was demolished. Townhomes now occupy the site. (Both, SHS.)

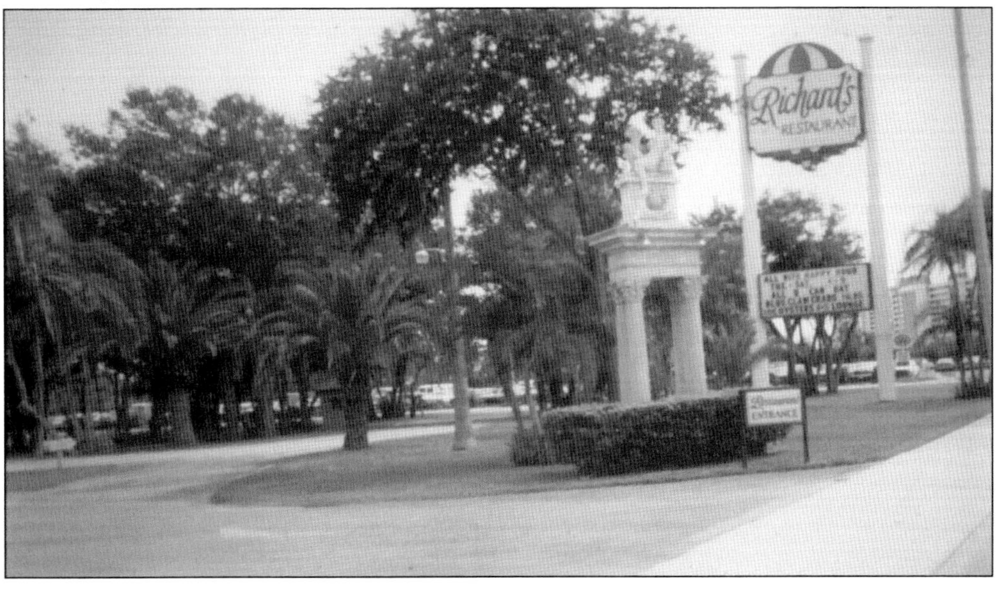

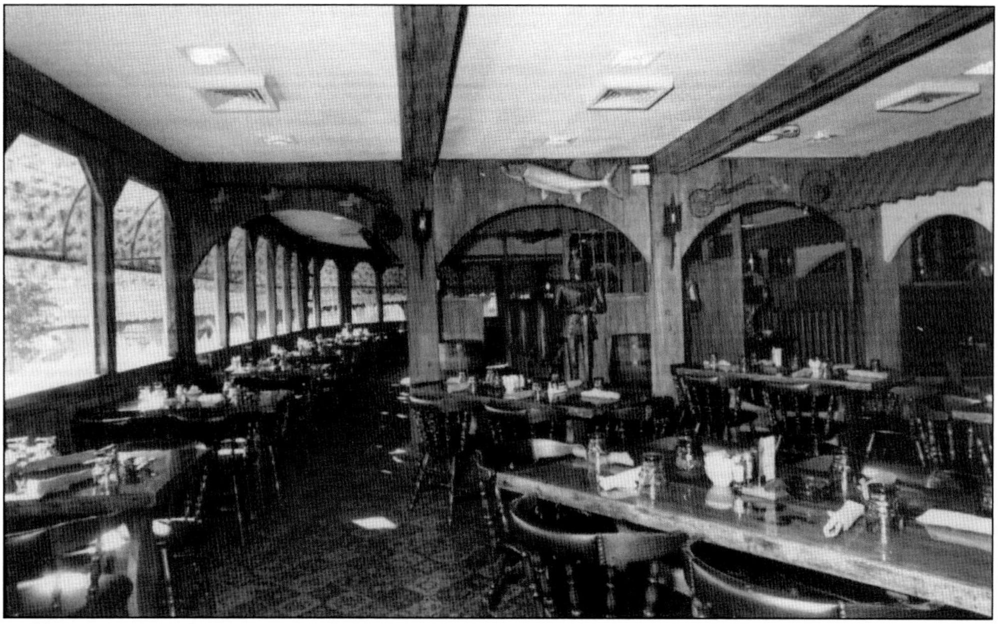

Baldassano P. "Bob" Spoto purchased the Fox and Hound Restaurant at 12999 Park Boulevard in December 1971. He moved down from the Chicago area in early 1972 and transformed the restaurant into Spoto's Stockyard Inn. The restaurant featured steakhouse and barbecue entrees and sat on a large lot that allowed for ample expansion. A fire on January 4, 1976, gutted part of the structure, but the Spoto family rebuilt the restaurant and, by the early 1980s, added banquet facilities that could accommodate 700 patrons. The restaurant closed again in April 1990. Spoto opened other smaller restaurants in the Seminole area in subsequent years. The large structure, shown in the advertisement below, burned to the ground in July 1993 after an arson incident. A shopping center rose upon the site in 1996. (Both, courtesy of the Spoto family.)

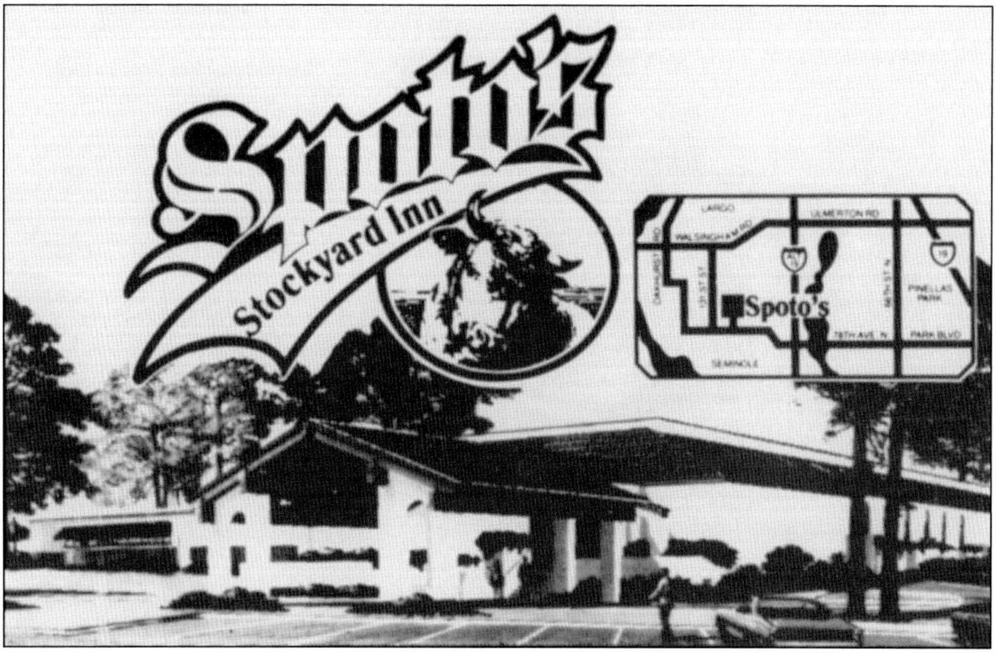

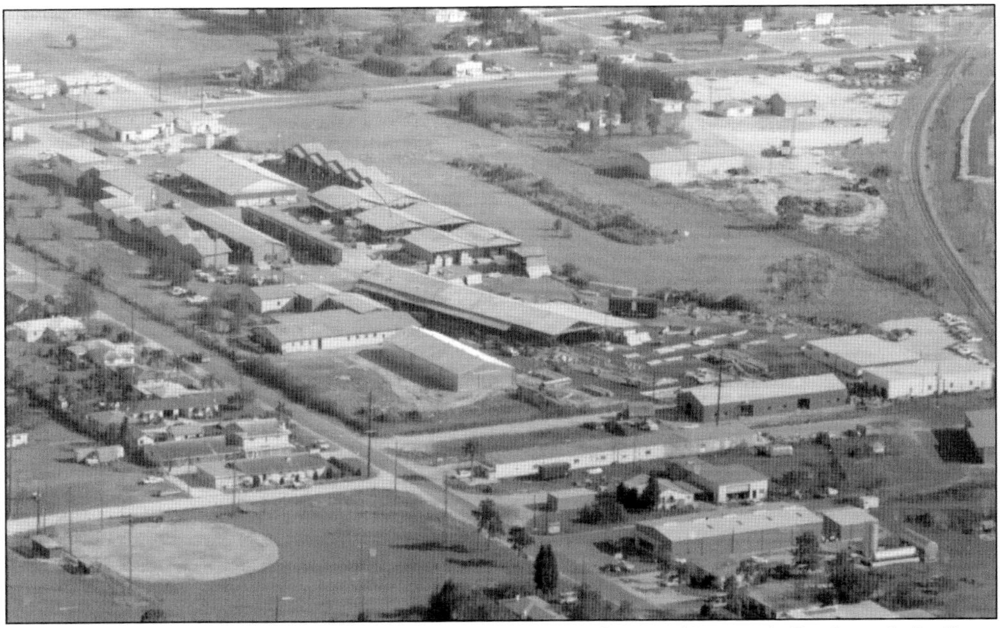

Located on a 13-acre tract south of Seventieth Avenue and west of Seminole Boulevard, Audlane Lumber & Builders Supply carried the materials needed to fuel the Seminole construction boom. Established in May 1957, the business occupied a large site near the railroad line, now the Pinellas Trail. Audlane closed and the Triangle Pacific Forest Products Corporation operated here in the early 1970s. An economic slump led to the store's closure in December 1975. Charles Haag, a restaurateur who launched his first Chief Charley's in Clearwater and a second in Dunedin, opened his third location here in August 18, 1978, when customers ordered their first meals in this 660-seat restaurant. Though the restaurant attracted large crowds for many years, soaring land values made it impossible to stay afloat, and the Seminole location closed in 1989. A complex now known as Beachway Seminole Condominiums took shape in the 1990s. (Above, HV; below, SHS.)

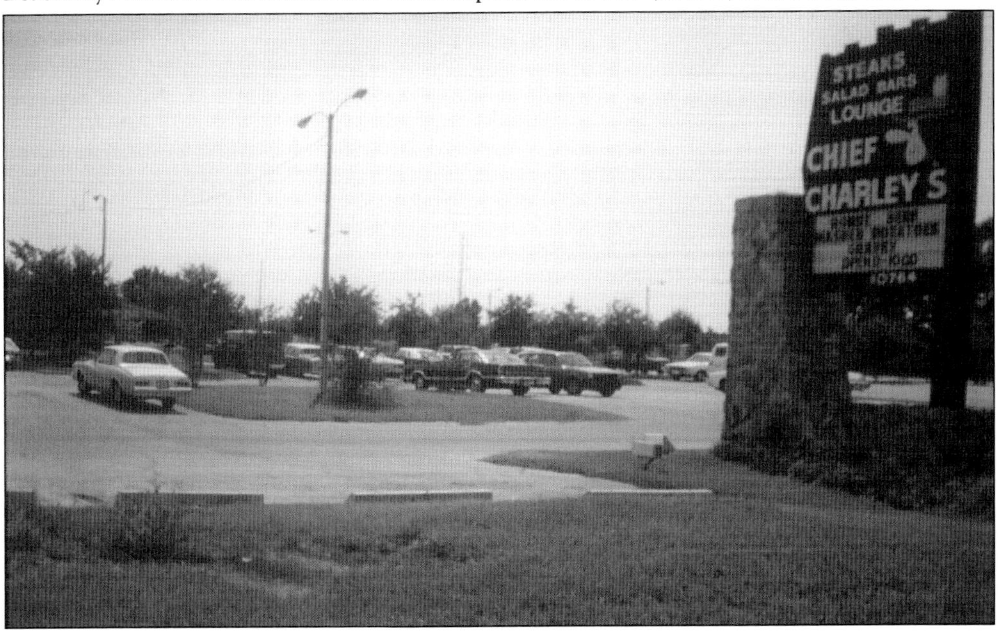

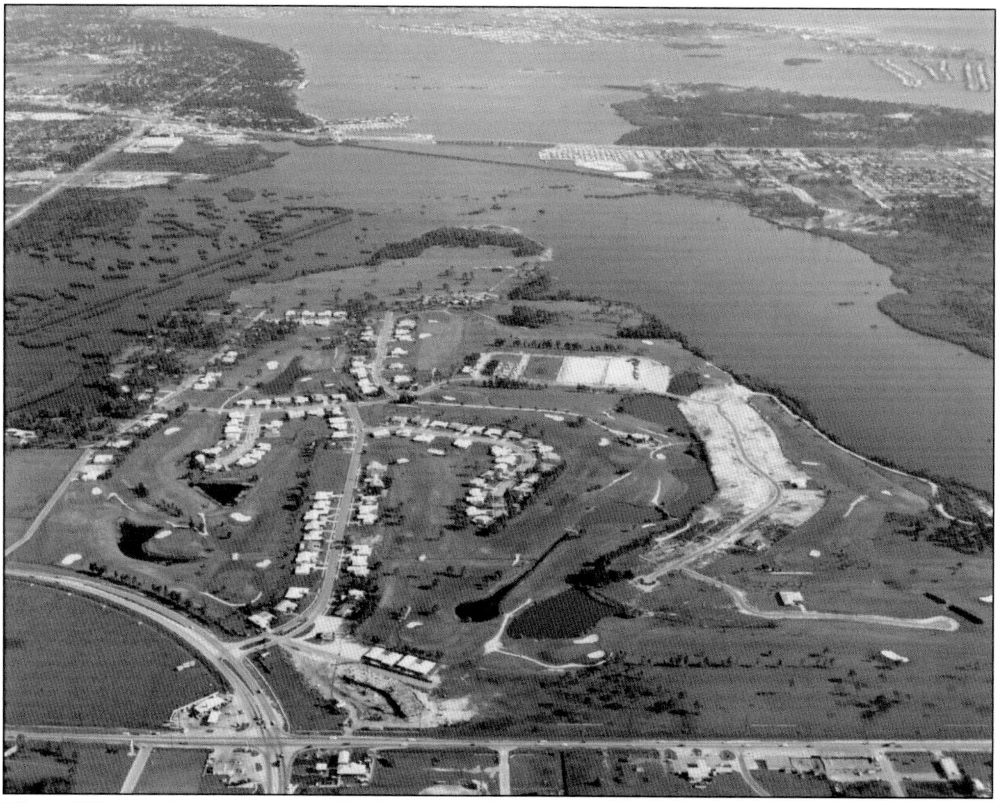

This 1970 aerial view looks south from the intersection of Park Boulevard and Starkey Road toward the Park Street extension across Cross Bayou and the Seminole Lake Country Club. The railroad trestle and bridge across Long Bayou, as well as developments at Bay Pines and Seminole Point, appear at upper center and upper right, with Treasure Island and Madeira Beach in the distance. (Swenningsen Collection.)

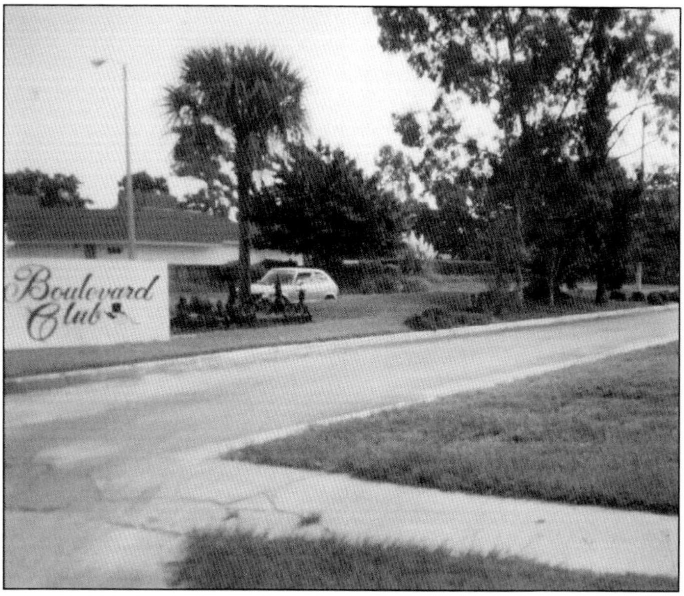

Development along the eastern side of Lake Seminole accelerated during the 1970s. As land values increased, some complexes transitioned from apartments into condominiums almost overnight. For example, in February 1978, the ownership of the 267-unit StarLight Park apartment complex, located at 7701 Starkey Road, decided to convert the property into a condominium known as the Boulevard Club with little notice. The condominium, shown here in 1983, still exists today. (SHS.)

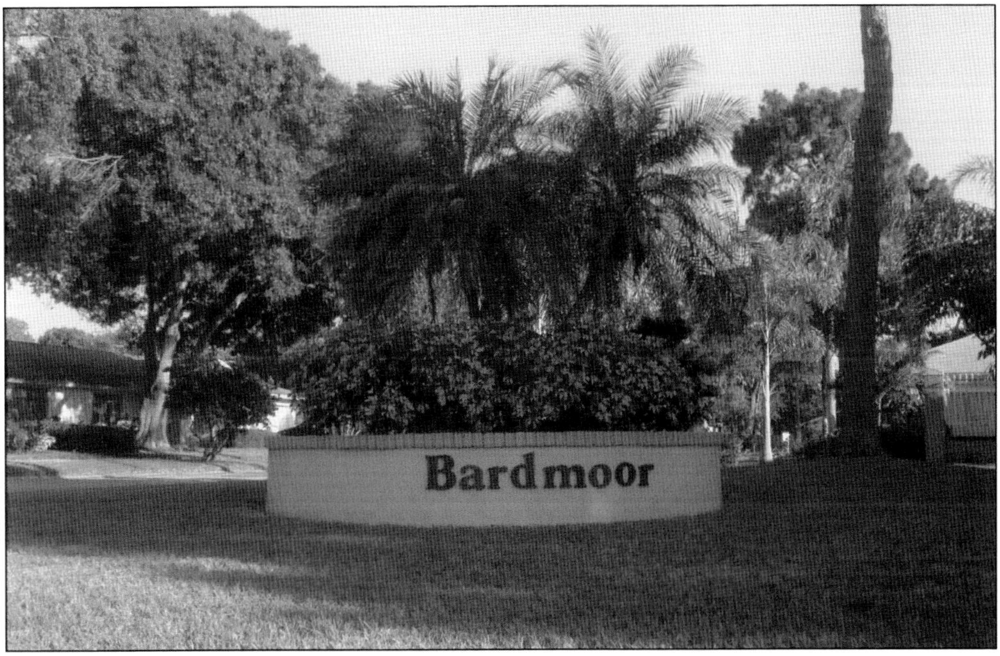

The upscale Bardmoor subdivision between Seminole, Largo, and Pinellas Park traces its origins to 1966. Oliver L. Bards of Cincinnati purchased more than 1,000 acres on the eastern side of Lake Seminole, east of Starkey Road and south of Bryan Dairy Road. The first substantial development began in the early 1970s, with additional planned communities in the ensuing years. (Author.)

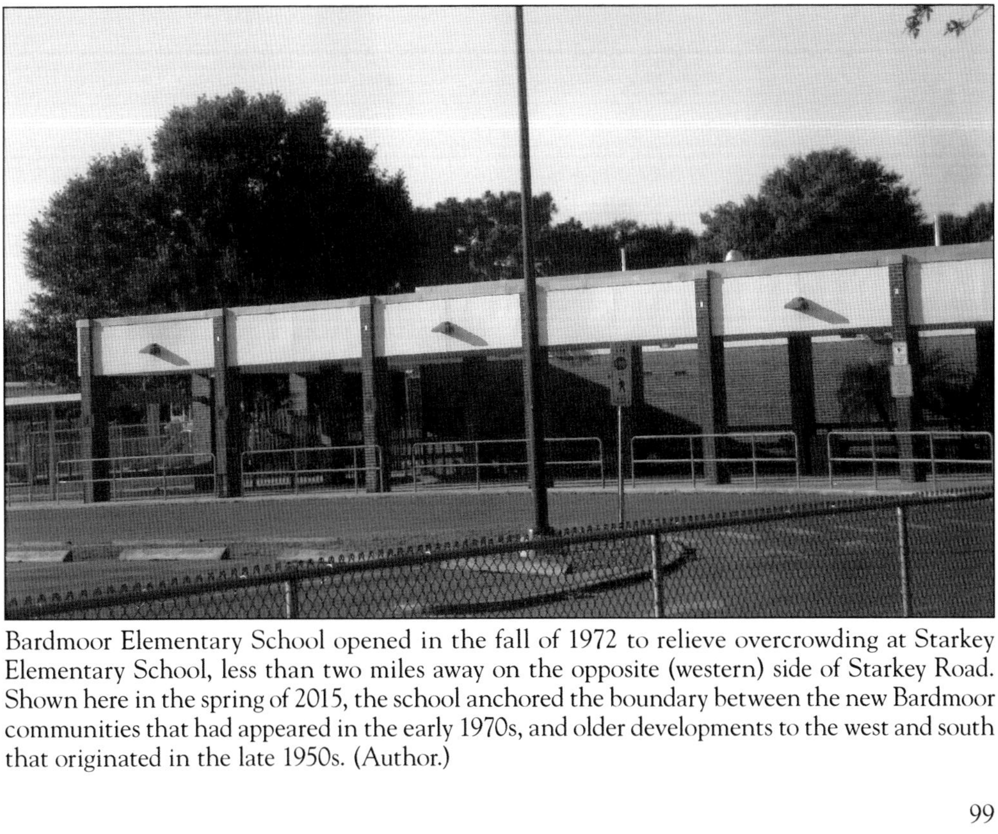

Bardmoor Elementary School opened in the fall of 1972 to relieve overcrowding at Starkey Elementary School, less than two miles away on the opposite (western) side of Starkey Road. Shown here in the spring of 2015, the school anchored the boundary between the new Bardmoor communities that had appeared in the early 1970s, and older developments to the west and south that originated in the late 1950s. (Author.)

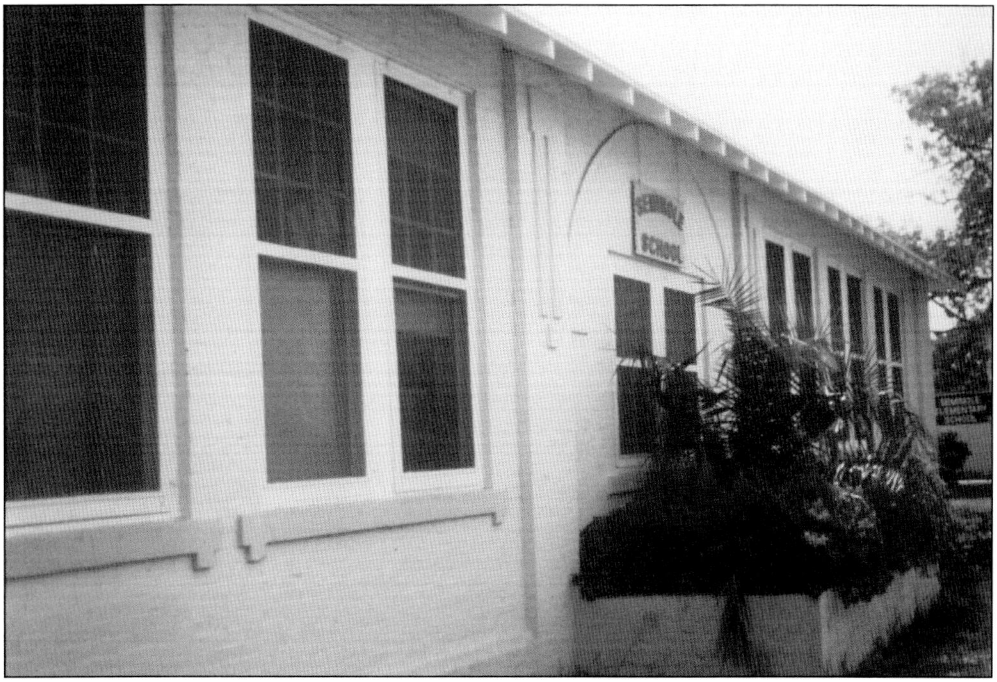

Seminole Elementary School, an educational anchor in the community since 1915, continued to serve students living in the areas closest to the original Oakhurst settlement. Shown here in the early 1980s, the school has operated continuously for more than a century. Other elementary schools, such as Bauder, Bardmoor, Madeira Beach, Oakhurst, Orange Grove, Southern Oak, and Walsingham, also meet the needs of students in the Seminole area. (SHS.)

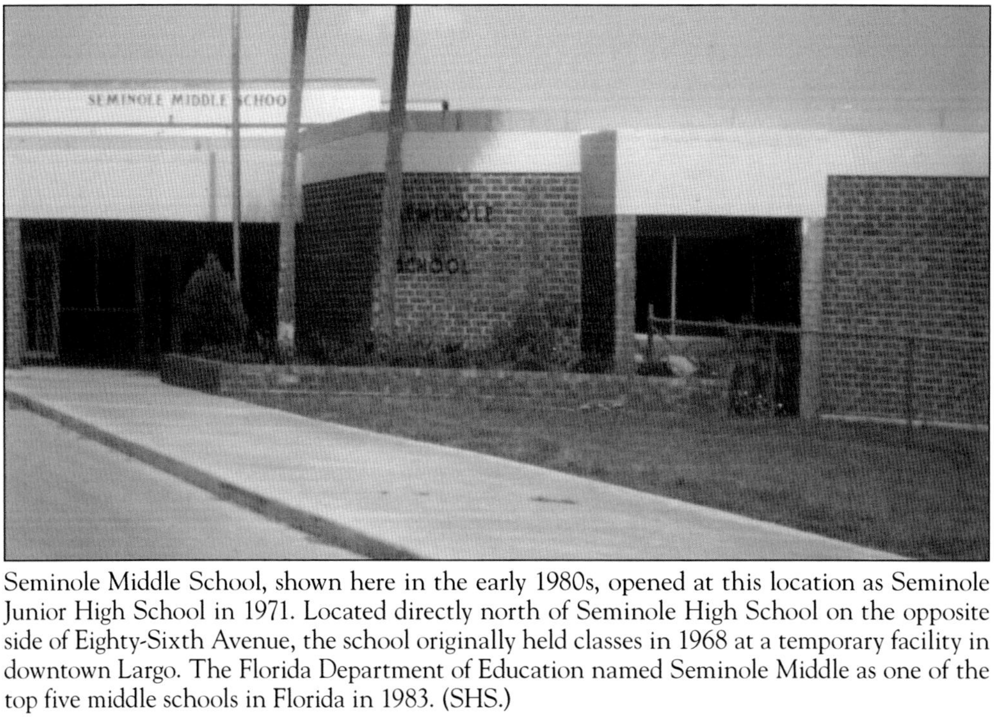

Seminole Middle School, shown here in the early 1980s, opened at this location as Seminole Junior High School in 1971. Located directly north of Seminole High School on the opposite side of Eighty-Sixth Avenue, the school originally held classes in 1968 at a temporary facility in downtown Largo. The Florida Department of Education named Seminole Middle as one of the top five middle schools in Florida in 1983. (SHS.)

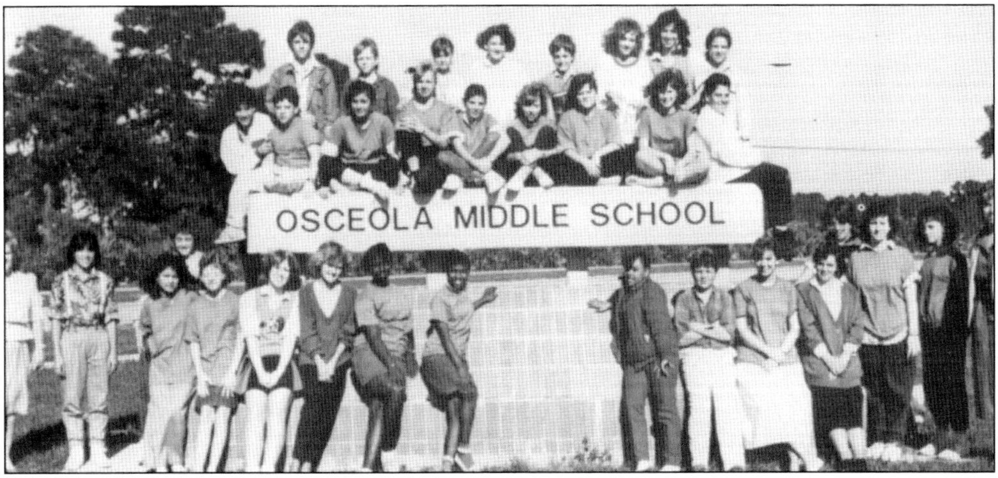

Osceola Middle School opened in August 1984 on 19.5 acres on the eastern side of Lake Seminole. Constructed to relieve overcrowding at Madeira Beach, Morgan Fitzgerald, and Pinellas Park Middle Schools, Osceola's student body selected "Chiefs" as their mascot. The image above shows student leaders from 1987. Most pupils who enrolled at Osceola Middle School prior to the early 2000s automatically attended Osceola High School. In recent years, however, magnet programs developed at both schools have allowed students greater options and geographical mobility. Known recently as a School of Technology and Innovative Instruction, Osceola Middle School began its third decade of service in the 2014–2015 school year. (Above, HV; below, author.)

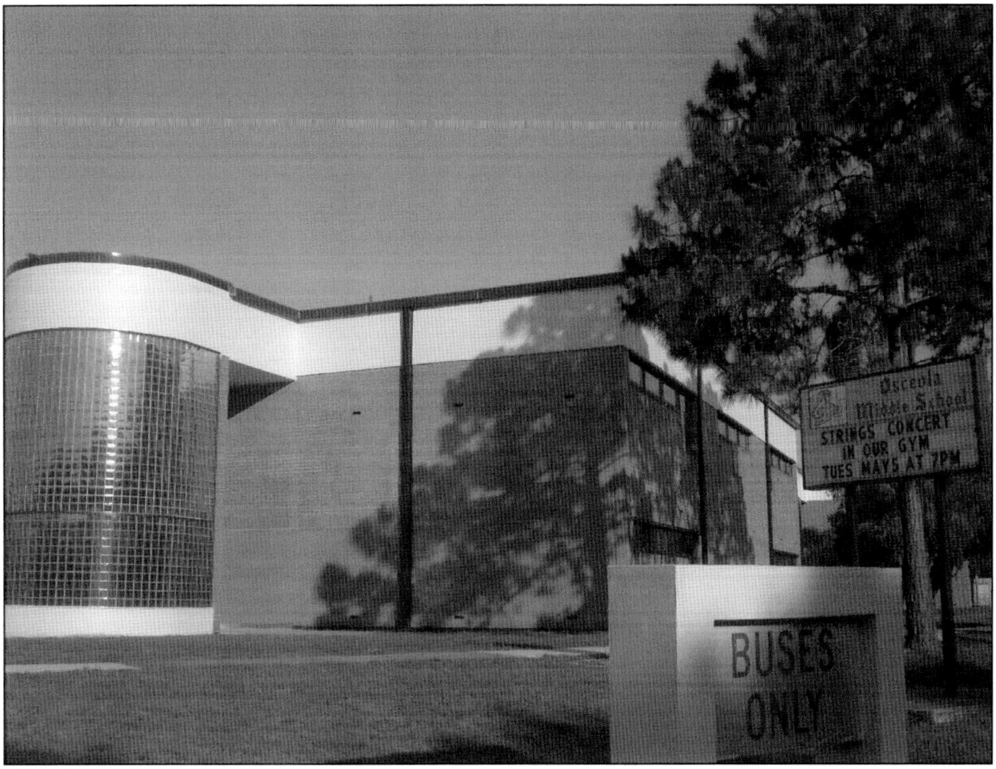

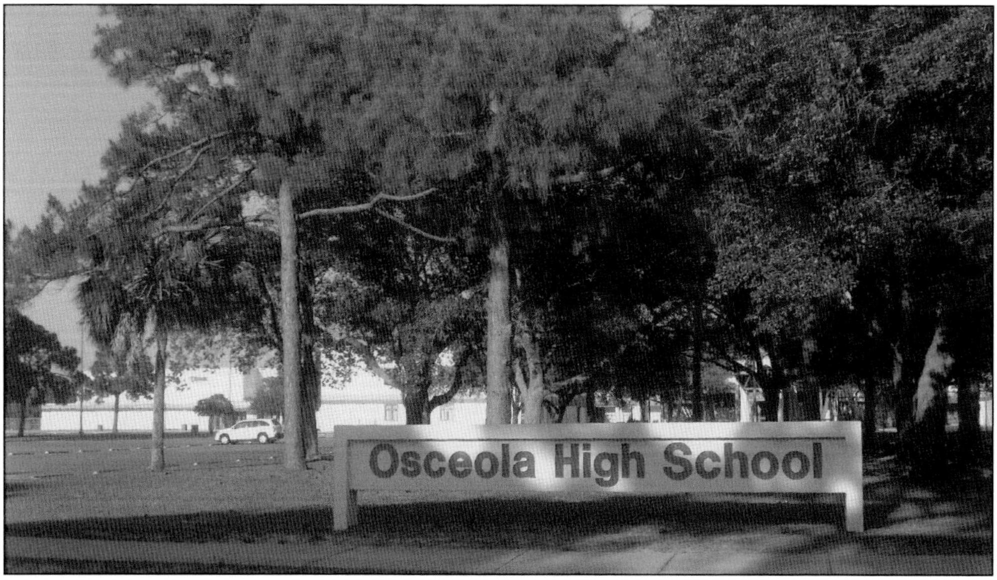

Osceola High School opened in the fall of 1981. The ground breaking for this new campus on more than 58 acres of former pastureland once owned by the Starkey family took place in December 1979. Bob Kalach, principal of Seminole High in 1980–1981, transferred across Lake Seminole to serve as the founding administrator at the school when it opened in the fall of 1981. Osceola High relieved overcrowding at Seminole High and also gave the Warhawks a new rival for high school sports, as Osceola's Warriors replaced the Packers of Largo High School during the 1980s. Known today as Osceola Fundamental High School, the institution transitioned to a back-to-basics curriculum with requirements for greater parental or guardian involvement beginning in 2006. (Both, author.)

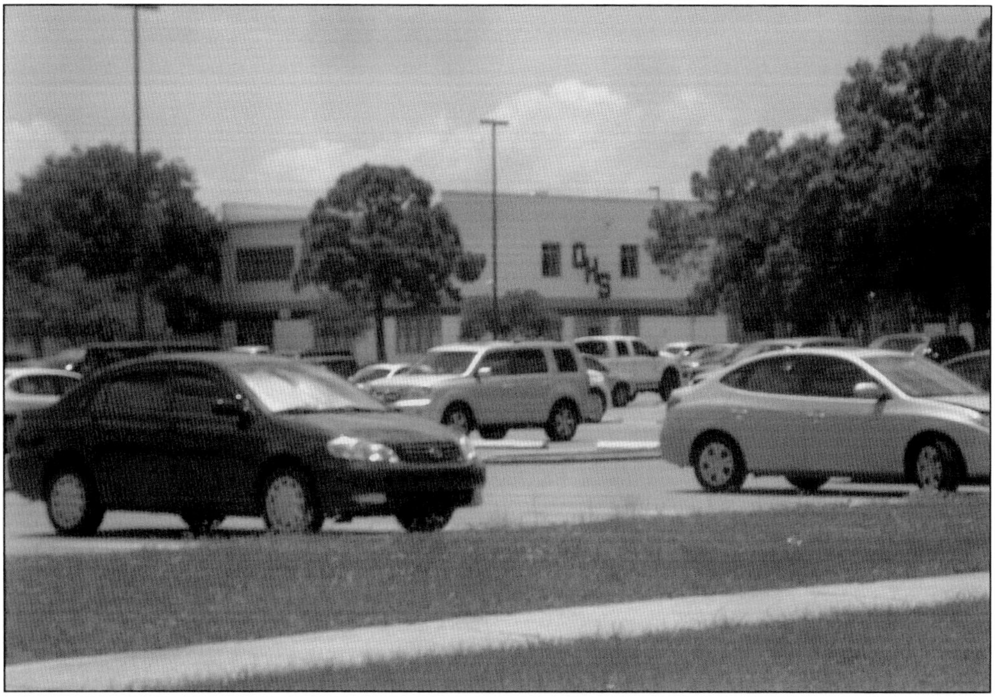

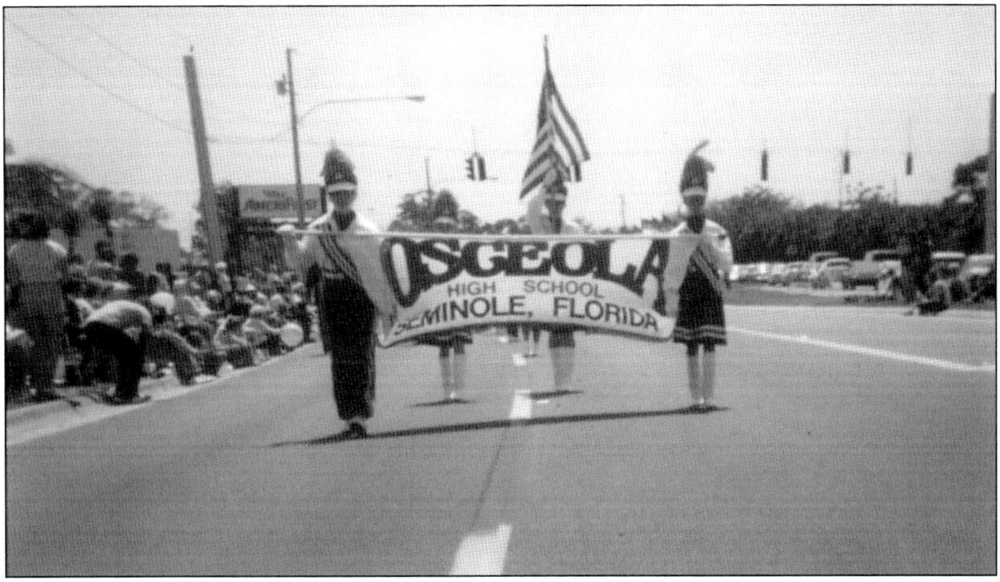

In these images from the early 1980s, members from the Osceola High School band participate in the annual Pow Wow, a civic event that began in Seminole in 1967. This parade route took floats and performers along Park Boulevard in front of Seminole Mall. During early years, the Pow Wow events often included barbecues and smaller gatherings, with a growing number of carnival rides and other activities added during the 1970s. In recent years, as the Pow Wow has continued to grow, many of the events have moved to the Seminole Recreation Center along 113th Street. The springtime carnival and parade excite young and old alike. (SHS.)

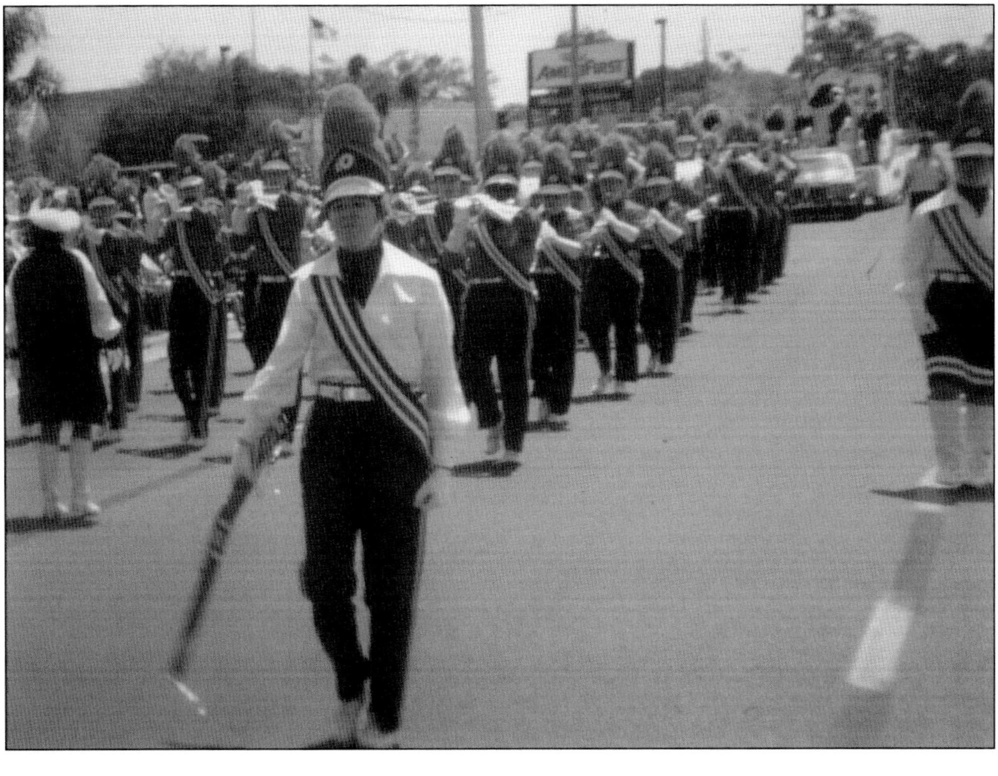

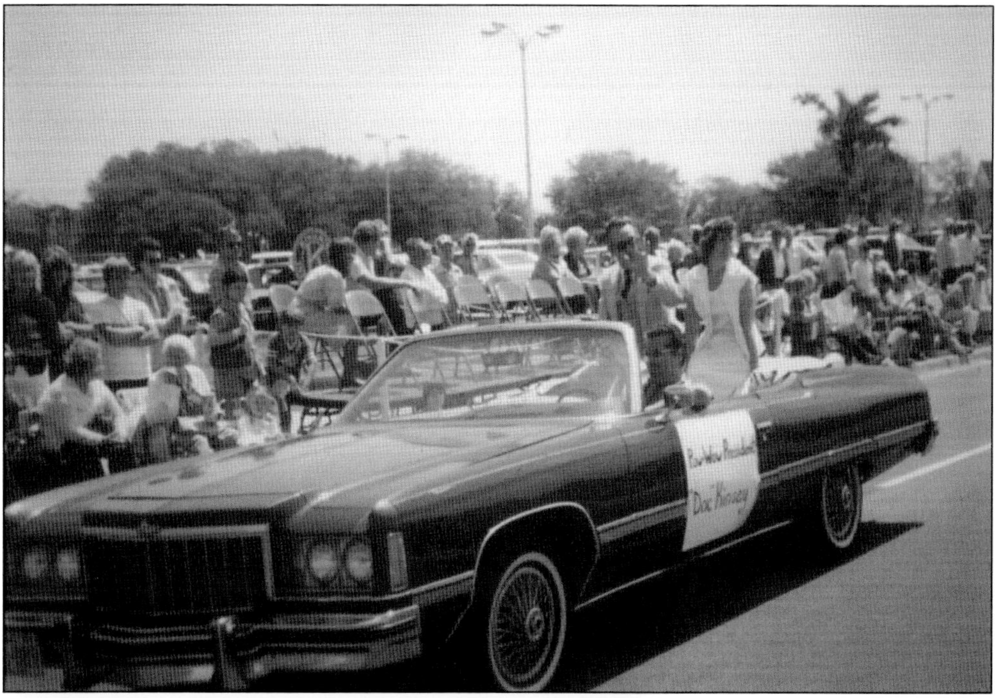

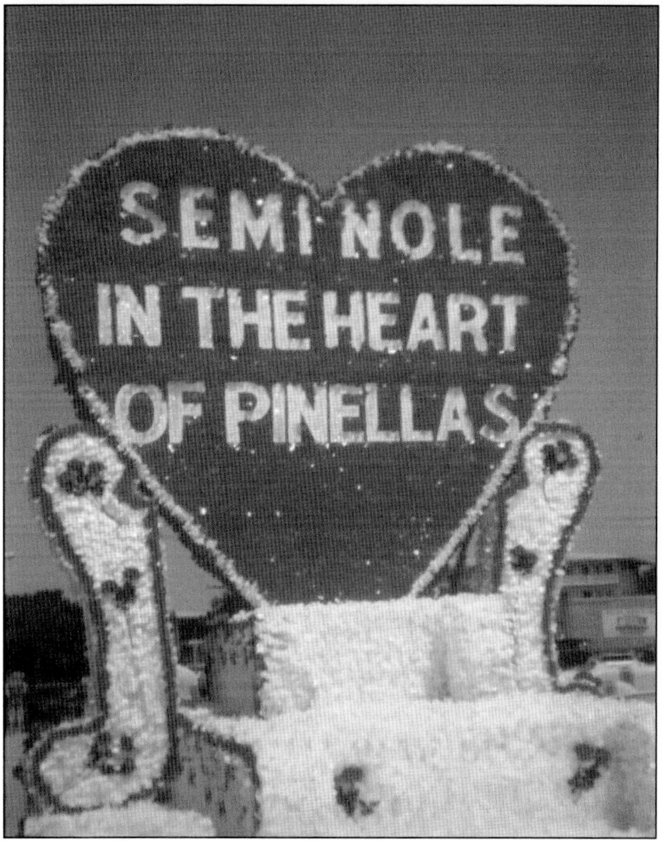

Pow Wows continued annually for 18 years. Holland Mangum, one-time mayor of Seminole, and Harold "Doc" Kinsey, shown above in the early 1980s, took the lead for many years. Service organizations and the local chamber of commerce also played important roles. For the first time since 1967, organizers failed to get the annual event off the ground in 1985. Organizers looked for new partnerships, and the Pow Wow celebrations resumed. Although the population within the municipal limits of Seminole did not surpass 5,000 until the early 1980s, many residents of adjacent unincorporated areas considered themselves residents of the "Greater Seminole Area" and became involved in community activities. (Both, SHS.)

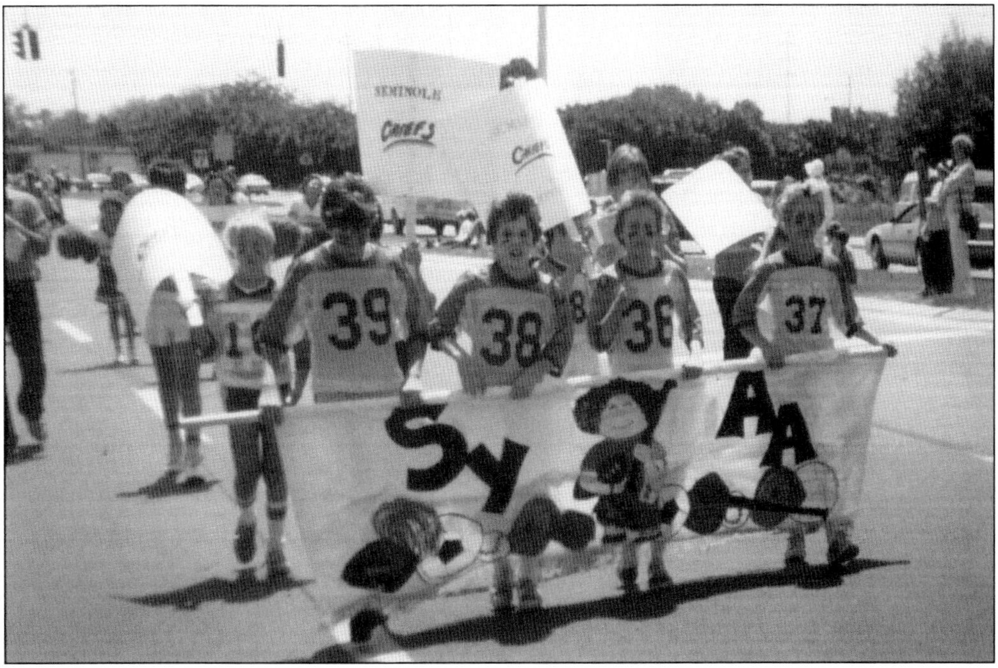

Above, members of the Seminole Chiefs represent the Seminole Youth Athletic Association (SYAA) at a Pow Wow in the early 1980s. As more families moved to the area in the 1960s, organizations such as SYAA tried to provide recreational opportunities and sports activities. During the late 1970s, the SYAA feared that it would lose a lease it had on a 20-acre site at Ninetieth Avenue and 121st Street that it had used since 1968. They maintained access to the site, shown below in 1983, and children and teenagers continue to enjoy baseball games and other events there in the 2010s. (Both, SHS.)

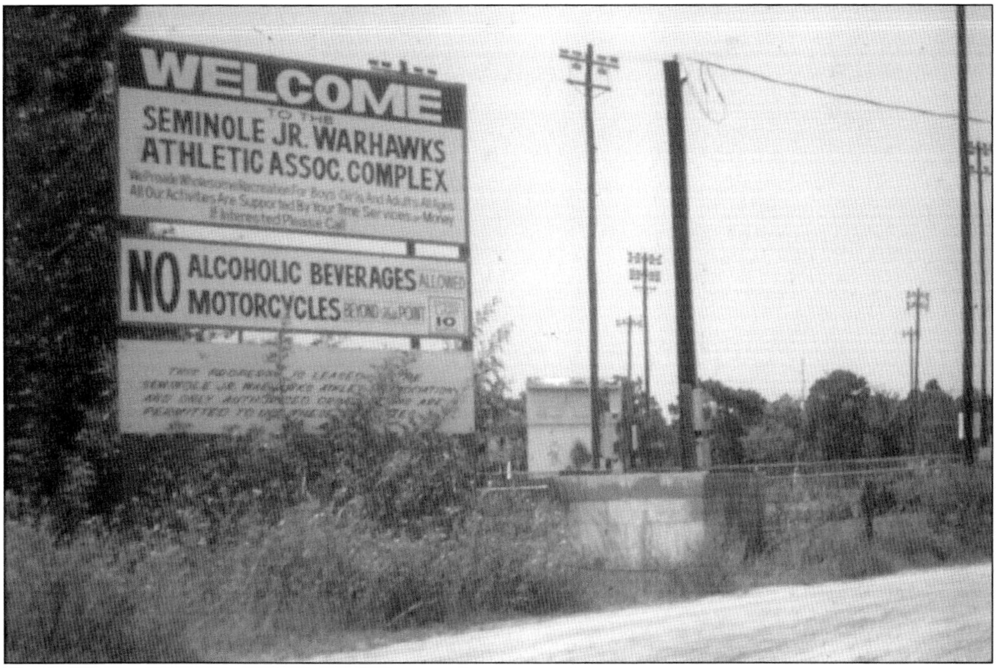

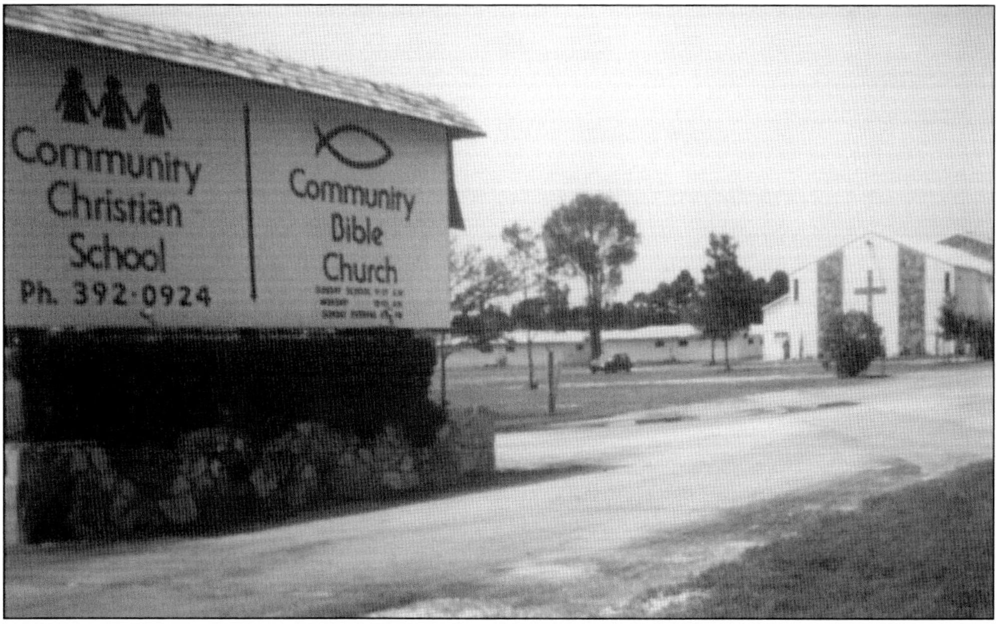

The Community Bible Church and Community Christian School trace their origins to the mid-1970s when a few families met for services at Seminole Elementary School. The congregation grew substantially by May 29, 1977, when church members held a ground-breaking ceremony for a 13,000 square foot building that included an auditorium easily accommodating 400 people. At the time, 113th Street did not reach Ulmerton Road, and much of the area north of Eighty-Sixth Avenue remained rural in character. The city purchased the church structure and adjacent facilities in 1992 with plans to expand recreational offerings. A renovated Seminole Recreation Center opened on this site on October 4, 2001, with indoor courts, exercise facilities, and meeting rooms. In May 2005, officials named this facility the Holland G. Mangum Recreation Center Complex to honor a former mayor. (Top, SHS; below, author.)

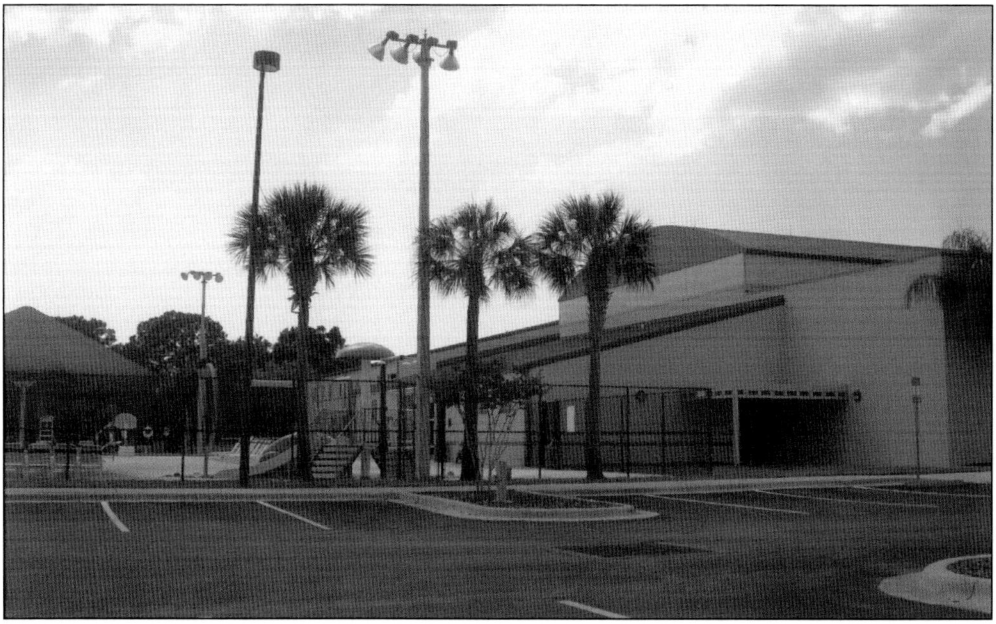

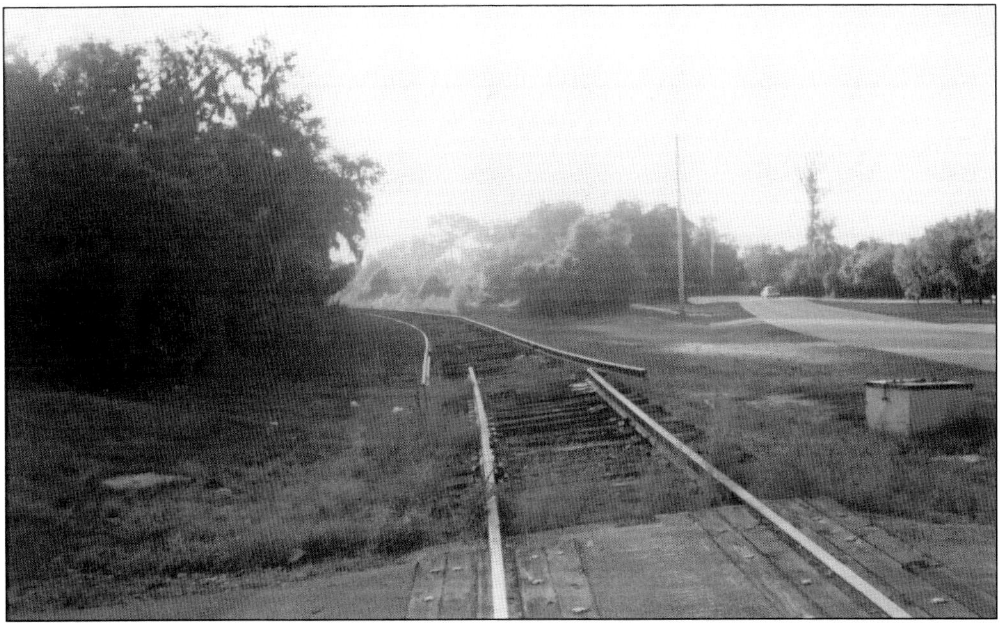

Passenger railroad service ended in Pinellas County in 1984. By the mid-1980s, crews had removed substantial sections of the old Seaboard Air Line (originally Tampa & Gulf Coast Line) tracks, including this section at the intersection of Old Oakhurst by the Seminole City Park. For a time, planners discussed transforming part of this right-of-way into a light rail system, but these proposals failed. (Lyn Friedt Collection, HV.)

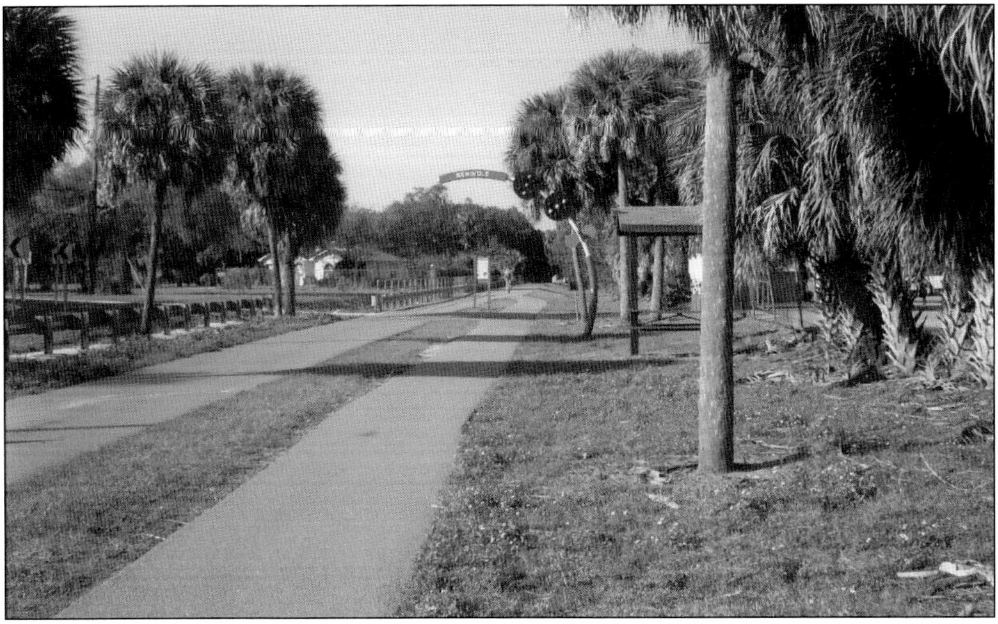

An alternative proposal involved transforming these abandoned lines, now in public ownership, into a recreational trail. The rails-to-trails movement had grown nationally in the 1980s. By the early 1990s, the first publicly accessible section of the Fred Marquis Pinellas Trail connected Seminole City Park to the Taylor Lake Park in southwestern Largo. The heavy use of this trail during the 1990s encouraged its continued expansion. (Author.)

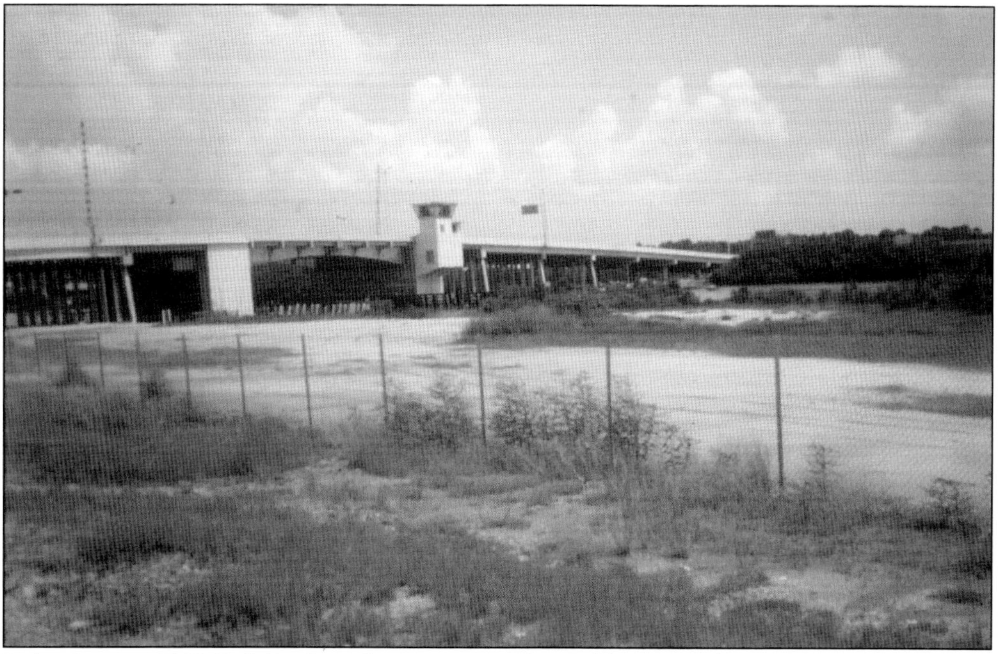

Before January 1982, Park Boulevard came to an end at Oakhurst Road. Since the 1960s, planners had discussed the possibility of extending the boulevard across the bay to meet Gulf Boulevard in Indian Shores. After acquiring the necessary parcels, site preparation began in November 1979, with ground-breaking ceremonies at the end of January 1980. The $14-million span opened two years later as a toll road, though the passage of the original "Penny for Pinellas" sales tax in November 1989 ended the tolls by the early 1990s. Discussions about developing the sensitive wetlands of Travatine Island on the Seminole side, just south of the bridge, led county officials to purchase that undeveloped area in December 1989. At about the same time, improvements on the Indian Shores side, shown below, included boat ramps that opened in June 1989. (Above, SHS; below, author.)

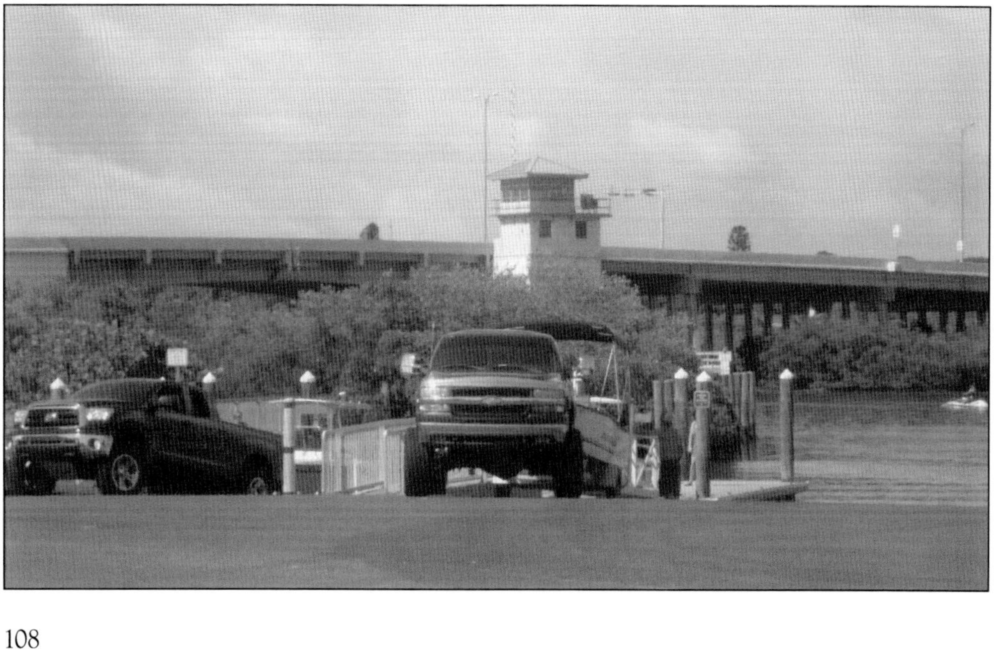

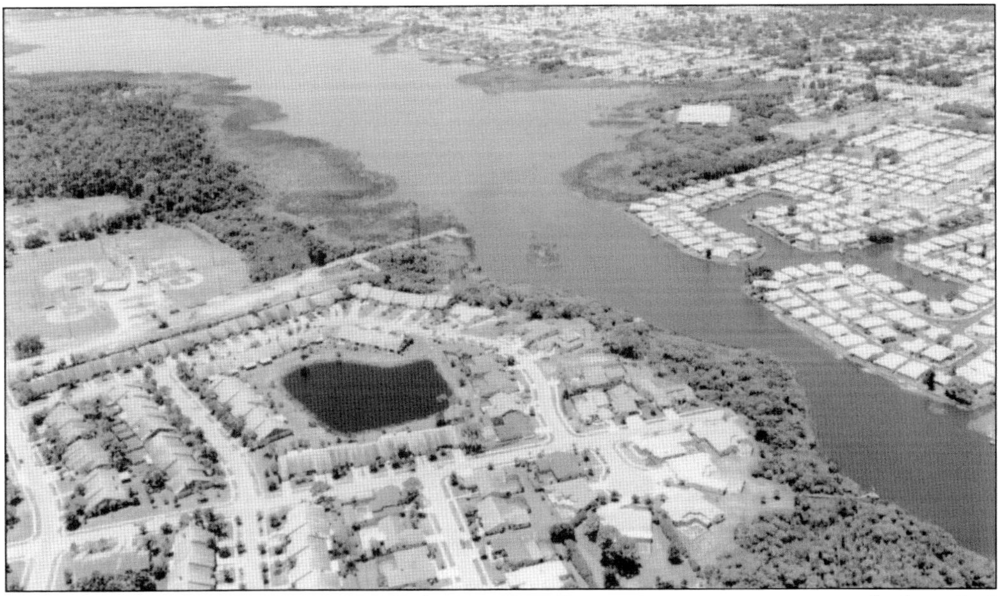

Traffic along both Park Boulevard and Ulmerton Road, important east-west arteries, had reached staggering levels by the 1980s. Planners envisioned development of a new roadway, County Road 296, to create another connection to allow those living on the western side of Lake Seminole easier access to Interstate 275. Conceptual planning for one segment, the Lake Seminole Bridge, began by 1987. Site preparation and construction moved forward after an extended discussion of environmental concerns. The view above looks south across Lake Seminole at the site of the bridge as crews cleared the approaches. The image below looks east toward the Cross Bayou Little League Complex and Osceola High School along Ninety-Eighth Street after the span opened in February 1994; an extension of Bryan Dairy Road connecting to 118th Avenue and Interstate 275 came later. (Both, HV.)

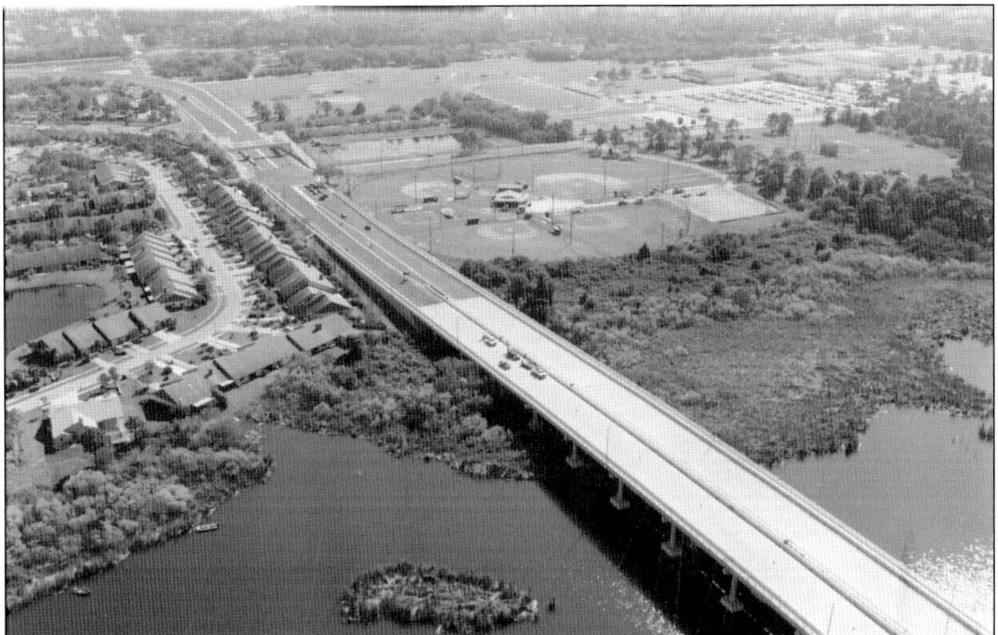

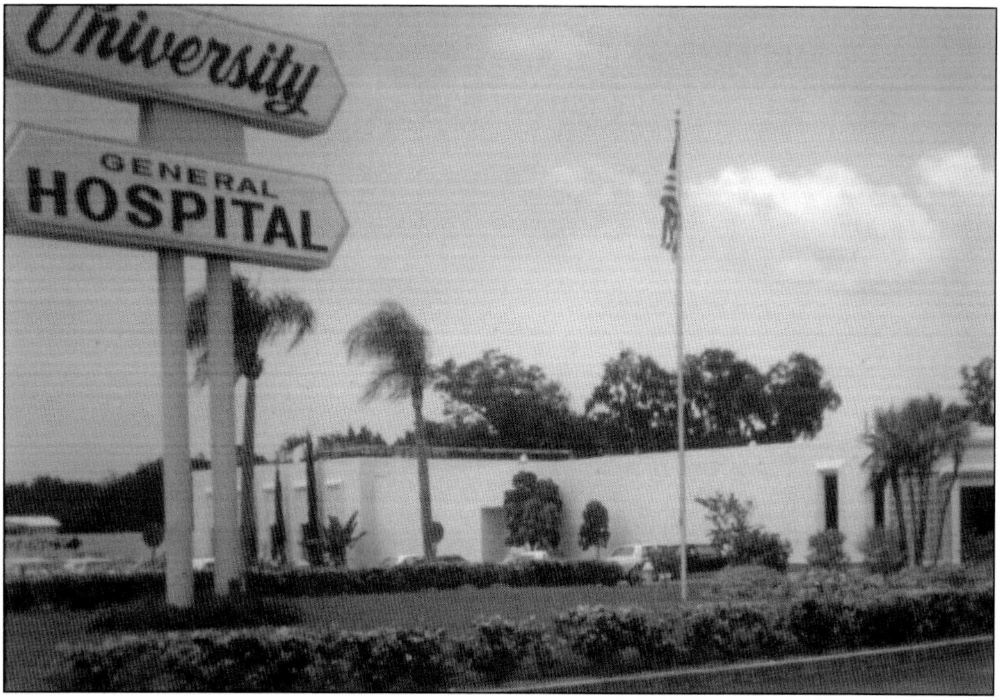

A tale of two nearby hospitals illustrates changes in the local landscape. Lake Seminole Hospital opened along the shore of Lake Seminole at 9675 Seminole Boulevard in February 1973. A little up the road, on the northwest corner of Seminole Boulevard at 102nd Avenue, Seminole General opened as a 140-bed facility in September 1975. Squabbling began immediately, as their similar names confused patients and families. Seminole General became University General Hospital (UGH), above, in March 1976. Lake Seminole later reopened as Women's Medical Center, struggled for years, and closed in 1996; University General closed the following year. In 2002, demolition of UGH began, and shoppers celebrated the opening of the Seminole Oaks shopping center in late 2004 (below). The Pinellas County Housing Authority acquired the former Lake Seminole Hospital site on April 30, 2013, for future development. (Above, SHS; below, author.)

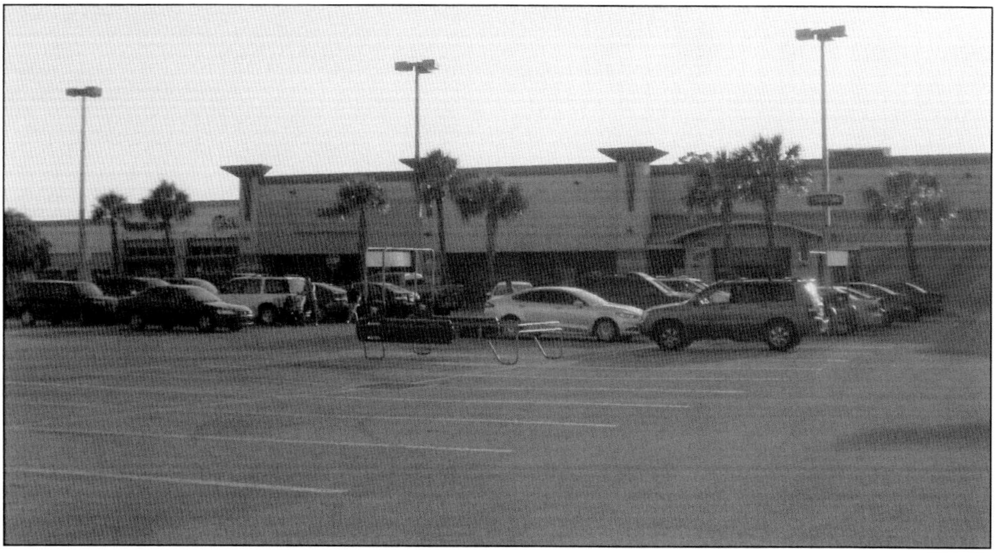

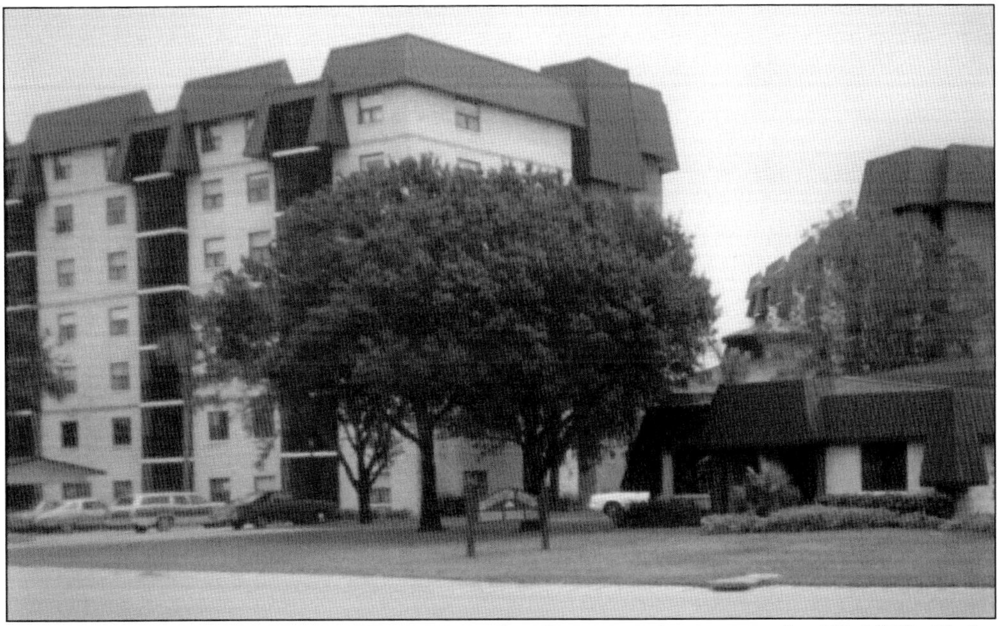

Though mobile home communities became popular alternatives for retirees after World War II, the increasing value of the land has forced many of them to close in recent years. Options for seniors have become more comprehensive since Seminole has incorporated. The opening of Freedom Square, shown here in the early 1980s, and similar communities allows residents to transition from independent living to facilities with full-time assistance without leaving home. (SHS.)

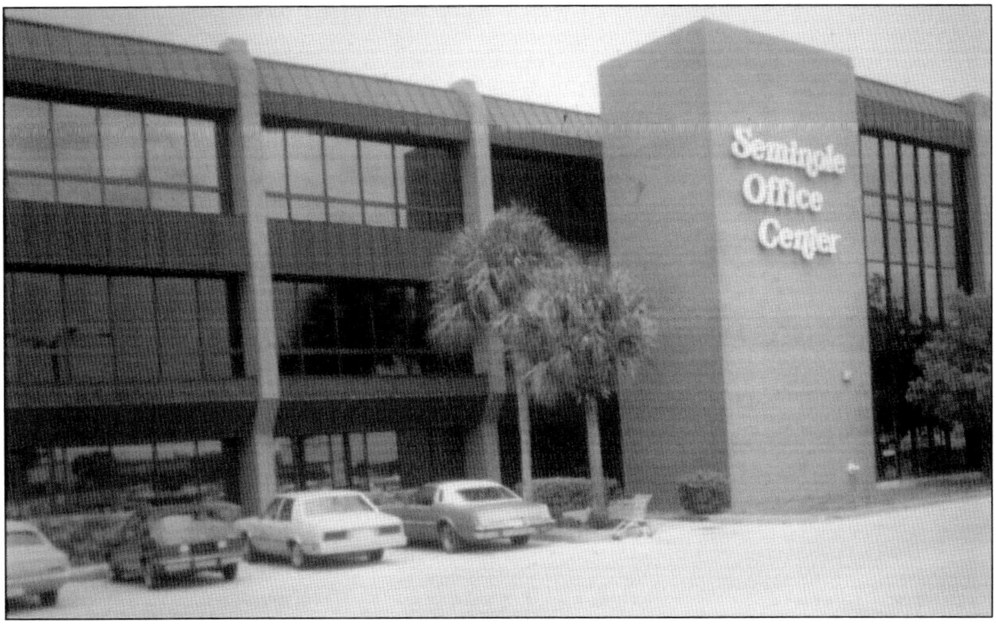

A growing community requires a comprehensive array of services. Touted as Seminole's first "prestige office building," the Seminole Office Center rose at the northwest corner of the Seminole Mall site adjacent to 113th Street. Frank Mudano, designer of the original Seminole Center, drew the plans for these buildings. Construction began in 1973, and offices opened in 1974. This image shows the structure in the early 1980s. (SHS.)

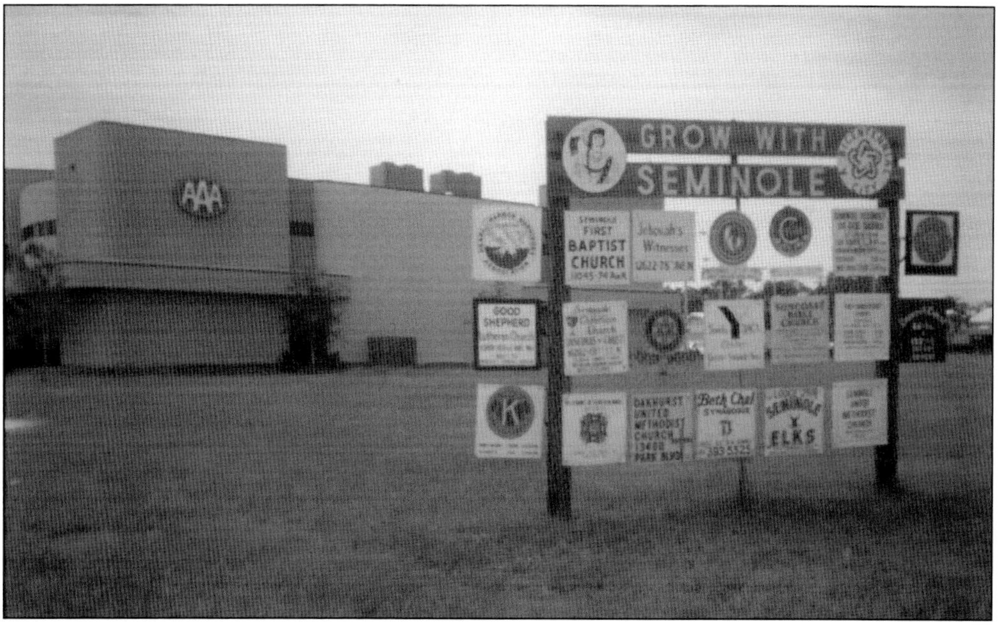

This "Grow with Seminole" sign greeted motorists driving south along Seminole Boulevard into the city during the early 1980s. A decade after the city first incorporated, officials mapped out plans to expand the municipal boundaries. Membership in the Seminole Chamber of Commerce had grown impressively since the opening of an expanded Seminole Mall in 1971. Residents expressed optimism about the area's future. (SHS.)

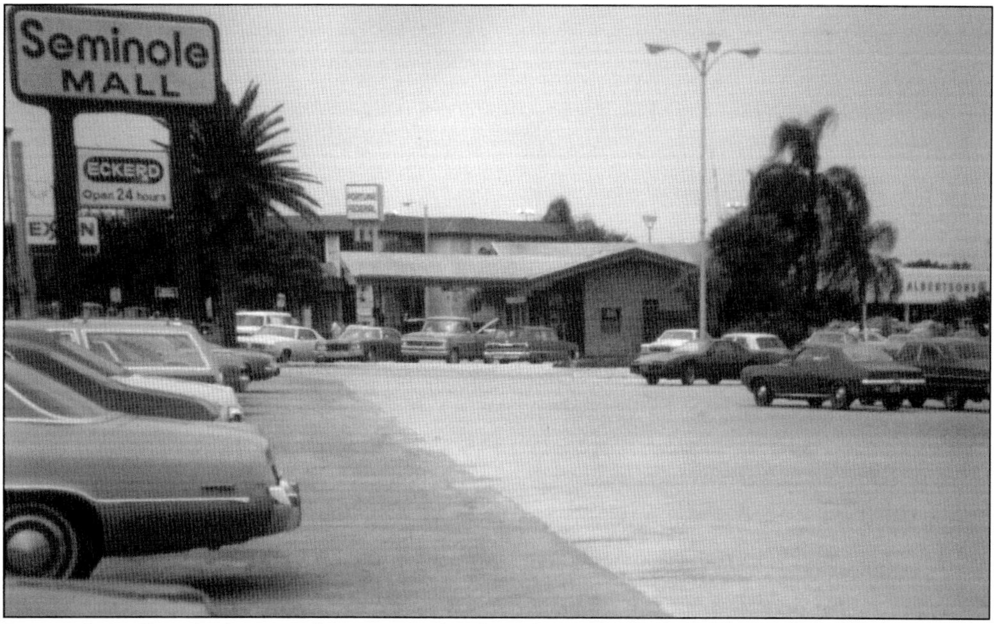

Seminole Mall took shape at the crossroads of 113th Street and Park Boulevard, shown here in the early 1980s with the Albertsons grocery store in the background. As the leaders of Seminole Center Inc., Jesse W. Johnson and Stuart S. Golding developed plans with Richard C. "Dick" Johnson, Jesse's son and an officer at the Bank of Seminole, in February 1969 to transform Seminole Center into Seminole Mall. (SHS.)

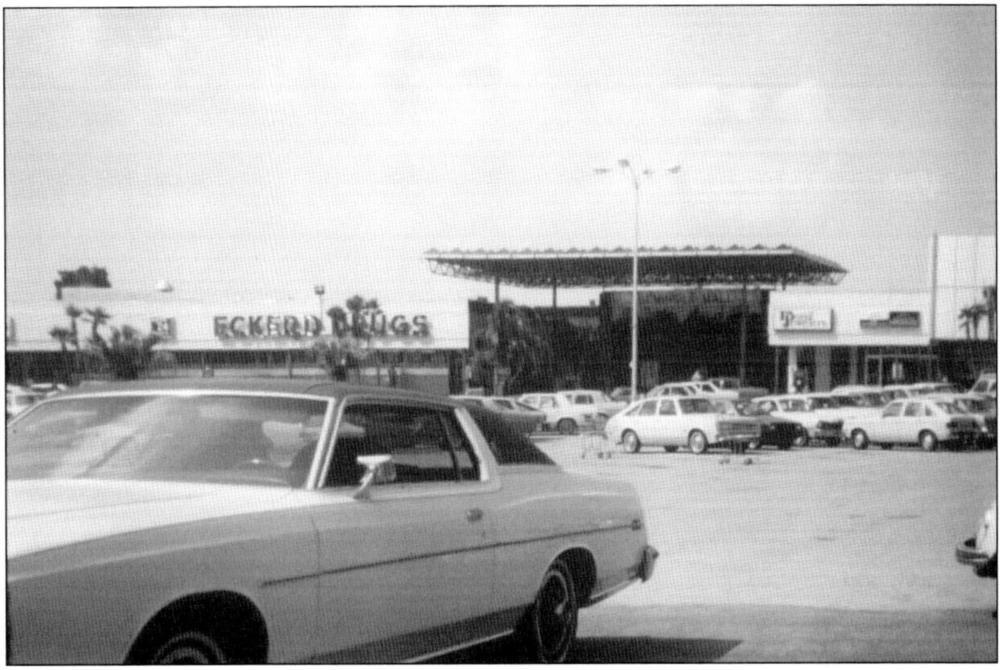

Expansion of the original shopping center occurred in 1970. On a 40-acre tract once used by Jesse Johnson for agricultural purposes rose a 340,000 square foot enclosed mall with 60 shops and parking spaces for 1,900 vehicles. A 117,000 square foot Woolco department store sat along the western side of the mall, where the Zayre department store appears in the 1983 image below. Most stores in the expanded mall opened in February 1970, with the Woolco opening a month later. At the height of the disco era in the late 1970s, the mall hosted occasional disco dance events for teenagers. Renovations in March 1986 gave Seminole Mall the distinction of having the first food court in a Pinellas County shopping center. Business in the mall remained vibrant into the new millennium. (Both, SHS.)

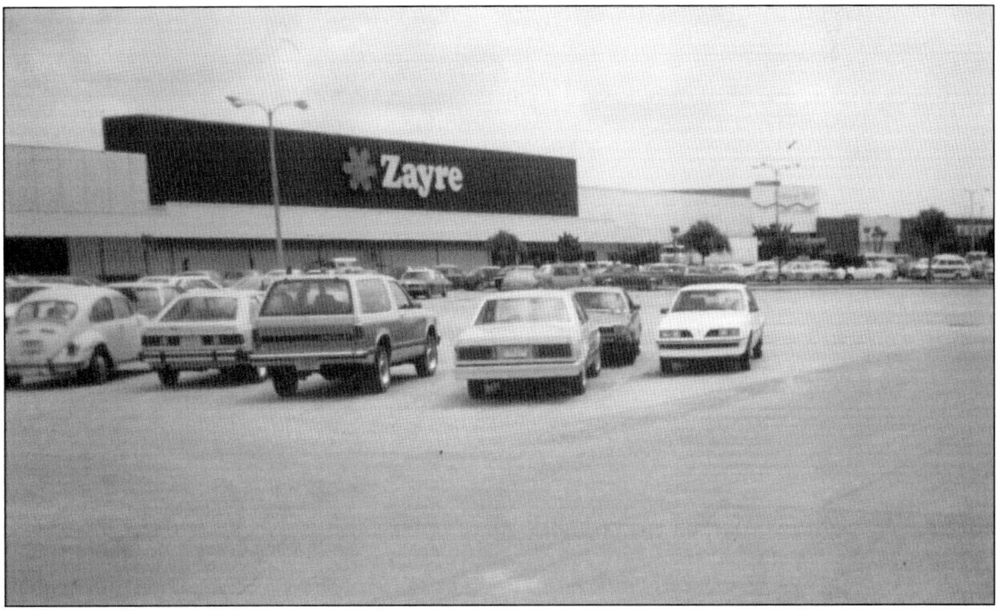

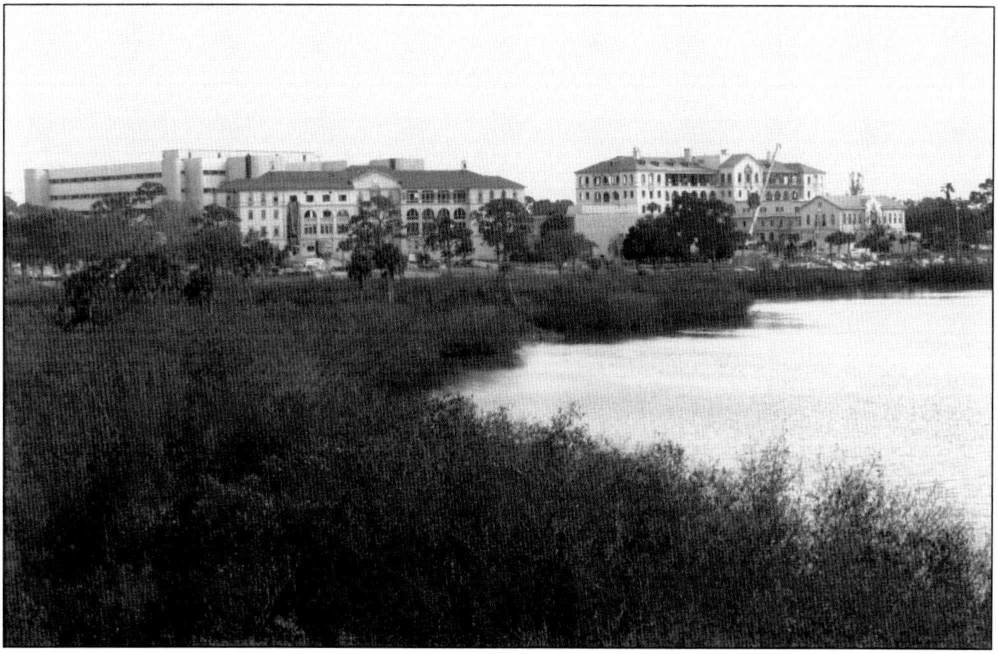

A variety of construction projects have reshaped the Bay Pines VA Hospital since the 1970s. New nursing care facilities opened in 1973 and expanded in 1980. Congressional appropriations for the large replacement hospital, Building No. 100, arrived in the late 1970s. Dedication ceremonies for this imposing structure, shown above on the left and below, took place in March 1983. Outpatient services have expanded throughout southwestern Florida, allowing the Bay Pines VA Healthcare System to serve in excess of 100,000 veterans across 10 Florida counties, a dramatic increase over the 159 veterans who first entered the hospital when it opened in 1933. (Above, HV; below, SHS.)

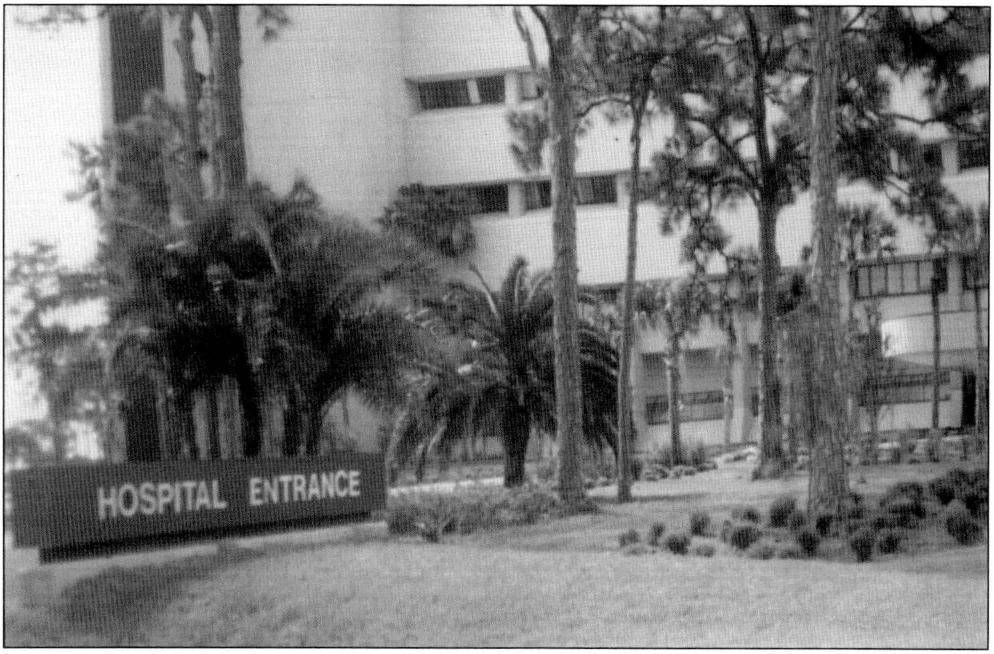

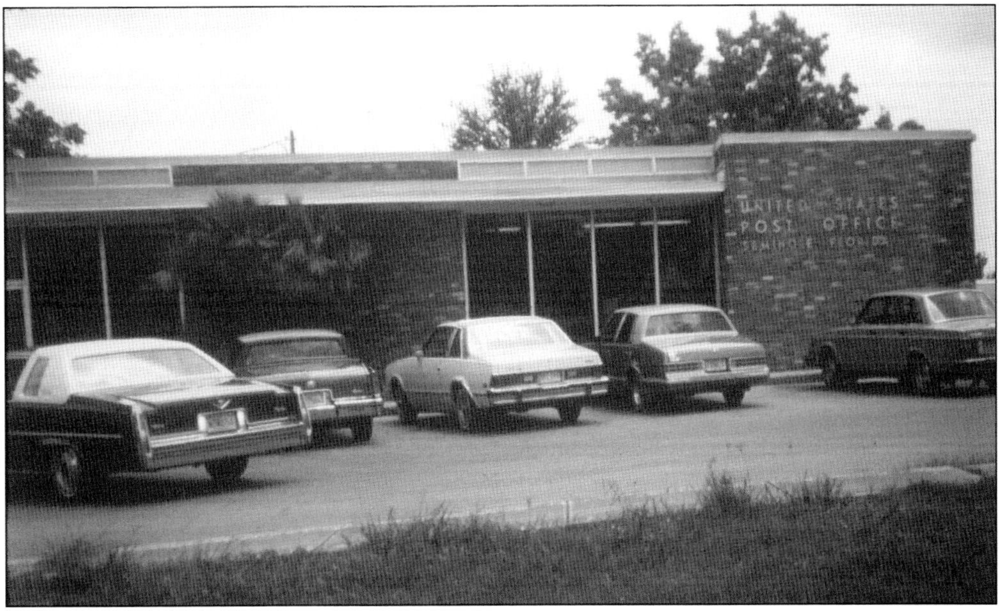

Congestion took its toll along Johnson Boulevard by the early 1980s. The first phase of the Freedom Square retirement and nursing home complex took shape adjacent to Seminole Mall and Johnson Boulevard in 1982. Located near the heart of Seminole, this community spanned more than 15 acres on land formerly owned by the Johnson family and included living spaces for active seniors as well as convalescents. The post office that residents had fought for and embraced two decades earlier drew regular complaints by the early 1980s, as customers fought over limited parking spaces and stood in long lines. The small library located at 11000 Johnson Boulevard since February 1971 had only 2,400 square feet of space and lacked room for expansion. As the city grew, residents demanded expanded facilities by the mid-1980s. (Both, SHS.)

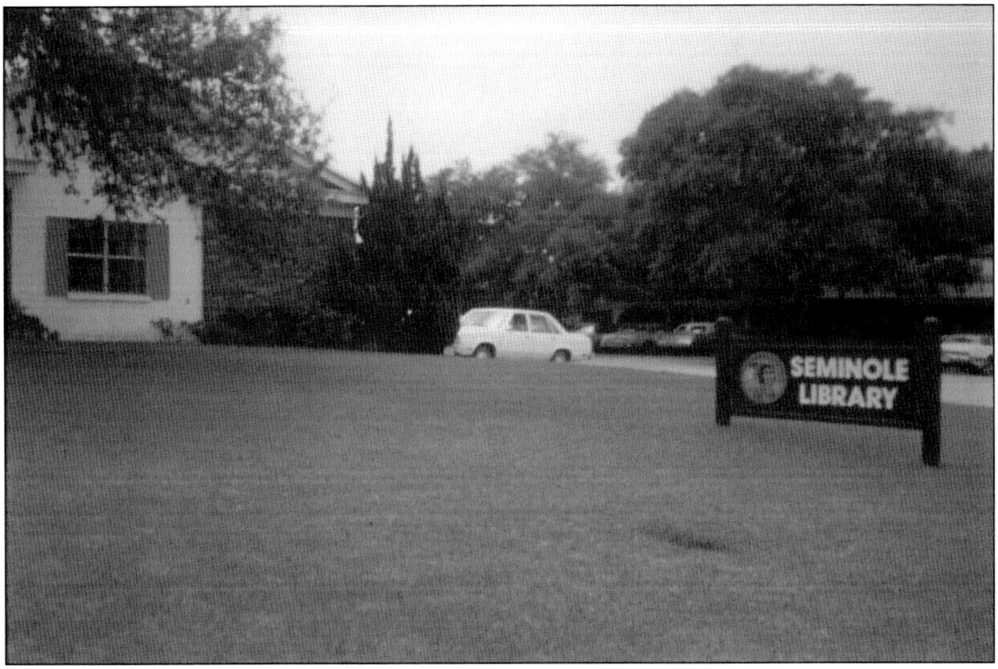

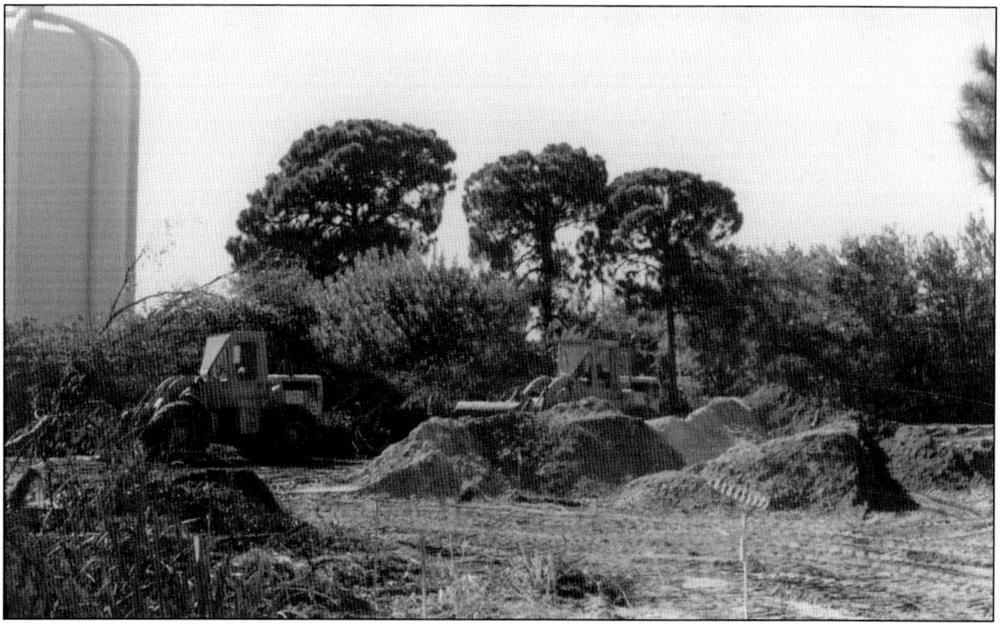

Work crews transformed one of the last undeveloped tracts of land in the heart of Seminole during the late 1980s. Located on the southern side of Park Boulevard across from Seminole Mall, this site became the home of the strip mall shops in the Park Collection. This view looks southwest from the land under development toward the water tower that rises above the city. (Lyn Friedt Collection, HV.)

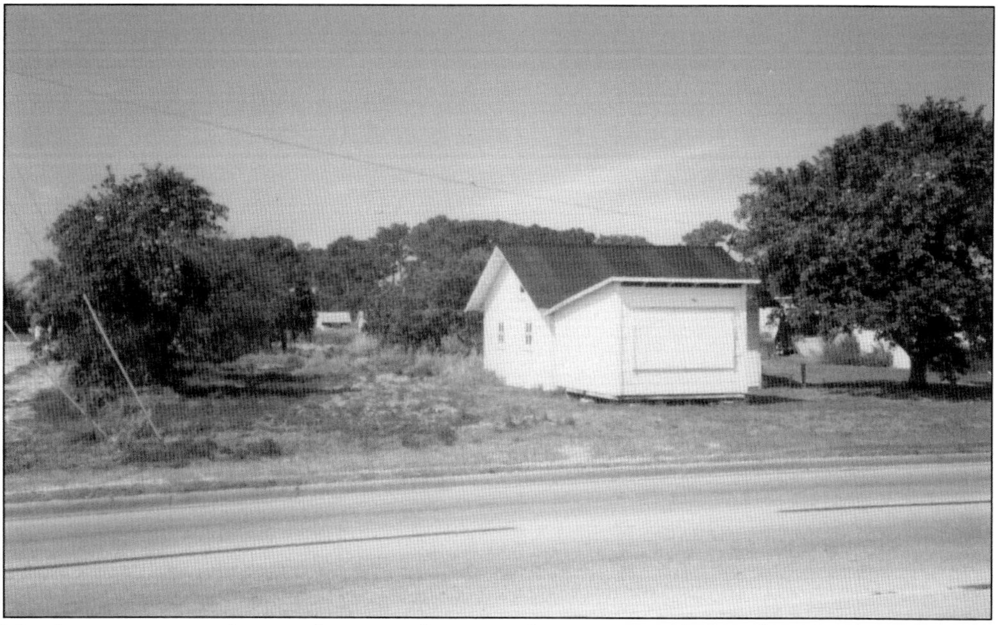

The last remnants of groves between the expanding municipalities of Seminole and Largo disappeared in the 1980s. The uninterrupted vistas of citrus trees from earlier years had transformed into miles of residential developments tucked along back streets behind businesses and asphalt parking lots. This view of 12260 Seminole Boulevard shows the last vestiges of a large grove and family home before a fast-food chain replaced them. (Lyn Friedt Collection, HV.)

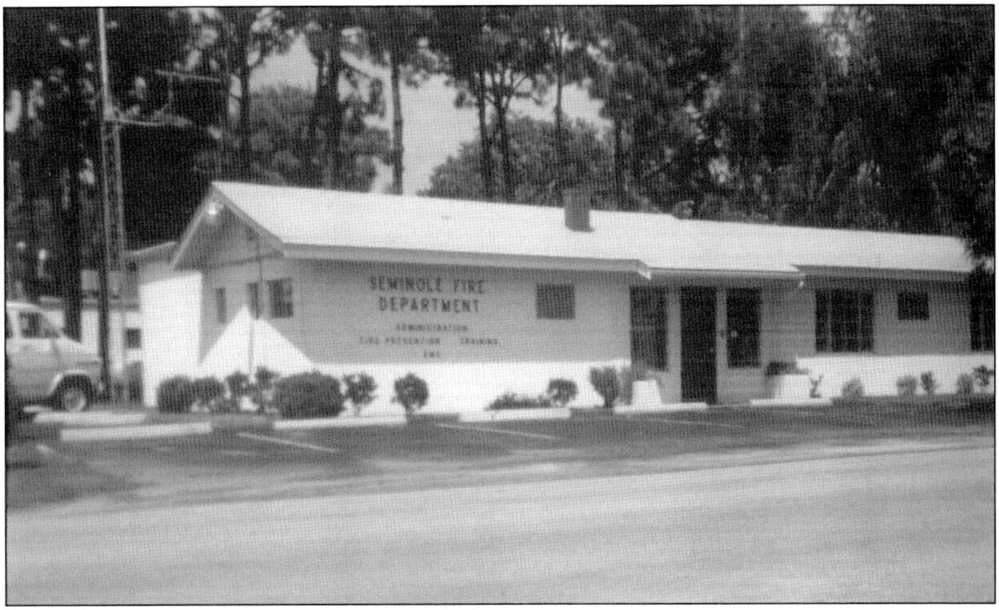

The Seminole Fire Department provides comprehensive life safety services on both sides of Lake Seminole, in both the city and unincorporated areas. The department had only seven paid firefighters in 1972, soaring to 25 paid firefighters in 1977. During the late 1950s, the department handled fewer than 100 calls in a year. This building along Seventieth Avenue near Duhme Road served as the headquarters during the 1980s. (SHS.)

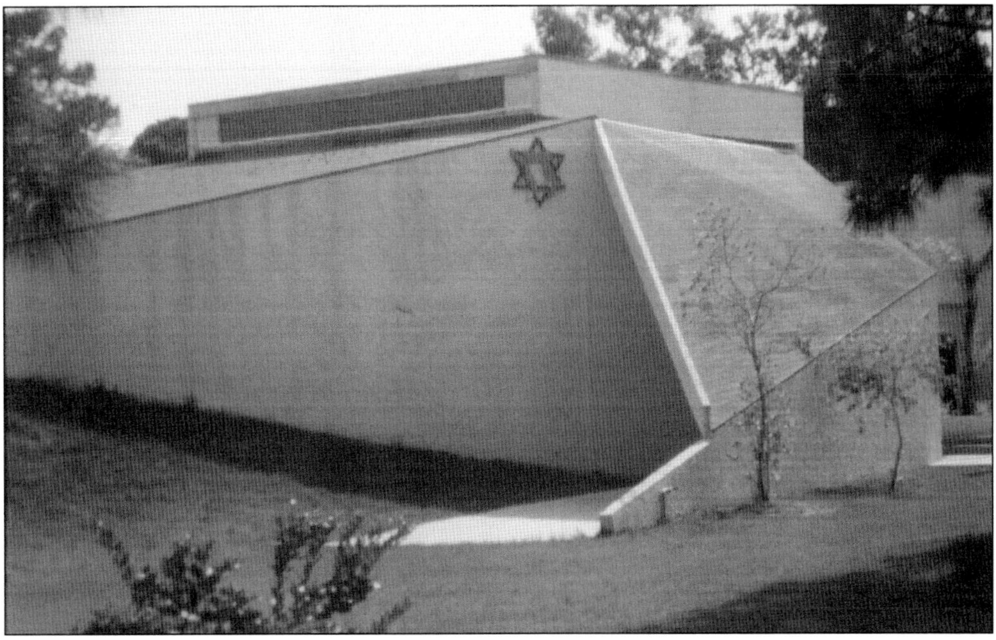

Nine Seminole area families formed Congregation Beth Chai in April 1975. Members of this conservative congregation sought a home for a synagogue. Construction began on this structure once located at 8400 125th Street in the fall of 1979. By the early 1990s, the temple struggled to meet mortgage payments. Soon, the congregation returned the land and left the building. The Temple Estates subdivision appeared at this site in 1993. (SHS.)

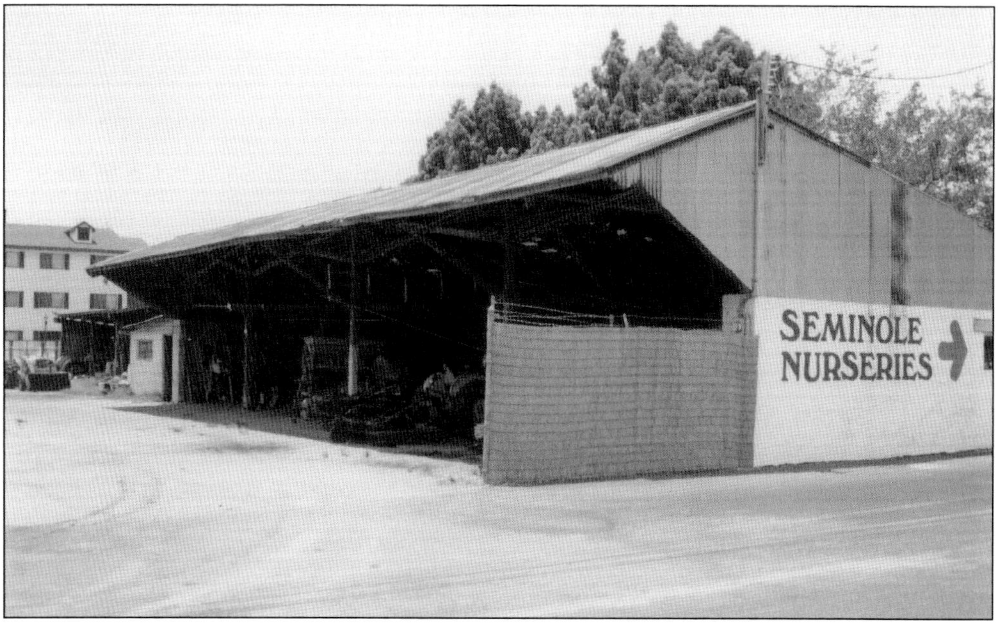

In the late 1950s, Jesse W. Johnson sold some of his land at Seminole Nurseries on Seminole Boulevard so developers could erect the first full-sized grocery store in the area, an A&P grocery store constructed in 1959. In recent years, that building became the Treasure Island Fun Center. Concrete and congestion replaced groves at the remnants of the nursery, shown here in November 1989. (Lyn Friedt Collection, HV.)

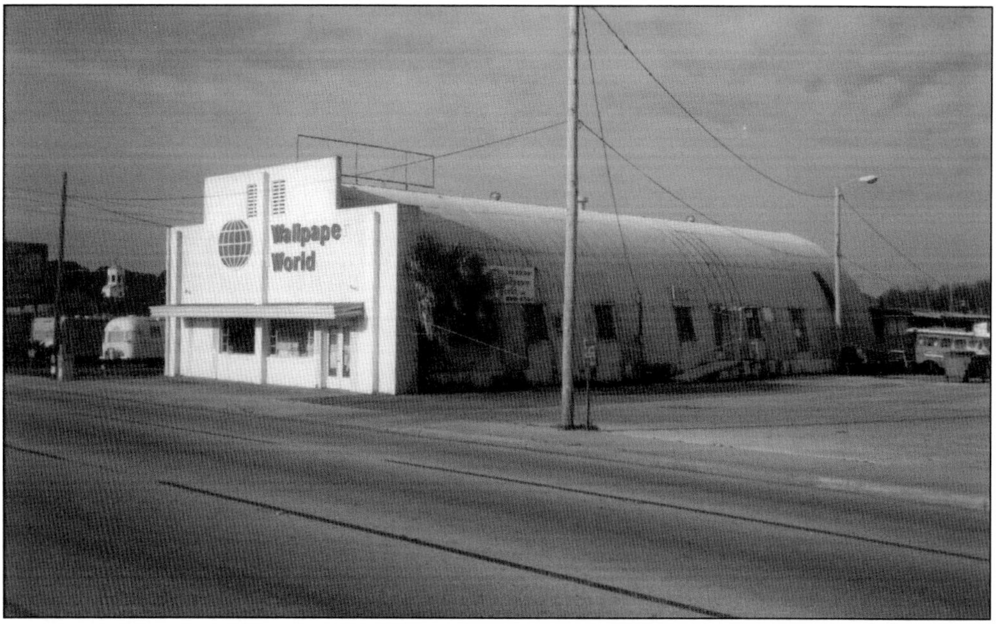

Shown in the early 1980s when it served as a retail outlet, this large metal building has sat at 5600 Seminole Boulevard since 1948. Paul and Katie Baker operated a fruit shipping business here until 1970. Immediately north of this site, members of the Campbell family owned the Jasmine Groves fruit stand. Ernest J. Bickley leased surrounding lands for a mobile home park in 1970. (Lyn Friedt Collection, HV.)

Five

A Mature and Diversified Community 2001–2015

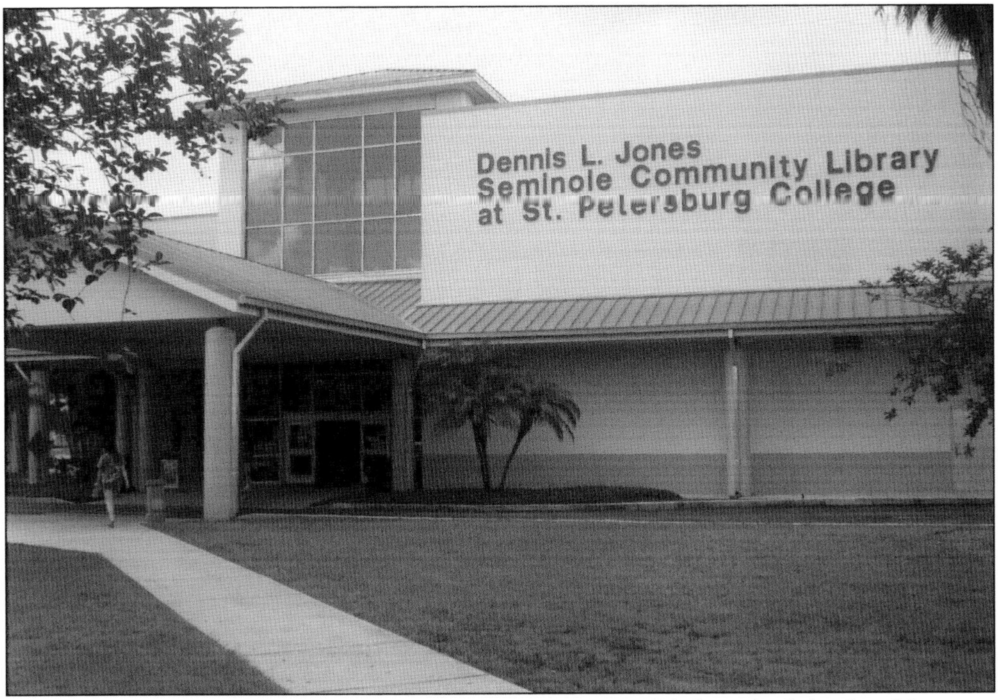

The Seminole Ridge Business and Professional Women's Club launched the first library in Seminole on July 12, 1960. The city began to manage the library in 1989. Since then, the library has benefitted from partnerships, shared resources, and other cooperative relationships. Soon after classes at St. Petersburg College Seminole Campus began, the city and college moved forward with plans for this joint-use facility that opened on August 10, 2003. (Author.)

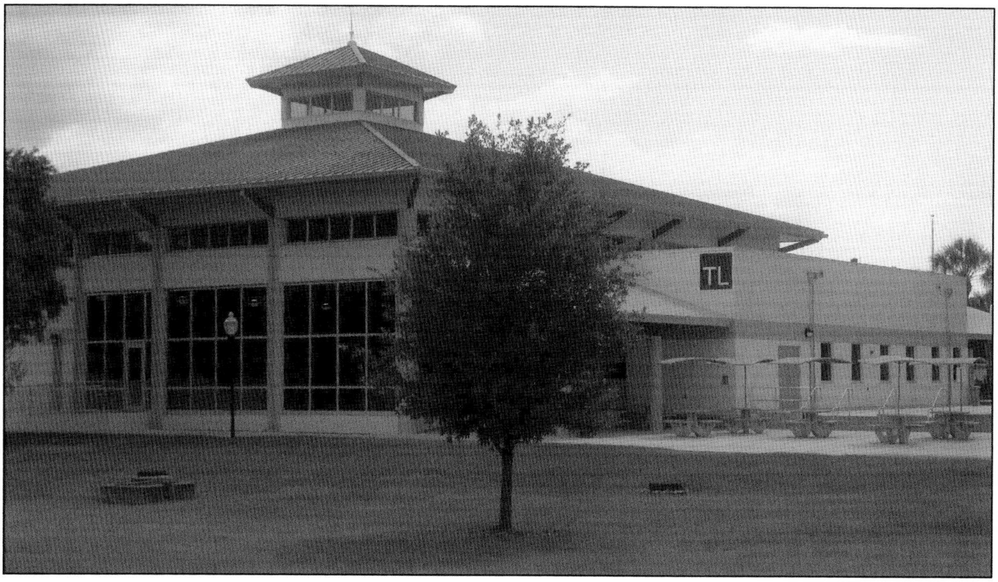

Partnerships define the Seminole Campus of St. Petersburg College. St. Petersburg Junior College, then a two-year institution, searched for land in the Seminole area during the late 1960s. Leadership at the time envisioned a campus at some point in the distant future, because the Seminole area remained largely agricultural in character. Planning for the development of the campus began in the fall of 1991, and ground-breaking ceremonies took place on September 3, 1997. The first classes under the leadership of founding provost James Olliver began in August 1998. Before the end of that decade, the Seminole Campus of the newly renamed St. Petersburg College entered into numerous academic partnerships with other higher education institutions. Students can enroll in undergraduate and graduate programs located at SPC Seminole and earn degrees in many fields. (Both, author.)

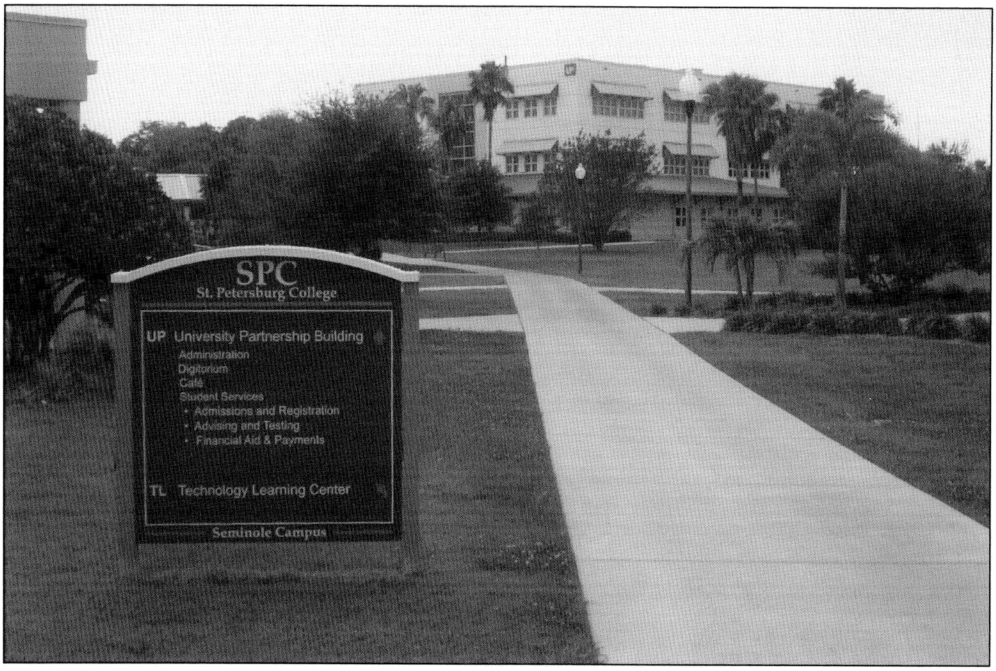

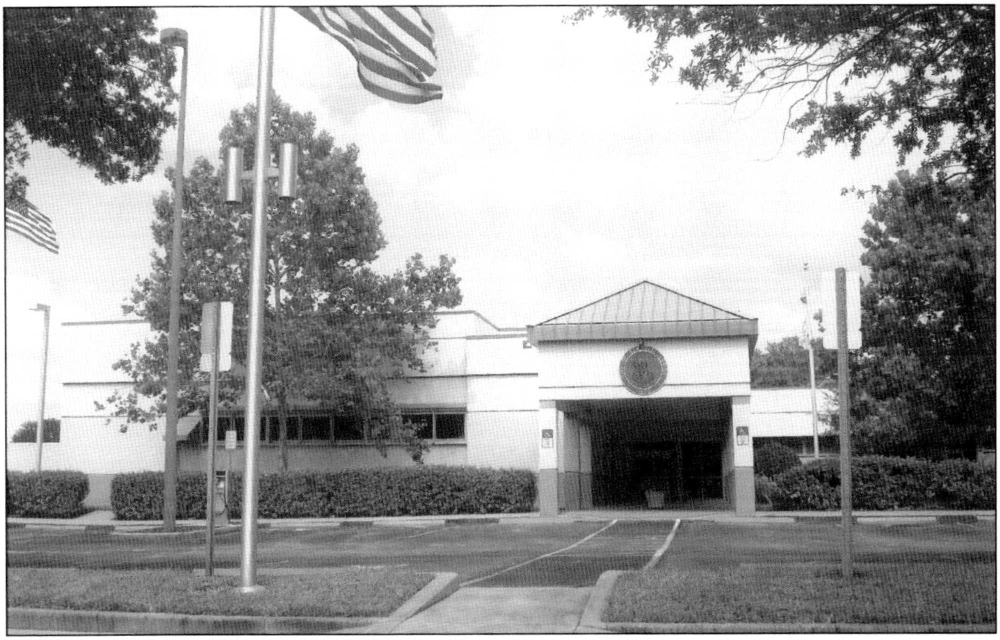

After more than 21 years at its Johnson Boulevard location, the Seminole Community Library expanded into a 17,000-square-foot facility at 9199 113th Street on August 3, 1992. A member of the Pinellas Public Library Cooperative, the library's extensive collections attracted large crowds during the 1990s. When the library moved across the street to the St. Petersburg College campus in 2003, crews converted the former library building, shown above in May 2015, into a renovated and enlarged city hall facility. Municipal offices and city council chambers moved to the former library on February 7, 2005. Just north of this building on the eastern side of 113th Street, a substantially larger Seminole post office (below) had taken shape in the mid-1980s, also replacing the smaller facilities once located along Johnson Boulevard. (Both, author.)

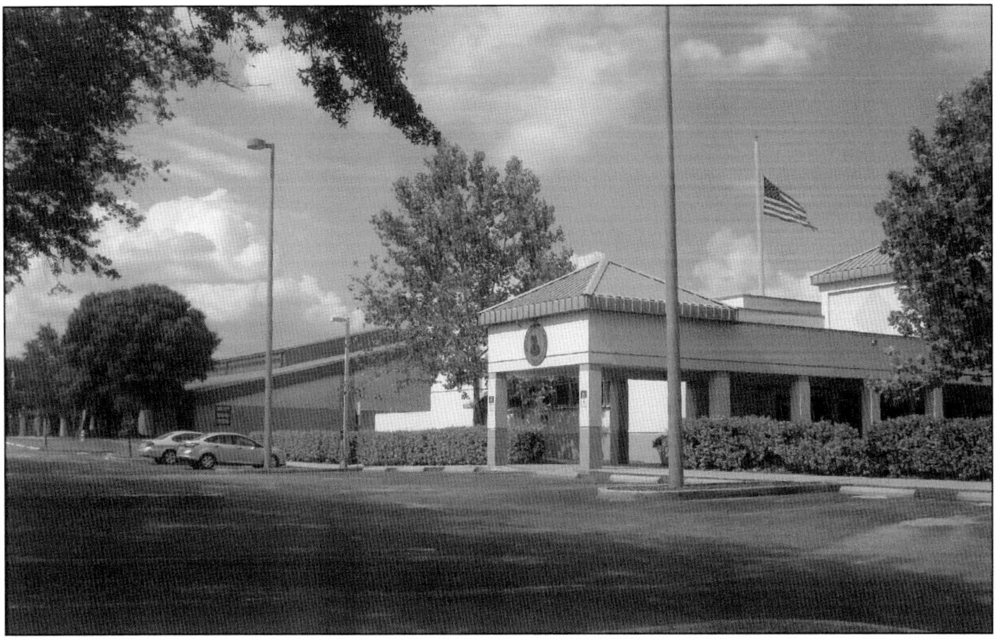

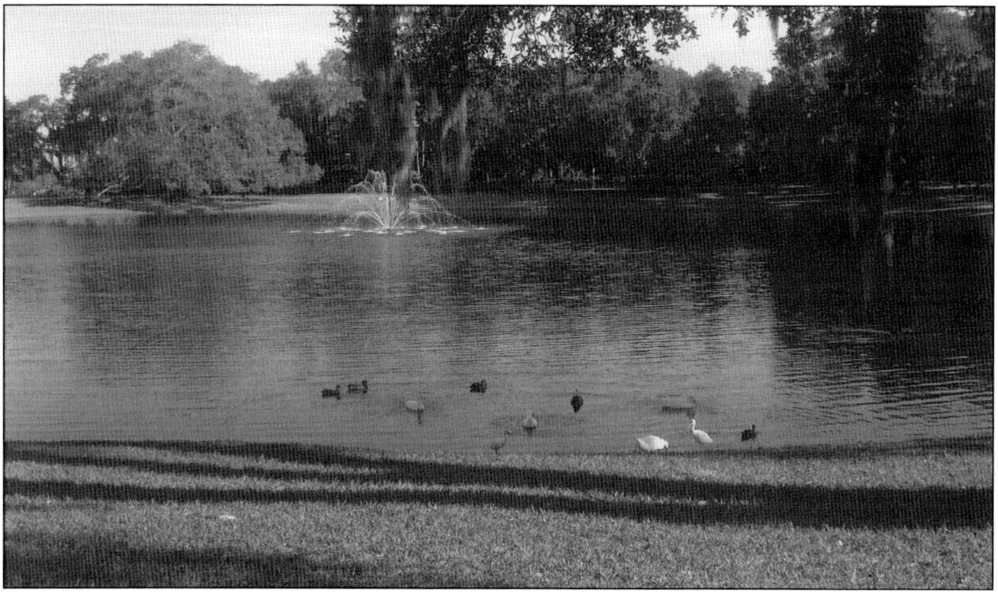

Seminole City Park remains a peaceful oasis in a well-developed, urbanized area. The park, formerly part of the Meares landholdings, possesses a strong sense of history. Located at 7464 Ridge Road, the park had served as the home of city hall since December 7, 1977. The renovation of the former city hall facilities allowed the Seminole Historical Society to move its headquarters to a dedicated space at Seminole City Park in the spring of 2015. Incorporated on June 28, 2004, the society had previously maintained its collection of documents and artifacts at the Seminole Recreation Center. Ironically, shortly after the city acquired the tract, discussions briefly ensued in 1974 about converting the former and long-since demolished Meares homestead into a historical museum. Facility improvements led to a rededication of the park on July 21, 2001. (Both, author.)

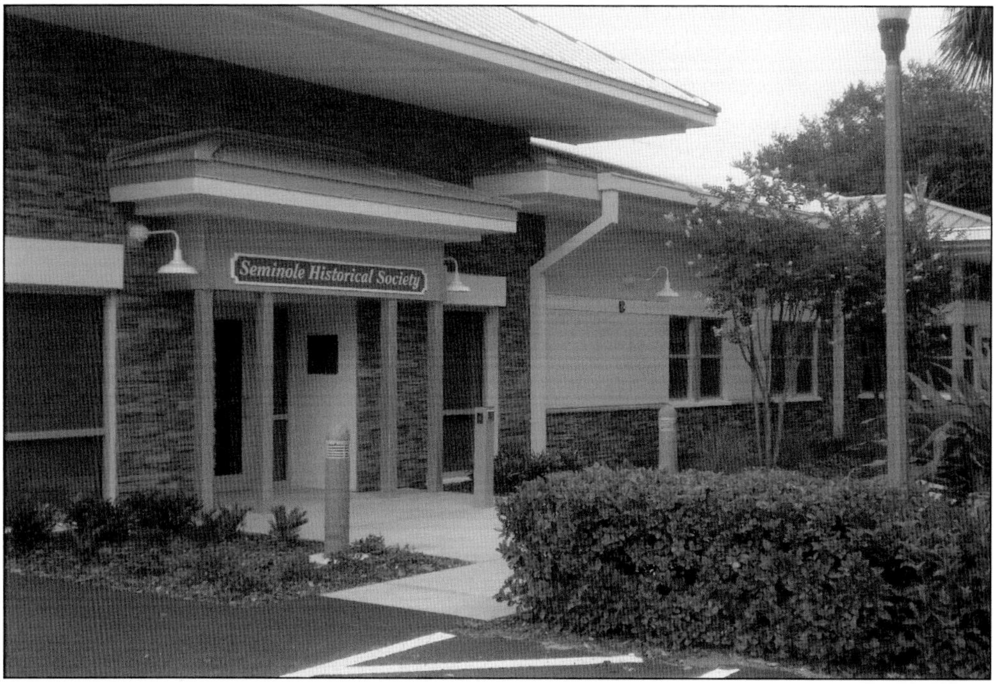

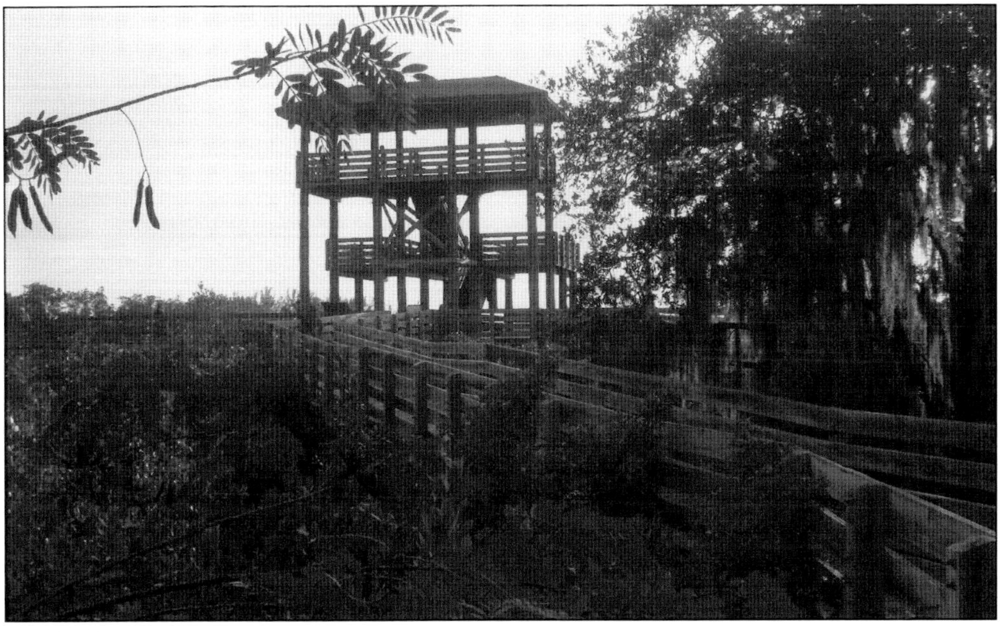

Boca Ciega Millennium Park, dedicated on April 7, 2001, served a utilitarian rather than recreational purpose during the latter part of the 20th century. For many years, Pinellas County's utilities division operated a pumping station on this land near the southern end of 125th Street, south of Oakhurst Road. Occasional floods or stresses on the system led to the pumping of untreated waste directly into Boca Ciega Bay primarily from the 1960s through 1980s, a time when the bay had already suffered a profound loss of fish and seagrasses due to dredging. Development of the park began in September 1999. Presently it is a county park with trails, boardwalks, picnic areas, playgrounds, a launch for kayaks and canoes, and an observation tower; the park, with its abundant native plants, has been listed on the Great Florida Birding Trail. (Both, author.)

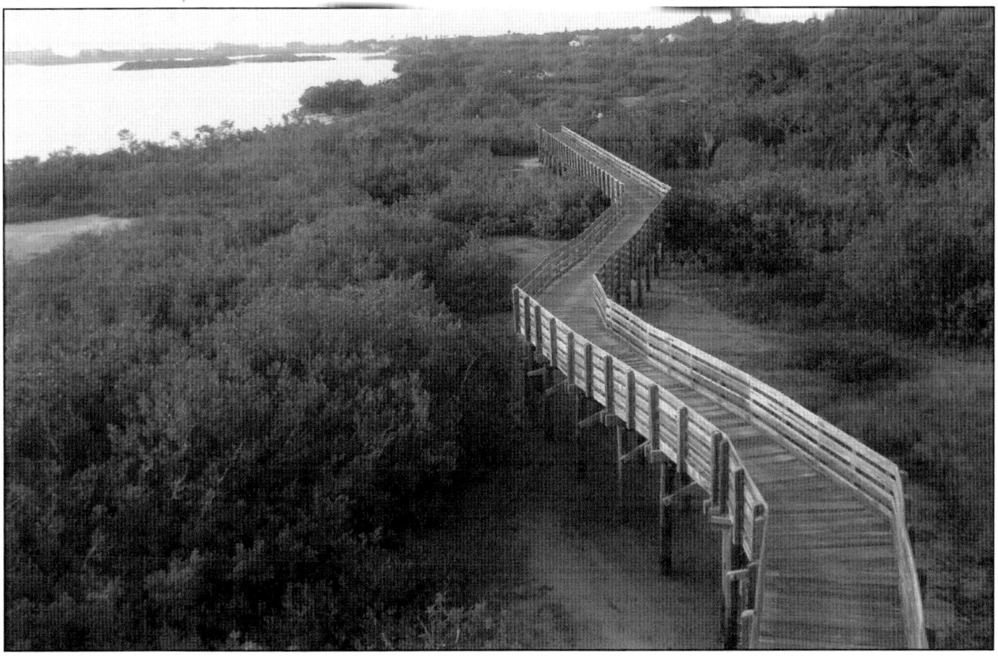

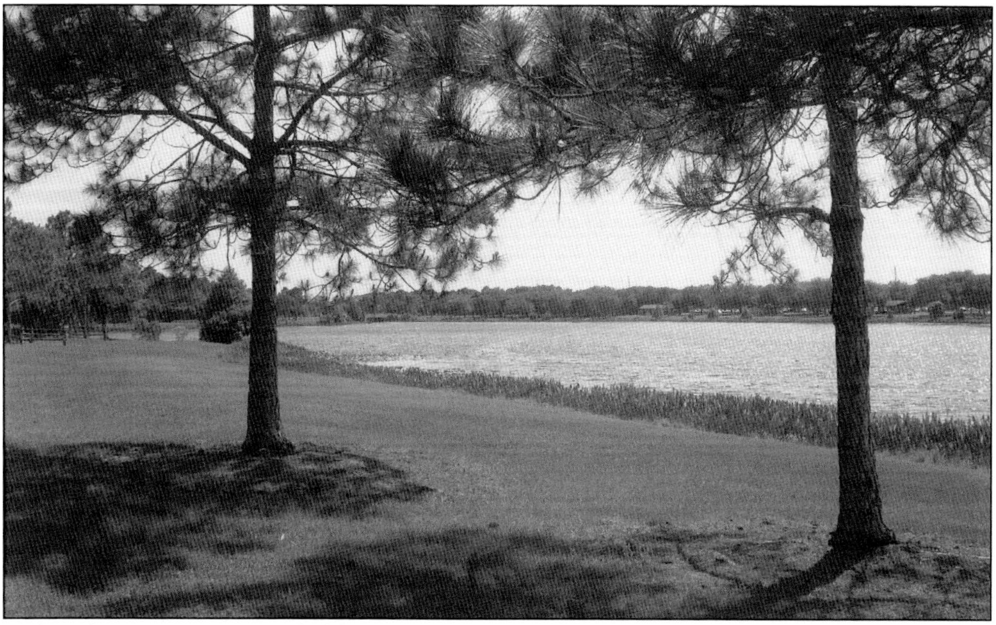

Walsingham Reservoir provided drinking water to early residents on the mainland. By 1937, pipes brought potable water from Lake Walsingham to island communities between Madeira Beach and Indian Rocks. Beginning in September 1962, sixty acres near the intersection of 102nd Avenue and 125th Street became home to the Suncoast Botanical Garden for two decades. The entire 354-acre reservoir opened to the public as Walsingham Park in the early 1990s. (Author.)

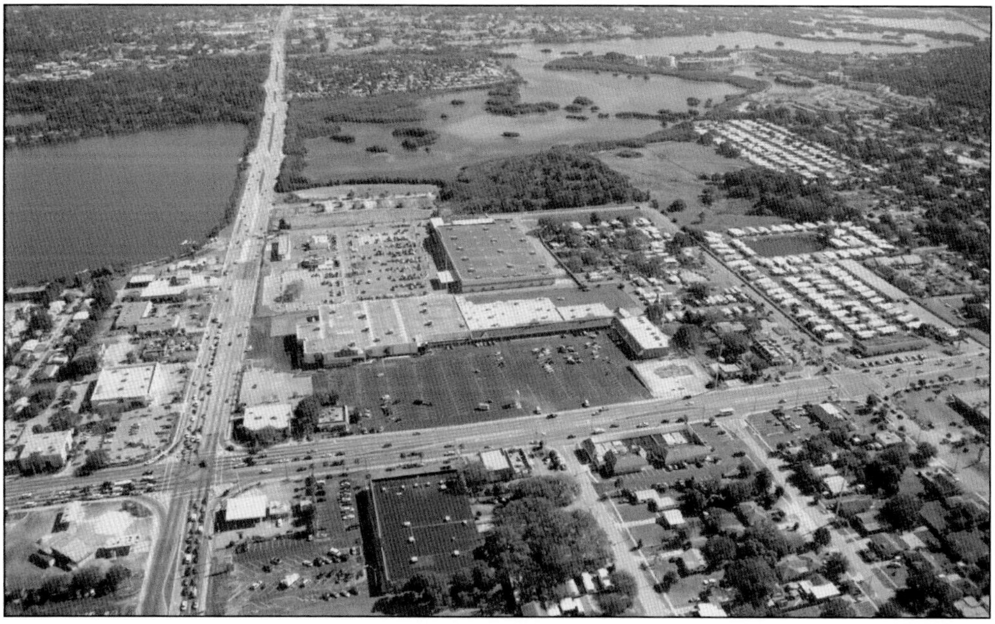

An eastward view of Lake Seminole and Long Bayou in January 2001 reveals the incredible development that the Seminole area has experienced since the 1970s. The intersection of Park and Seminole Boulevards is at lower left. Few undeveloped parcels remain, and those that do often sit within conservation boundaries or public parklands. Commercial enterprises and high-end residential areas have replaced mobile home communities. (USFSP.)

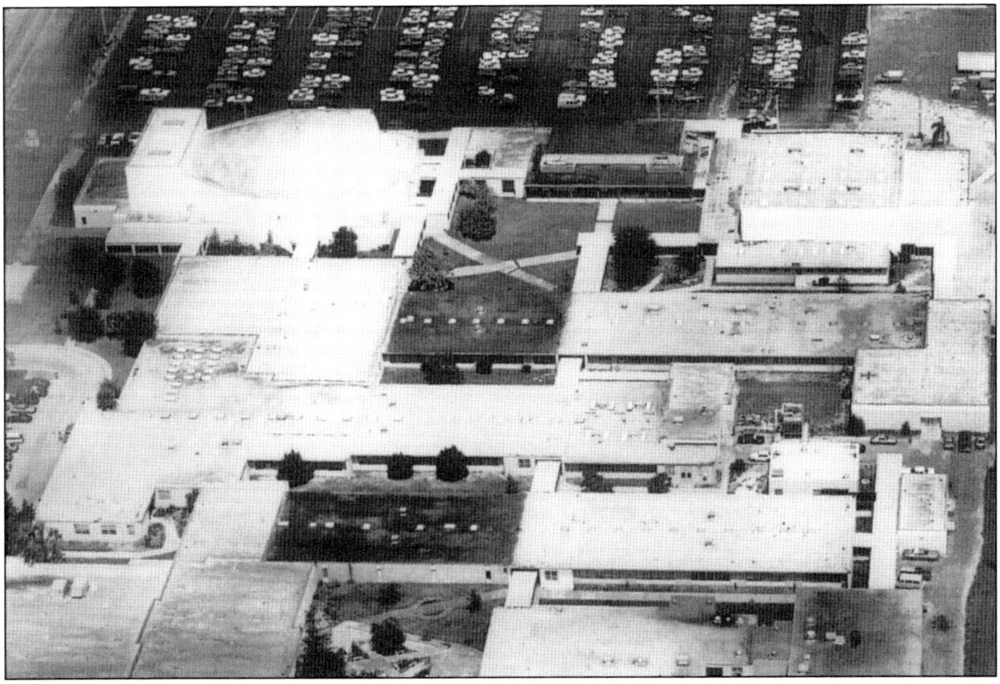

A view above the Seminole High School campus in 2003 offers a sharp contrast to the newly opened school surrounded by countryside shown on page 72. Although telephone service had not yet arrived to the area when the school first opened in 1962, present-day Warhawks enjoy an education that embraces technology. More than 90 percent of graduates enroll in higher education institutions. (Courtesy of Patricia Landon.)

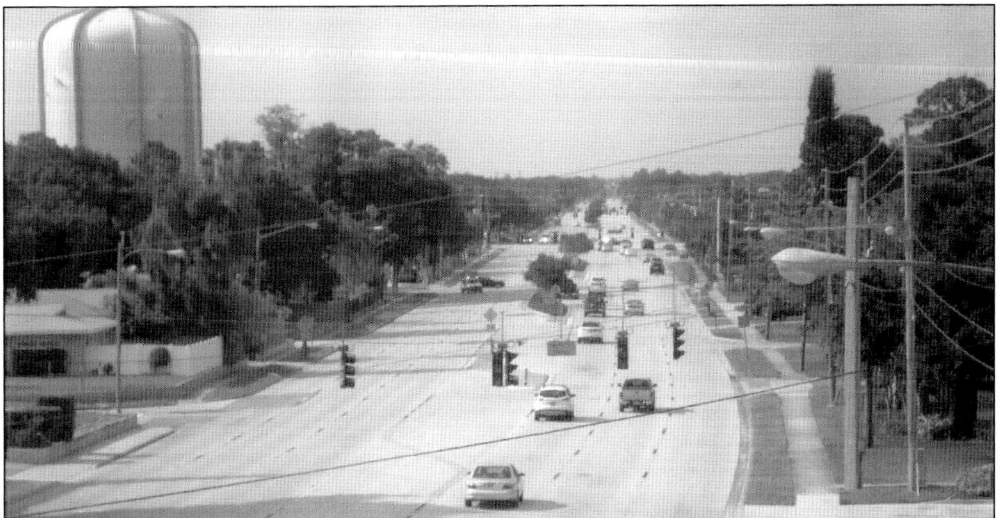

The Seminole area continues to grow. Since the 1990s, the city has embarked upon an ambitious plan to annex large tracts of unincorporated land north toward Largo, east toward Pinellas Park, and southeast on the other side of Cross Bayou toward St. Petersburg and unincorporated areas of western Lealman. Although less than 18,000 lived within Seminole's municipal limits in 2013, the greater Seminole area claims a substantially larger population. (Author.)

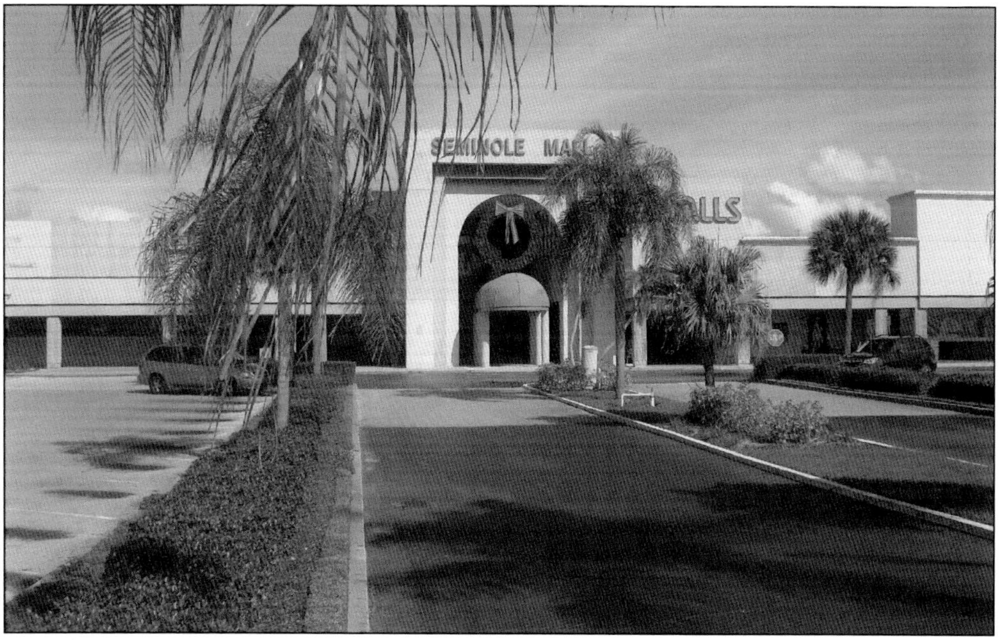

By early 2015, Seminole Mall began to show its age. Nearly a half century after it opened and almost 45 years after it served as the site for the city's inception, Seminole Mall no longer attracted throngs of crowds the way it had years earlier. The food court closed long ago, with little interest in the mostly vacant area except a seldom examined plaque commemorating the city's formation on November 15, 1970. A series of managers and developers have failed to bring life into the mall, which sold for an inflated price of $35.7 million in 2006 and only $14.6 million in 2012. Empty lots in December 2014, above, and the demolition of the movie theater complex in early 2015, below, represent the passing of an era. A new chapter of Seminole's history begins tomorrow. (Both, author.)

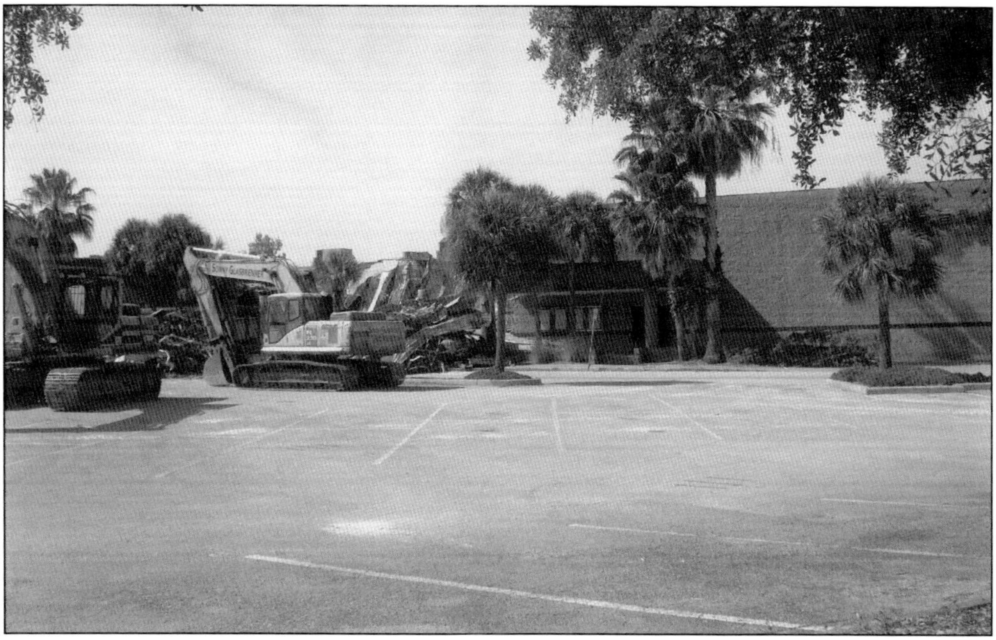

BIBLIOGRAPHY

Campbell, F. Leon. *A History of Seminole Pioneers*. Undated, typewritten manuscript in possession of the Seminole Historical Society.

Costrini, Patricia Perez, ed. *A Tradition of Excellence: Pinellas County Schools, 1912–1987*. Clearwater, FL: School Board of Pinellas County, 1987.

Gagel, Katherine. *A Prehistoric and Historic Survey of the Bay Pines Veterans Administration Property, Bay Pines, Pinellas County, Florida*. Tallahassee, FL: State of Florida, Bureau of Historic Sites and Properties, 1976.

Gallagher, John C., and Lyman O. Warren. "The Bay Pines Site, Pinellas County, Florida." *Florida Anthropologist* 28 (September 1975): 96–116.

Largo Area Historical Society. *Largo, Florida, Then 'Til*. Largo, FL: Bicentennial History Book Committee, 1979.

Miller, Marian. *The Campbells Are*. N.p.: n.p., 1998.

Pinellas County. *The Golden Anniversary of Pinellas Schools, Celebrating 50 Years of Educational Progress*. Clearwater, FL: Pinellas County Board of Public Instruction, 1962.

Schnur, James Anthony. *Largo*. Charleston, SC: Arcadia Publishing, 2011.

———. *Madeira Beach*. Charleston, SC: Arcadia Publishing, 2013.

Starkey, Jay B. *Jay Starkey's Things I Remember, 1899–1979*. Brooksville, FL: Reprint by Southwest Florida Water Management District, 1980.

Wingham, Erma Kyle. *History of Seminole United Methodist Church, Seminole, Florida, 1890–1990*. [Cover title: *Harvest of a Hundred Years*]. Seminole, FL: Seminole United Methodist Church, 1990.

In addition to the publications above, those wanting additional information about the history of the Seminole area should contact the Seminole Historical Society and the Archives and Library at Heritage Village.